A4 PACIFIC
LOCOMOTIVES

A4 PACIFIC LOCOMOTIVES

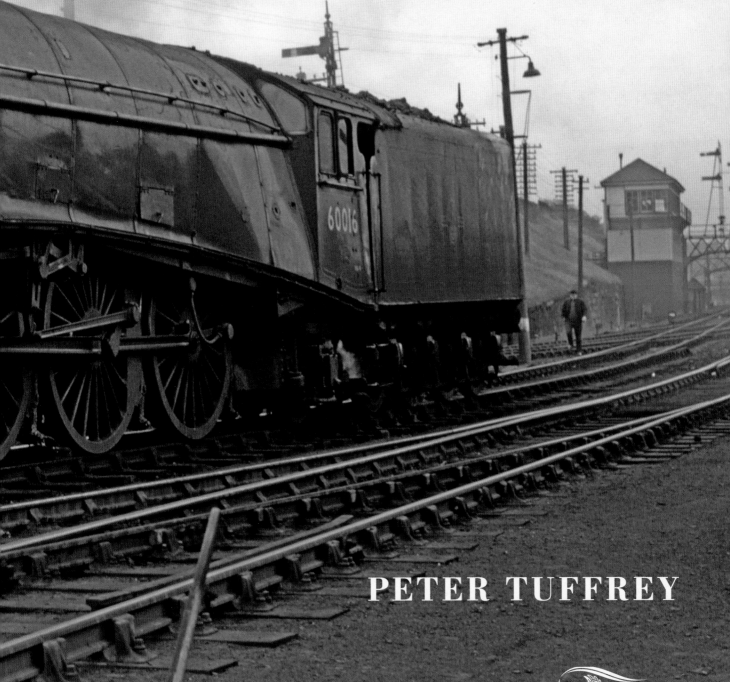

PETER TUFFREY

First published 2016

ISBN 978 07110 3847 9

Published by Ian Allan Publishing Ltd, Addlestone, Surrey KT15 2SF

Printed in Bulgaria

Visit the Ian Allan Publishing website at www.ianallanpublishing.com

Acknowledgements

I am grateful for the assistance received from the following people: Jack Beeston, Ben Brooksbank, Doug Brown, Paul Chancellor, David Clay, Marian Crawley, Nick Grant, Peter Jary, John Law, Hugh Parkin, Derek Porter, Bill Reed, Andrew Warnes, Sue Warnes. Special thanks are due to my son Tristram for his help and encouragement throughout the project.

Photographs

Unless otherwise stated, all photographs in this book are from the collections of either Malcolm Crawley or Ben Burrell. Every effort has been made to gain permission to use the images. If you feel you have not been contacted please let me know: petertuffrey@rocketmail.com. Photographs credited 'IAL' are from the Ian Allan Library.

Information

I have taken reasonable steps to verify the accuracy of the information in this book but it may contain errors or omissions. Any information that may be of assistance to rectify any problems will be gratefully received. Please contact me by email petertuffrey@rocketmail.com or in writing: Peter Tuffrey, 8 Wrightson Avenue, Warmsworth, Doncaster, South Yorkshire, DN4 9QL.

PAGE 1 'A4' class Pacific No 60034 *Lord Faringdon* is serviced alongside Stanier 'Black Five' No 44718 at Glasgow St Rollox shed before returning home to Aberdeen on 22 August 1965. Rising behind are two blocks of the Red Road housing development, which was begun in 1964 and completed in 1971. *Bill Reed*

PGAES 2-3 No 60016 *Silver King* was fresh from being taken out of storage when caught here at Aberdeen Ferryhill Junction on 16 April 1964, having been reinstated about a month earlier. The engine is just north of the engine shed, and the junction signal box can be seen in the background. *Bill Reed*

RIGHT No 60019 *Bittern* at Aberdeen Ferryhill on 2 June 1966 during the last summer in traffic. *Bill Reed*

CONTENTS

INTRODUCTION

Arguably, no class of locomotive has captured the public's imagination more than Sir Nigel Gresley's 'A4' class Pacifics. For just over 80 years their exploits have been followed by successive generations and this shows no sign of diminishing. Why is this? The streamlining has caught many people's eye, especially when compared with that applied to contemporary engines. Also, the 'A4s' were predominantly used on both the LNER's and BR's prestige trains, in addition to those run for special occasions, giving the class an 'elite' status that inevitably draws followers. Furthermore, there are dozens of achievements of haulage capacity and many relate to speed, not least the world record for steam traction, which was attained by No 4468 *Mallard* in 1938 and made the 'A4s' famous across the globe.

The journey to the introduction of the 'A4s' began in the midst of the First World War when Gresley accepted the task of designing a new locomotive for express passenger traffic. The Great Northern Railway's 'A1' class Pacifics would not appear until 1922, as Gresley developed the final specifications on several other designs first. These included the use of a large boiler supplying steam to three cylinders with valves operated by a conjugated motion. There were some initial flaws, but these would be addressed and the 'A3' class appeared in the late 1920s.

The GNR, and the London & North Eastern Railway after Grouping, used the Pacifics on the principal expresses. These were generally loaded above 400 tons but the average speed was quite low and made journey times longer than was necessary. This was highlighted in 1928 when the first non-stop journey was made between King's Cross station and Edinburgh Waverley in a time of 8 hours 15 minutes. Reports at the time noted that much of the journey was drawn out so as not to run too far in front of schedule.

Soon after this event the global economy fell into the Depression and passenger numbers declined on many railways, including the LNER, but the downturn particularly affected the freight traffic that was very important for the company. In America, the railroads were also challenged by the rise of the motor car, investment in highways and in air travel. To fight back, the Chicago, Burlington & Quincy Railroad, as well as the Union Pacific, designed and introduced diesel-powered railcars that would travel at high average speed between densely populated areas. Similar schemes were set in motion in France and Germany and all met with success, forcing the railway world to take note.

The LNER was particularly impressed with the 'Flying Hamburger' from Germany, and approached the manufacturers of the railcar to provide details of a similar unit. After close inspection of these, Gresley and the Board decided to put their faith in steam being up to the task. New motive power with a light train formation was authorised for an express service between King's Cross and Newcastle called the 'Silver Jubilee'. In order to achieve the high speed necessary, Gresley tweaked his successful 'A3' design and turned to streamlining to save power. This was a relatively new concept to railway engineering but, as was typical of Gresley, he did not hesitate to be bold and use the feature, believing that economies would be made in the coal and water consumption.

The first 'A4' class locomotive – No 2509 *Silver Link* – was ready for service in early September 1935 and on the maiden run several records were broken including the highest speed achieved by a steam locomotive. When the 'Silver Jubilee' began there was widespread public interest as people lined the route – waiting both at stations and trackside to see the 'A4' storm past – and there was heavy publicity, which was increasingly becoming a tool to be exploited.

The 'A4s' and the 'Silver Jubilee' were an immediate success and the decision was taken to perpetuate the class for general expresses. Two more high-speed trains were also introduced in 1937 between London and Edinburgh and Leeds and King's Cross, and accelerations were made to normal services. As a result of these changes improvements had to be made to the braking systems then in use. Trials were conducted with new brake valves and on one of these test runs 'A4' No 4468 *Mallard* – fitted with a Kylchap exhaust system – reached 125mph, becoming the fastest steam locomotive in the world.

The role of the 'A4s' changed dramatically after the outbreak of war in 1939 as the weight of trains increased substantially and the operating conditions deteriorated rapidly. Nevertheless exceptional demonstrations of the engines' capabilities were made and the 'A4s' 'did their bit' for the war effort.

The Pacifics were under threat shortly after the end of the war as the LNER looked to introduce diesel locomotives, but nationalisation of the railways in 1948 saw any desire to do so lost. A range of standard types was decided upon by the new British Railways and the 'A4s' were involved in trials all over the network to determine the best attributes of the competitors to be culled for these. The class succeeded in producing some of the best figures of the express engines participating – at the expense of several failures – but in the event BR did not adopt many of the ex-LNER engines' features.

Heading into the 1950s the railways were slow to recover and the standards of service experienced before the war did not start to return until the middle of the decade. BR struggled to attract

staff for maintenance duties and many classes, including the 'A4s', suffered as a result. Coupled to rising costs, the situation caused BR to implement a wholesale replacement of the steam fleet and the introduction of diesel units. A few years would pass before their presence began to be felt, and in the meantime the 'A4s' reached the peak of their careers as middle big-end bearing problems were addressed and Kylchap double blastpipes and chimneys were fitted to all class members, removing steaming problems and increasing efficiency.

Despite this, the diesel takeover thundered on and with the introduction of the 'Deltics' in 1961/62 the 'A4s' lost their place as the prime motive power between King's Cross and Edinburgh after more than 25 years at the top. Famous names and star performers such as *Silver Link*, *Silver Fox*, *Seagull* and *Walter K. Whigham* were soon in the scrapyard, but some 'A4s' found employment in Scotland, being used for expresses between Glasgow and Aberdeen.

As many steam locomotives were withdrawn, concerned people stepped in to buy them from BR, which also set aside a number of engines. No 4468 *Mallard* was the obvious choice, while No 60008 *Dwight D. Eisenhower* and No 60010 *Dominion of Canada* were sent by BR to American and Canadian museums respectively. The first 'A4' to be purchased was No 60007 *Sir Nigel Gresley*, by the A4 Locomotive Society, and the engine was followed soon after by No 60009 *Union of South Africa* and No 60019 *Bittern*, both being bought by private individuals. No 60007 was fully restored to LNER livery and number (4498) and began working specials in 1967, while No 60009 was placed on a short section of private line at Lochty, Fife. No 60019 was also briefly used before the steam ban was imposed by BR in 1968 and the engine (along with No 4498) was put into storage.

ABOVE No 60025 *Falcon* has just backed on to a southbound express at Grantham on 12 September 1958. The engine was just over a week out of works, where a Kylchap double chimney had been fitted. *Bill Reed*

Steam returned to the network in 1971 but was limited to certain sections, and restrictions were placed on the speeds allowed. *Sir Nigel Gresley* would subsequently become a regular on the many railtours organised, as would *Union of South Africa* when the engine returned to the main lines in 1973. The locomotives would travel all over the country – at least where steam was welcome – and deliver excitement to those who had not seen them in their pomp on the East Coast Main Line, as well as to a new generation of enthusiasts. Unfortunately, *Bittern* proved to be too costly to operate and after a brief return in the early 1970s would not run again for over 30 years.

Mallard has been the focus of two big events to celebrate the anniversary of the achievement of the speed record. For the 50th year in 1988 the locomotive was partially restored and ran a number of railtours that were highly successful. On the 75th anniversary the engine was displayed alongside all surviving 'A4s', as No 60008 and No 60010 were repatriated especially. The popularity of the events organised by the National Railway Museum was unprecedented and attracted not just enthusiasts but the general public – demonstrating that the 'A4s' still have that magic they possessed in 1935.

Peter Tuffrey
Doncaster, April 2016

GAINING SPEED, 1911-1934

Herbert Nigel Gresley was appointed Locomotive Engineer of the Great Northern Railway in 1911, taking up the position on 1 October. He had previously been Carriage & Wagon Superintendent for the company and because of this he was seen as somewhat of an unlikely successor to outgoing Locomotive Engineer H. A. Ivatt. The latter had been in harness since 1896 and had produced several successful designs, not least the express passenger 4-4-2 Atlantic locomotives.

Gresley's first task was dealing with the pressing need for mixed traffic and heavy freight engines as the company struggled to cope with the existing motive power. The first to emerge was 'H2' class 2-6-0 No 1630 in August 1912, and this was based on the Great Western Railway's recently introduced '43XX' class, which in turn had been inspired by American practice. A novelty of the 'H2' design was the use of outside cylinders and Walschaerts valve gear. Gresley followed this with the 'O1' class 2-8-0 two-cylinder freight locomotives, the first – No 456 – appearing from Doncaster in December 1913. These two classes were followed by the 'J23' 0-6-0T (for shunting duties) and a larger boiler version of the 'H2', classified 'H3', before Britain became involved with the First World War in 1914.

For Gresley the conflict brought a lot of munitions work to Doncaster and reduced the time he had for strictly locomotive matters. In the periods he could dedicate to his primary role, Gresley was deciding how he would progress his designs after the cessation of the conflict. Generally speaking, this involved increasing the number of cylinders used in order to provide greater power for the increasingly heavy loads. In anticipation of even longer passenger trains, Gresley based a proposed design on the Ivatt Atlantic locomotives but with a Pacific or 4-6-2 wheel arrangement and four cylinders. As an experiment Ivatt Atlantic No 279 was taken into Doncaster Works in October 1914 and fitted with a new front end featuring four 15-inch-diameter cylinders with 8-inch piston valves that were operated using Walschaerts valve gear; the inside valves were operated using a rocking shaft connected to the outside motion.

RIGHT Herbert Nigel Gresley (later Sir) pictured c1930.

The locomotive was tested in June 1915, but the results appear to have been unconvincing for Gresley and no further development was carried out. Gresley was either spurred on by this or had already discarded the use of four cylinders because in November 1915 he submitted a patent for a design of conjugated motion that was to be used with three cylinders.

In 1925 Gresley delivered a paper to the Institution of Mechanical Engineers on 'The Three-Cylinder High-Pressure Locomotive', which dealt at length with the use of three cylinders on contemporary locomotives and the advantages for using such an arrangement. In Britain, J. G. Robinson of the Great Central Railway and Sir Vincent Raven of the North Eastern Railway were the principal protagonists in this area, applying the layout to freight and express passenger designs respectively, and with varying degrees of success. Gresley goes on to state that he had been an admirer of the use of three cylinders for the following reasons: reduced tyre wear owing to a uniform turning movement at the rail; steadier running at high speed and reduced hammer blow; a more even draught action, reduced coal consumption and boiler stresses; and lower permissible factor of adhesion, allowing a higher tractive effort. With regard to his valve gear for

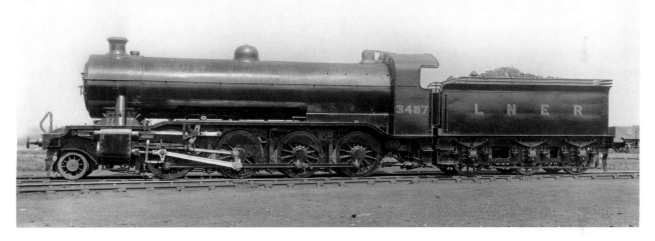

operating the middle valve, Gresley said: 'The author had for some years appreciated the advantages to be gained by this system [three cylinders], but felt that if two instead of three main valve gears could be used, as in the two- and four-cylinder engines, one of the principal objections, which from time to time has been urged against three-cylinder engines, would be removed.'

A patent was accepted for Gresley's conjugated valve gear in October 1916. In the meantime, the frames had been ordered for a locomotive in which the system would be fitted. This engine was to be a 2-8-0 freight type with the same boiler as the earlier 'O1' class. The new locomotive was slow being erected and did not appear in traffic until May 1918, being classified 'O2' and numbered 461. The conjugated valve gear took the form of rocking shafts that were driven by the outside valve gear. The two shafts for the middle valve were of unequal length – the right shaft was longer than the left – to give the correct rate of movement for the valve. Unfortunately, there were several problems with this design. The cylinders had to be inclined at 1 in 8 for the centre cylinder to clear the first pair of coupled wheels (Gresley abhorred any cylinders driving on to the first

TOP Gresley continued to push forward his ideas on locomotive design with the 'O1' class 2-8-0s.

ABOVE No 3487 was the first of 15 'O2' class engines constructed at Doncaster after the Grouping.

coupled axle), with the outside pair following suit to allow the crank angles to be set at 120 degrees. The rocking shafts had seven pins and joints that outnumbered those of an independent set of inside valve gear and these would often be worn and in bad condition, leading to poor engine performance. The arrangement was heavily criticised by the contemporary technical press and other engineers for this reason.

While developing this valve gear Gresley also designed a simpler form, which was similar to a design patented, but lapsed, in 1913, submitted by Harold Holcroft, who worked for the GWR, where the rocking shafts were replaced by levers. These had not been used on No 461 because they would have been at the same inclination as the cylinders, which was undesirable. Nevertheless, following the 'O2' class engine's first month in service, tests were conducted with the GWR dynamometer car between No 461 and 'O1' No 456. The results and subsequent experience in service were enough for Gresley to later say, '…the improved results obtained in the matter of fuel consumption, maintenance costs and general reliability were such that no more two-cylinder engines have been constructed for this service, and the three-cylinder type has been adopted.'

Holcroft and Gresley met in early 1919 and discussed the solution to the employment of the simple version of the gear. Simply, this was to incline the centre cylinder only and have the middle crank displaced from 120 degrees by an angle equal to the difference between the outside and inside cylinders. This principle was embodied in the following 10 'O2' class locomotives, which were ordered from the North British Locomotive Company in March 1919 and at work by May 1921. Meanwhile, Gresley introduced an improved version of the 'H2'/'H3' 2-6-0s in March 1920. 'H4' class No 1000 was equipped with a 6-foot-diameter boiler, which was the largest then employed by a British locomotive, and Gresley's new valve gear. No 1000 was extensively tested, and during one run the centre valve overran causing damage to the steam chest cover as a result of coasting in full gear with the regulator shut. The root cause of this was imperfection in the set-up of the gear, which was multiplied as the speed grew. As a means to solve the issue Gresley ordered that the maximum cut-off be reduced from 75% to 65%, thereby limiting the valve travel in full forward gear from $6^3/_8$ inches to $5^3/_8$ inches. Drivers were also told to alter their methods so that 25% cut-off was selected when steam was shut off.

While these developments were taking place Gresley still had a large new engine in mind to replace the Ivatt Atlantics on the GNR expresses. From the original Pacific design of 1915 the proposal had evolved to an engine with a 2-6-2 wheel arrangement, which was produced in mid-1918. No further action was taken and as time progressed the Pacific design again found favour. A new drawing was produced in April 1920 showing the principal features of three 20-inch-diameter cylinders, and a 6ft 5in-diameter boiler reducing in size to 5ft 9in and working at 180lb per sq in. The firebox had a grate area of 41.25sq ft and a short combustion chamber. Two oddities of the design were the Ivatt cab and a six-wheel tender, but these were soon discarded in favour of an enclosed cab, which was along the same lines as the Great Eastern Railway type, and an eight-wheel tender with a 5,000-gallon water capacity and space for 8 tons of coal. The only negative point to be aimed at the design before experience was gained in service was that the 8-inch-diameter piston valves were quite small for the cylinder volume and restricted the steam flow by causing back pressure when exhausting to the blastpipe.

The small valves were the result of the complicated front-end layout, which limited the space available. Two locomotives were ordered in January 1921 and the first, No 1470 *Great Northern*, was sent into traffic on 11 April 1922.

An important aspect of the design was the boiler. In his Inaugural Address as Chairman of the Leeds branch of the Institution of Locomotive Engineers, Gresley reiterated his adoption of the large boiler policy that had been begun by Ivatt several years previously. He said: 'The power of an engine depends upon its capacity for boiling water. The boiler is therefore the most important feature, but many engineers still compare the power of an engine by tractive force alone and ignore the boiler. Tractive force is useless unless the boiler is able to supply the necessary steam for long and continuous service.' While Ivatt's parallel boiler was very good, Gresley seems to have been deterred from adopting this design and was perhaps swayed towards the type used on the Pennsylvania Railroad's impressive 'K4s' Pacifics after becoming aware of their remarkable performances. This class was based on a prototype that had been constructed by the American Locomotive Company in 1910 and had then undergone thorough trials on the road and in the Altoona test plant in order to determine the optimum dimensions of the class, such as those for the boiler. When the Pennsylvania Railroad began producing the design in numbers the boiler was equipped with a combustion chamber – not used in the prototype – 19-foot-long tubes, and the boiler's diameter reduced from 7ft 5in to 6ft 6½in. The firebox was also of the wide type.

With the promise of a plentiful supply of steam to the cylinders, Gresley stated that his new Pacifics could haul trains of 600 tons, which was a heavy load at the time, at express schedules. On 3 September 1922 Gresley's assertion was put to the test when the second 'A1' class Pacific, No 1471 (later named *Sir Frederick Banbury*), was sent from King's Cross to Grantham and back with 610 tons (20 carriages) behind the tender. The engine headed out to Finsbury Park (2½ miles) in 7 minutes 30 seconds and covered another 2½ miles to Wood Green in a further 4 minutes 15 seconds. No 1471 managed to accelerate from 34 to 38mph up the 1 in 200 to Potters Bar (12¾ miles from King's Cross) and the total time to this point was 24 minutes. The speed reached 58½mph at Knebworth, after 7 minutes 30 seconds were taken for the 8.3 miles from Hatfield at an average speed of 66mph. A little further on at Stevenage a signal check halted progress but the engine was soon accelerating from 43mph to 56½mph at Hitchin, then a high of 73½mph was achieved at Biggleswade. No 1471 completed the 58¾ miles from King's Cross to Huntingdon in 69 minutes. On the 11½ miles from Essendine to Stoke summit (where the line rises at 1 in 200 to the highest point between London and York) the speed averaged 46mph and

ABOVE The 'A1' Pacific was the culmination of Gresley's work with the GNR. No 1471 *Sir Frederick Banbury* poses on an unidentified turntable.

RIGHT The British Empire Exhibition was used to showcase the 'A1' Pacific for the newly formed LNER. No 4472 *Flying Scotsman* – the first built for the company – was present in 1924 and 1925.

arrival at Grantham was made in 122 minutes from King's Cross. With this performance being particularly good for the time, the GNR had no hesitation in ordering 10 more Pacifics before the company ceased to exist.

The Railways Act 1921 – also known as the Grouping Act – drastically reduced the number of railway companies operating in Britain at the time to four, later being collectively known as the 'Big Four'. The GNR was amalgamated with the Great North of Scotland Railway, North British Railway, North Eastern Railway, Great Eastern Railway and Great Central Railway to form the London & North Eastern Railway. This company was the second largest of the four, the others being the London Midland & Scottish Railway (the biggest), the GWR and Southern Railway (the smallest). Of the engineers in contention for the Chief Mechanical Engineer's position on the LNER, Gresley, while being the youngest, had made the biggest impact prior to the event with the introduction of his Pacifics. The other two CMEs in the frame were Sir Vincent Raven of the NER and J. G. Robinson of the GCR. Both had enjoyed distinguished careers up to this point, but

both men were reaching the age for retirement. Therefore without too much surprise Gresley was appointed CME in early 1923, taking charge of 7,392 locomotives, approximately 21,000 carriages and 300,000 wagons.

One of the first new locomotives to be completed for the company was 'A1' Pacific No 1472 in February 1923; the engine was later renumbered 4472 and named *Flying Scotsman*. Of the Pacifics in service No 1472 was chosen to represent the LNER at the British Empire Exhibition being held at Wembley in 1924. The locomotive was specially prepared and was in immaculate condition when put on display in the Palace of Engineering. The general public were suitably impressed by No 4472 (by then renumbered) but were left somewhat confused when moving on to the GWR's exhibit featuring the recently constructed 'Castle' class locomotive No 4073 *Caerphilly Castle*,

LEFT No 4474 *Victor Wild* performed creditably in the exchanges with the GWR.

ABOVE *Pendennis Castle* and No 4475 *Flying Fox* in the yard at King's Cross shed during the exchanges of 1925.

RIGHT Collett 'Castle' class 4-6-0 No 4079 *Pendennis Castle* under close attention at Doncaster shed in 1925.

which had a prominent notice proclaiming that the engine was the most powerful in Britain at the time. This was true, as the tractive effort was 31,625lb compared to 29,835lb of the 'A1', but the public found this hard to believe given the difference in size between the two locomotives. From this discrepancy emerged the 1925 exchange trials of the two classes between the LNER and GWR, and with the event came an enthusiasm and interest for the railway from the public that had not been seen since the 'Races to the North' of 1895.

On 27 April 1925 'A1' No 4474 (later *Victor Wild*) travelled to Paddington to work the 10.50am 'Cornish Riviera Limited' to Plymouth, returning the next day with the up train. Driver A. Pibworth and Fireman E. Birkwood were on the footplate and were aided on the unfamiliar road by a pilotman. Competing against them was Driver Rowe and No 4074 *Caldicot Castle*, which began on the up service on the Monday. Driver Pibworth stuck to the timetable as far as possible. Despite Fireman Birkwood struggling to adapt initially to the Welsh coal, he managed to bring the consumption down from a 50lb average on the first down train to 40.4lb on the final up run with an overall average of 48lb per mile. Driver Rowe took the competition to a different level and ran his engine considerably harder, setting up a couple of line records and gains of up to 15 minutes in the process. The coal consumption was not too adversely affected by such performances and a high of 46.8lb was recorded on one run compared with a low of 38.8lb, while the average was 42lb per mile.

No 4079 *Pendennis Castle* was sent to King's Cross to run from there to Grantham on the 10.10am, returning with the 3.07pm on Monday, Wednesday and Friday, and working the 1.30pm King's Cross to Doncaster and 6.21pm return on Tuesday, Thursday and Saturday. No 4475 (*Flying Fox*) was competing for the LNER on the first day, but fell victim to overheating and was replaced by No 2545 (*Diamond Jubilee*). Driver B. Glasgow was in charge of both the 'A1s', which performed poorly over the period and had an average coal consumption of 59lb between King's Cross and Grantham and 55.3lb on the other journey, producing an overall average of 57.1lb per mile. No 4079 with Driver Wood and Fireman Pearce astonished many on the LNER with very good performances on the line, coping easily with the 480-ton train used for the tests and the hard Yorkshire coal. The coal consumption between King's Cross and Grantham was 57lb, and 49.8lb for the King's Cross to Doncaster trains, the total average being 53.4lb per mile.

While the question of which class of engine was the most powerful was not answered on the tests, the differences in economy between them was there for all to see. This was especially the case when the GWR published specific details of the runs when there was an agreement in place between both companies not to disclose them before a mutually agreed period. This only added to the general disappointment felt by Gresley over the performance of his engines, but he was convinced that better displays could and would be given by the 'A1s'.

BELOW No 2559 *The Tetrarch* was converted to long-travel valve gear in January 1930. The engine is seen at Doncaster shed in 1936, during an allocation that lasted from July 1934 to March 1938.

Prior to the trials Gresley's Technical Assistant, Bert Spencer, had attempted to persuade the CME to accept a proposal to alter the valve gear from short travel to long travel. The use of the latter had largely been shunned due to concerns over increased wear, but this objection was only relevant when concerning long travel of slide valves, which had only relatively recently been replaced by piston valves. G. J. Churchward of the GWR was quick to seize upon this fact and his designs had been fitted with long-travel valve gear since the early years of the 20th century. Therefore his engines, and the company's subsequent designs, had an improved flow of steam in and out of the cylinders and shorter cut-offs could be used. While 'Castle' No 4079 *Pendennis Castle* was at Doncaster for the 1925 trials the opportunity was taken to measure the valve setting of the locomotive; No 4082 *Windsor Castle* was similarly treated when at Stockton for the Railway Centenary parade in July 1925. With the measurements in hand Doncaster Works – without Spencer's involvement – was ordered to convert No 4477 *Gay Crusader* with a 1^5/$_8$-inch steam lap and a valve travel of 5¾ inches, increased from 4^9/$_{16}$ inches. Extensive tests were carried out in August 1925 but the improvement was only slight and not enough to warrant significant expenditure on altering the whole class. Spencer would not be moved on his position, arguing that the setting as applied to No 4477 was inaccurate due to short-cuts taken, such as using the existing motion components.

Gresley finally relented in late 1926 and allowed No 2555 *Centenary* to have the valves set by Spencer with ^{1}/$_8$-inch lead steam, 1-inch lap and no exhaust lap, maximum valve travel 5¾ inches; the centre cylinder retained ^{1}/$_{16}$-inch additional lap. Greater attention was paid to the set-up of the motion as the upper arm of the combination lever was increased in length. When Spencer was satisfied that the valve events at 15% cut-off would be at their optimum level, No 2555 was altered in March 1927. After the engine was tested against No 2559 *The Tetrarch*, the saving in coal was recorded as being 12lb per mile over the original valve gear – down from 50lb to 38lb, or just over 1½ tons if a normal journey was made between Doncaster and King's Cross. Gresley appears to have been quite astonished by the result and had to accompany the engine on a journey before he was convinced that the alteration was worthwhile; the water consumption was also recorded as 9lb less per drawbar horsepower hour than normal less than normal. On 14 May 1927 authorisation for the modification of the whole 'A1' class was given to Doncaster and the engines were altered from November 1927 to May 1931.

Gresley changed his mind about using a higher boiler pressure before the fruition of this work was reached, although the reason he did is unclear. He was perhaps swayed, again, by the performance of the 'Castles' and by other engines, such as R. E. L. Maunsell using 220lb boilers on the SR 'Lord Nelson' class and Sir Henry Fowler's 'Royal Scot' class on the LMSR, which used 250lb per sq in. Gresley had previously dismissed the use of such pressures because of the first cost being higher and the maintenance requirements being greater, thus outweighing potential benefits in fuel consumption and efficient use of steam. He had attempted to side-step the issue of raising the pressure by increasing the temperature of the steam by superheating further using an increased number of elements. An 'E double'-type superheater with 64 elements was fitted to No 2562 *Isinglass* and 'P1' class 2-8-2 No 2394 in order to achieve this. In the event the temperature was only 31°F higher than the standard arrangement, leading to the rejection of the equipment. In the early part of 1927 Gresley instructed Doncaster Works to produce a new design for the Pacific boiler with a 43-element superheater, then almost immediately amending these orders to increase the pressure to 220lb per sq in. This was soon completed and five boilers ordered. No 4480 *Enterprise* was the first 'A1' to be fitted with the diagram 94HP in July 1927, then being reclassified 'A3'. The number of tubes was reduced to 125 of 2¼-inch diameter and the elements were of ^{17}/$_{32}$-inch diameter with 43 flues 5¼ inches in diameter. The total heating surface was slightly reduced to 2736.6sq ft but the superheater surface area was increased from 525sq ft to 706sq ft. With the cylinders remaining at 20-inch diameter, the nominal tractive effort was increased to 36,465lb. The following conversion, No 2544 *Lemberg* in December 1927, had the cylinders lined down to 18¼-inch diameter for a closer comparison with the 'A1' class and the tractive effort became 30,362lb. The weight of the engine was increased by the new boiler by 3.8 tons to 96 tons 5 cwt, and the adhesion weight was increased by over 6 tons to 66 tons 2 cwt.

Contemporary observer and writer on locomotive performance C. J. Allen recorded an immediate change in the working of the 'A3' locomotive, also with the revised valve gear arrangement, when riding on the footplate of No 4480 soon after conversion. He compared the working to 'A1' No 1473 *Solario* shortly after construction, where the engine was generally given partially opened regulator and cut-off set around 45% when working normally. No 4480 saw the cut-off reduced to 15% for the easier sections and not much higher than 20% on the remainder of the line.

Despite this immediate change the question of economy had a more elusive answer. Trials between the 'A3' class Pacific and an 'A1' were not organised until February 1928, when No 2544 was used against No 4473, both having run about 5,000 miles since the last general overhaul. The services for the tests were the 11.04am King's Cross to Doncaster and 4.00pm return. No 4473 went first on 13 February, performing six round trips, followed by No 2544, which only worked five returns due to the dynamometer car being required elsewhere. The average

ABOVE No 2562 *Isinglass* was the last 'A1' Pacific to be built at Doncaster Works in July 1925.

weight that No 4473 handled from Doncaster was 435 tons and from King's Cross to Peterborough 491 tons, then 331 tons to Doncaster. *Solario* had to work against adverse weather conditions and this caused a higher coal consumption figure of 38.83lb per mile or 3.08lb per drawbar horsepower. No 2544 had a slightly lighter train on average from Doncaster at 428 tons, while heading down to Peterborough the figure was 506 tons, reduced to 348 tons for Doncaster. The coal consumption figure was 35.37lb per mile and 3.12lb per drawbar horsepower. In terms of average speeds No 2544 was roughly 2mph faster than the 'A1' class locomotive. Despite these close results Gresley had already made his decision to perpetuate the 'A3' class as approval for 10 new engines had been given in August 1927. The first frames were in the New Erecting Shop at Doncaster on 24 February 1928 – the last day of the comparative tests. A further 17 new 'A3s' would be constructed up to 1935 and the remaining 'A1s' were converted when the original boilers required replacement. The cylinder diameter of the 'A3s' was standardised at a 19-inch nominal diameter, the tractive effort becoming 32,909lb. The boiler was slightly modified for the new engines as 125 small tubes were present, which increased the heating surface to 2,736.6sq ft, and the superheater heating surface was 3sq ft greater than originally.

On 11 July 1927 the LNER introduced a relief train to the 'Flying Scotsman' service between King's Cross and Edinburgh Waverley stations, leaving the former at 9.50am (except Tuesdays, Wednesdays and Saturdays) and heading to Newcastle non-stop in 5 hours 30 minutes for the 268 miles; the first train was hauled by No 4475 *Flying Fox*. This overtook the previous British record for a non-stop train, which had been held by the 'Cornish Riviera' express since the early years of the 20th century. In the following summer the LNER went further by making the 'Flying Scotsman' non-stop between the English and Scottish capitals in a time of 8 hours 15 minutes. This slow running time was restricted through an agreement reached between the East and West Coast railway companies after the 'Races to the North' in 1895, when a lot of hard and dangerous running had been made to reach Aberdeen in the quickest time. By the late 1920s this restriction was outdated given the power of the engines at the disposal of the LNER and the LMSR in the form of the 'A1' and 'A3' Pacifics and 'Royal Scot' 4-6-0s, but remained in force nevertheless.

In 1928 the non-stop 'Flying Scotsman' became the longest such journey in the world by regularly completing 392¾ miles, but in order to achieve this feat of endurance Gresley saw fit to provide a means of connection between the footplate and the train in order to change the crews about halfway through the journey. In late 1927 he devised the corridor tender, which featured a passageway running along the right-hand side, 18 inches wide and 5 feet high, to achieve the switchover. Other improvements included the addition of space available for a further 1 ton of coal. Ten corridor tenders were ordered along with the ten 'A3s' of 1928, but only three of these were paired with the new type of tender; a further three went to the conversions to 'A3', with the other four going to 'A1s'. The construction of the first tender was performed by Doncaster in the impressive time of 50 days from the arrival of the plans to engine No 4472 *Flying Scotsman* being in receipt of the new tender. The other engines coupled were Nos 4476, 2573, 2580, 2546, 2569, 2556, 2565, 2744 and 2745 in numerical order beginning with tender No 5323 and ending with No 5332. An interesting point is that the weight displaced by the presence of the corridor had to be balanced, and weights were provided beneath the floor. As a means to publicise the non-stop run, both No 4472 and No 4476 *Royal Lancer* were put on display with the corridor tenders at King's Cross and the connection was open to the public.

The first non-stop 'Flying Scotsman' ran on 1 May 1928 with No 4472 taking the down train and No 2580 *Shotover* heading south. At King's Cross a large crowd of people gathered to see the departure at 10.00am. Prior to this the engine and train had been inspected by the Lord Mayor of London Sir Charles Batho, who was accompanied by the Chief General Manager of the LNER Sir Ralph Wedgwood. The train weighed 386 tons tare, 400 tons gross, with Driver A. Pibworth and Fireman W. Goddard of King's Cross shed on the footplate first, being relieved past York by Driver T. Blades and Fireman W. Morris of Gateshead; Locomotive Inspector Bramall was also present. The running was quite leisurely and the highest average speed on the down train was 54.5mph and the lowest 44.9mph between Doncaster and York. Arrival was made at 6.02pm with a large crowd cheering in the train; officials of the Scottish Area, such as Mr A. C. Stamer, the Assistant CME, were on hand to greet the travellers, which included Gresley. An estimated 2 tons of coal remained in the tender at this time, approximating to a coal consumption of 34lb per engine mile; the water consumption was about 2,500 gallons per 100 miles.

A similar ceremony was presided over at Waverley by General Manager, Scotland, Mr J. Calder, with Edinburgh's senior Magistrate Bailie Hay and his daughter inspecting the train. The latter presented Driver Henderson and Fireman R. McKenzie of Haymarket and Driver J. Day and Fireman F. Gray of King's Cross with rosettes of black and white (the city's colours) and silver badges of the arms of Edinburgh. Driver Henderson also accepted a similarly decorated horseshoe for luck. The journey was completed 1 minute early without any incidents occurring. The highest booked average speed was 49.3mph between Edinburgh and Berwick, while the lowest was 44.6mph on to Newcastle. The crews were greeted at King's Cross by Chairman of the LNER William Whitelaw and Sir Ralph Wedgwood. The warm reception was not confined to the two ends of the East Coast Main Line, but at numerous points along the route where many people gathered to watch the trains go past. A. J. Mullay, in *Non Stop! London to Scotland Steam*, records that by 25 September 250 journeys between the capitals had been completed and the total mileage was 98,165. Only one late arrival occurred on 14 August when a vehicle on the line caused the down train to be over half an hour late.

Not to be outdone by such a service, in 1927 the LMSR had run the 'Royal Scot' train (from Euston to Glasgow) between Euston and Carnforth (236 miles) non-stop before extending this to Carlisle (299 miles) in the winter timetable for 1927/28. To steal the LNER's limelight in 1928 the LMS ran two non-stops on 27 April from Euston to Glasgow and Euston to Edinburgh – the journey length for both being about 400 miles. 'Royal Scot' class No 6113 *Cameronian* took the former and Midland Railway 4-4-0 No 1034 the latter, both arriving just before time. The performance of the crews is worthy of highlight for the fact that there was no relief for them on the footplate for the length of the 8-hour journey. With such a feat of endurance becoming a regular occurrence being impossible, this was a one-off that the LNER hierarchy and staff presumably thought little of.

At the time of Grouping the financial prospects of the LNER had been average at best. A number of the constituents were in a poor state and the NER was the only one in a strong position. In the first year the total receipts from traffic of £68.8 million were considered poor after operating expenses were deducted to leave £14 million in net revenue. The actual amount needed to cover share and loan obligations was £500,000 more, and this sum had to be found from a contingency source. Passenger revenue accounted for £17.5 million and 240 million passenger journeys (excluding season tickets) were completed during the year; these would prove to be the best results the LNER recorded up to nationalisation of the railways in 1948. In 1924 a small drop in business occurred before a real slump was felt in 1925. The catastrophic year was 1926 when the prolonged miners' strike then the General Strike caused the number of passenger journeys to fall to 190 million and only £14.8 million was taken in receipts. A similar story was encountered with freight traffic; the total receipts from this were £48.6 million and the net revenue was £4.6 million. Passengers came back in 1927 and this continued to 1929 before the effects of the Wall Street crash and the Great Depression began to be felt. The company had 214 million passenger journeys with £14.3 million received, contributing to the total revenue of £55.6 million and net revenue of £13 million. In 1931 the lowest drop in passenger numbers occurred when only 189 million journeys were made in comparison with 206 million the previous year; total receipts were just £47.2 million. The lowest pre-war passenger figure came in 1932 with only 182 million journeys being made – a loss of 58 million from the 1923 figure – and passenger receipts were £11.5 million. The LNER's fortunes would improve the following year with the public using more services, adding 5 million journeys to the previous year's total, and the recovery continued to 1935 when 201 million ordinary passenger journeys were made. In 1937 a return to the 1929 figure

ABOVE The Chicago, Burlington & Quincy Railroad's 'Zephyr' railcar revolutionised the company's services.

occurred, but in 1938, with the mini-recession that took place, 18 million passenger journeys were lost. Freight receipts reached a low of £26.5 million in 1932 but again an upturn was experienced and £31.1 million was taken in 1937. Many areas of industry were served by the LNER, such as the Yorkshire coalfield and the steelworks of Tyneside, making the company more susceptible to economic pressures on these than was the case with other railways.

The company's position was not helped by the Government restrictions on rate setting, as competitive prices for services could not be offered. This was also the case for the other three companies and left the railways vulnerable to competition, a position that was gainfully exploited by the burgeoning road haulage industry. The LNER attempted to cope with this, and the many financial crises in the 1920s and 1930s, by saving money and cutting costs wherever possible. For example, in 1929 the company claimed that £1 million had been saved as the result of economical driving methods employed by the footplate crews. Additionally, there were cuts in staff levels and wages, although in the latter instance these cuts were revoked when the financial position of the company allowed. The LNER sold several assets during the 1930s, including Tyne Dock for £800,000. The Government assisted to a degree by abolishing passenger duty in 1929, but this was done with the proviso that the vast majority of the money saved would be reinvested in works schemes; the annual duty was approximately £1.5 million. The second half of the 1930s saw the formation of the Railway Finance Corporation, which was authorised to raise £26,500,000 for improvements of the railways. This was guaranteed by the Treasury and a further £3 million was provided by the 'Big Four' companies. The

LNER received £6 million at first, then an additional £4 million in 1937. The money was spent on the Woodhead route electrification scheme, station and line improvements and new rolling stock, including 43 locomotives.

The situation was not unique to Britain as tough operating conditions were to be found all over the globe. For instance, in America the railway companies faced increasing threats from both air and road travel and their fares were also Government controlled. The rise of the motor car had a considerable impact on the industry during the 1920s, as between the end of the First World War and 1928 the number of new car registrations jumped from 3.5 million to 29 million. During this period the number of passenger journeys was halved. In 1938 *The Engineer* reported that at the annual meeting of the American Society of Civil Engineers Mr L. I. Hewes (an expert in road construction) had said that in the last 10 years road use had increased by 73% and the number of trucks had grown by 47% compared with 22% for the car. Air travel in America began to grow in the mid-1920s as the Government attempted to improve the fortunes of the aircraft industry by subsidising companies to the effect of $100 per passenger carried. A further loss to the railroads was the carriage of mail, which became increasingly the preserve of airlines that could cover the great distances involved in North America much more quickly and easily than the railroads. In the 1930s the American Post Office invested some £10.5 million in switching mail carriage from the rails. In the Great Depression

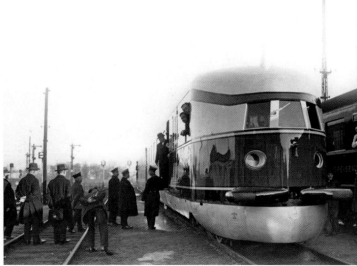

ABOVE LEFT Following closely behind the Burlington was the Union Pacific, with M10000 and the record-breaking M10001, shown here.

ABOVE RIGHT Deutsche Reichsbahn's high-speed railcar the 'Flying Hamburger', which impressed the LNER officials and Gresley.

the railroads were particularly hit and roughly 1 million employees had to be dismissed, corresponding to 40% of the total workforce. By 1935 16 American railroads were bankrupt, while another 89 were close to the same fate.

Because of these pressures some railroad companies attempted to economise as far as possible. Others sought to make an improvement to their services while still keeping costs down. This latter was the route taken by the Chicago, Burlington & Quincy Railroad, which was under the direction of former Civil Engineer Ralph Budd. He had come to the company in 1932 with the remit of turning around the fortunes of the railroad after a quarter of the freight traffic and a third of the passenger traffic had been lost. While looking for an idea Budd became aware of Edward Budd (no immediate relation) who was a pioneer in the use of steel for car bodies and had branched out to construct an experimental lightweight stainless steel railcar. The two joined forces to design a similar rail vehicle in late 1933 and the first 'Burlington Zephyr' appeared in April 1934. The carriages were constructed entirely of stainless steel and fabricated through welding. There were three carriages, which were articulated and accommodated 72 passengers along with mail and luggage compartments; there was also an observation car at the rear. For traction a diesel engine of 600 horsepower was employed and coupled to an electric generator, which then powered traction motors coupled to the axles. For the first trip a long, non-stop journey of 1,015 miles between Denver and Chicago was scheduled for 26 May 1934 and several members of the press were invited. The total time for this to be

completed was 13 hours 5 minutes 44 seconds and an overall average speed of 77.6mph was recorded; the maximum speed attained was 112½mph over a distance of 3 miles. The run was quite a publicity coup for the railroad and thousands of people lined the route to catch a glimpse of the new vehicle. Additionally, the train was displayed at the Chicago World Fair and toured the country subsequently. A feature film, called *The Silver Streak*, featuring the 'Zephyr' was also made.

The Union Pacific built a similar train, M10000, which entered service slightly earlier in February 1934 and employed a distillate oil engine, as the preferred diesel engine had not yet been fully developed by the manufacturer. Again this was a 600-horsepower unit and the train was of three articulated carriages with the front serving as a power car/luggage compartment, while two passenger cars provided accommodation for 116 passengers. The material used for construction was aluminium alloy, which meant that at a total weight of 85 tons the whole train was considerably lighter than a standard formation of nearly 1,000 tons. Later in the year a second train, M10001, was constructed with a diesel engine and was in the headlines for making a long-distance journey between Los Angeles and New York (3,259 miles) in 56 hours 55 minutes. Both of the trains toured the US extensively after their construction before entering revenue-earning service, and were seen by millions of people.

Part of the attraction to these trains was the unique external appearance – they were streamlined. Several industrial designers, such as Raymond Loewy, Norman Bel Geddes and Otto Kuhler, had contributed to this movement during the 1920s and had applied the style to several products, from clocks and toasters to cars and buses. The application of streamlining to locomotives was as much for publicity purposes as any aerodynamic considerations. The benefits were mainly in the individuality gained by certain railroads in using the

ABOVE Gresley and Bulleid travelled with Bugatti on his petrol railcar between Deauville and Paris.

made his name constructing racing cars and luxury vehicles. A venture in this latter area had caused him to diversify and build a railcar design for submission to the État. Bugatti's Type 41 car was an extremely expensive model aimed at the European aristocracy, but he had started the project in the late 1920s at the time of the great financial calamity. A total of five were constructed before plans for others had to be abandoned, but several petrol engines were already in stock. Bugatti chose to use four of these engines in his railcar, providing a total of 800 horsepower and top speeds of well over 100mph; seating was for 52 passengers. Being well aware of the reduction in air resistance required at high speed through experiments conducted with his racing cars, Bugatti adopted his most successful 'wedge-shaped' front, which was taken from the Type 32 racing car of 1923. The railcar was so successful on the test run, reaching 107mph, that several more were immediately ordered. Elsewhere in France, the Nord Railway followed the lead of the Bugatti cars and received two railcars consisting of three vehicles in 1934 for services between Paris, Lille and Tourcoing. The engines were Maybach 820-horsepower diesel units. Streamlining was also incorporated.

The application of streamlining was certainly partly based on publicity, which was needed in the climate of the time, but there was a definite scientific argument for the modification of the designs of rail vehicles in order to reduce the resistance that the air placed on them in traffic. This was not a new idea as Reverend Samuel Calthrop had patented a design for a locomotive and train in 1865 that was covered in a smooth metal skin in order to reduce the losses of power to the air. This came to naught and only sporadic effort was made on the subject by rail engineers in France and the USA until a more serious approach was taken in the late 1920s and early 1930s.

One man who drew attention to the subject in Britain was F. C. Johansen, who worked at the National Physical Laboratory

practice, therefore a train would be distinct from a competitor and more likely to be used by the consumer because of the inferences that the style created – modernity and the prosperity of the company (M10000 cost over $200,000).

Across the Atlantic similar problems were being experienced in Europe and were tackled in several countries. In Germany the Deutsche Reichsbahn developed a streamlined railcar, the 'Fliegender Hamburger' or 'Flying Hamburger'. This project had taken several years to complete and the railcar had been specially tested in a wind tunnel to find the best design to reduce air resistance when travelling at high speed – edges were rounded off and skirting covered the wheels and undercarriage. The train was put to work on the Berlin to Hamburg line running the 178 miles in 138 minutes at an average speed of 77.4mph with a maximum speed of 100mph. Two Maybach diesel engines were employed (each developing 410 horsepower) and connected to electric traction motors. The two carriages were articulated and formed a large saloon with a bar in the centre; a cold buffet was provided for the 102 passengers (usually businessmen who were targeted as the clientele). The railcar first ran on 15 May 1933 and was met with great acclaim.

In France the État (State Railway) went down a similar route and introduced high-speed railcars on the Paris to Deauville route. These were manufactured by Ettore Bugatti, who had

RIGHT The wind tunnel was an important tool that the railways only began to use in the 1930s. Pictured is the LMSR's example, installed at Derby Works, which could emulate wind speeds up to 100mph.

ABOVE 'A3' Pacific No 2795 *Call Boy* leaves King's Cross with the 'Flying Scotsman'. The locomotive was a favourite on the train in the late 1920s and early 1930s.

and conducted wind tunnel tests there for both his own research and for the LMSR and LNER on the air resistance of trains and locomotives, also extending to smoke deflection. In an article written by him in *The Engineer* of 10 February 1928 he commented on the method of experimenting with model trains in a wind tunnel, the results to be gained from these and the benefits of the railway companies doing so. In the piece he says that the use of scale models is desirable in industries where full-scale tests or the extrapolation of principles is problematic and prohibitive due to costs. He points to the ship-building industry and aeronautics as two that have benefitted from many useful tests and the valuable conclusions drawn from them, with their application to full size being quite satisfactory. Johansen suggests the railways could benefit from the wind tunnel as the difficulty in creating the correct conditions for testing on the track is insurmountable, as is the task of segregating the effect of air resistance from the other forces acting on the train. Johansen comments that further investigation is necessary because the air resistance rises quite considerably as the speed of the train increases, and as higher speeds are being attempted all the time attention on the subject is justified because there was very little data to be consulted. He gives the example that at 60mph a train's air resistance accounts for 36% of the total resistance, and the horsepower used by the locomotive to overcome this is 346. To illustrate the potential saving that further investigation could cause, a simple calculation is presented, showing that if 6lb of coal per

drawbar horsepower hour was used and the cost of coal was 30 shillings per ton, over an hour's work at this rate 28 shillings is spent on overcoming the air resistance. Johansen writes that several problems will have to be overcome, not least the 'scale effect' (the different value of variable forces acting on the model and extrapolated up to an actual train), for reliable data to be gained from wind tunnel tests on locomotives. The author notes that through tests on other objects, such as an airship, the inaccuracy due to the 'scale effect' was found to be in the region of 10%. Yet under the same conditions the ships and aeroplanes had been tested, with no ill effects experienced by the finished designs. The 'scale effect' might have a bearing on a full-size finished train, but when the air resistance is measured against changes in the shape of the train more reliable results are produced. If a modification to the form is accompanied by a 20% reduction of the air resistance, a reasonable assumption is that this will be realised at full scale. This is because the resistance coefficient is markedly affected by velocity and weight values whereas there is little change manifested by alterations in form.

The feature that was perhaps directly responsible for the popularity of the various diesel railcars, on the part of the passengers, was the high speed at which they travelled. This often beat, by some distance, the time taken by steam locomotives hauling the expresses of the time. In 1932 the agreement between the LMSR and LNER was finally discarded and from 18 July the timing for the LNER's premier train was reduced to 7 hours 30 minutes. The section times were pressed closer to a 60mph average speed, this being near to the requirement for the sections between King's Cross and Peterborough and York and Darlington. The 27 miles between Hitchin and Huntingdon were allowed 22 minutes and the average speed needed for this to be completed successfully was 73½mph. No 4472 *Flying Scotsman* again handled the first down train (383 tons), finishing the journey 3 minutes 30 seconds ahead of time. The down train (315 tons) was hauled by No 2795 *Call Boy*, which arrived early by just 1 minute. There was evidently still room for improvement on the times as observers noted that the train was still keeping time easily. The timings north of Newcastle remained generous as 2½ hours were scheduled for the 124½ miles at an average speed of 49.8mph. Before the 'Flying Scotsman' accelerations, the 7.50am Leeds to King's Cross (unofficially known as the

'Breakfast Flyer' and aimed at businessmen) had 11 minutes removed from the timings between Grantham and King's Cross, making the 105½-mile trip in 1 hour 40 minutes at an average speed of 63.3mph with around 300-315 tons. This increase in speed made the train the fastest non-stop over 100 miles in Europe.

The LMSR was also quick to cut service times, with 15 minutes discarded from the Euston to Manchester schedule, the new timing being 3 hours 15 minutes. The 5.20pm from Liverpool with one stop was allowed 3 hours 45 minutes, but the new schedule had 25 minutes removed and two stops were made. The 'Royal Scot' had 15 minutes less to complete the journey between the two capitals. The GWR was not content to be left out. In 1932 the 'Cheltenham Flyer', having run the 77 miles between Swindon and Paddington at an average speed of 66.2mph in 70 minutes from 1929, was accelerated to complete the same section in 65 minutes at an average speed of 71.4mph

After the inauguration of the 'Flying Hamburger' in May 1933 the LNER Board authorised an expedition to Germany in order for some of the company's senior engineering officials to report back on the new marvel and advise on the possibility of a similar train being used on the East Coast Main Line. Gresley's assistant, O. V. S. Bulleid, led the party on their expedition the following month, when restricted access was given to the train and a meeting was held between Dr Maybach and Bulleid. Gresley inspected the train himself in early 1934 and he later commented on the journeys he made in his Presidential Address to the Institution of Mechanical Engineers in 1936: '…I was so much impressed with the

BELOW No 2750 *Papyrus* was posed for this picture with the dynamometer car and train after breaking the world speed for steam traction.

smooth running of the train at a speed of 100mph, which was maintained for long distances, that I thought it advisable to explore the possibilities of extra high-speed travel by having such a train for experimental purposes on the London & North Eastern Railway. I accordingly approached the makers of the train and furnished them with the full particulars as to the gradients, curves and speed restrictions on the line between King's Cross and Newcastle.' Gresley goes on to describe some details of the submission: 'The train, weighing 115 tons, was to consist of three articulated coaches and to be generally similar to the German train. The times for the complete journey were given as 4 hours 17 minutes in the up direction and 4 hours 15 minutes 30 seconds in the down. The train provided seating for 140 passengers.' Gresley states that this was unsatisfactory to the LNER and that: 'My Chief General Manager suggested that with an ordinary Pacific engine faster overall speeds could be maintained with a train of much greater weight, capacity and comfort.'

The test was scheduled for 30 November 1934, running between King's Cross and Leeds. Driver Bill Sparshatt and Fireman Webster were on the footplate of No 4472 *Flying Scotsman*, which had run 44,176 miles since last the overhaul. A light train of 145 tons was formed from the dynamometer car, a first class corridor, dining car and brake van (roughly equalling the seating provided by the 'Flying Hamburger'), and left at 9.08am. The start was vigorous and Finsbury Park was passed in 4 minutes for the 2½ miles. The speed was 71½mph as *Flying Scotsman* passed Wood Green while heading up the 7 miles to Potters Bar, and here the speed had only dropped to 67½mph. Passing Hatfield at 83mph No 4472 continued at a similar pace on to Peterborough, recording 93½mph at Hitchin and completing the 27 miles to Huntingdon in 18 minutes 9 seconds at an average speed of 89.2mph; 20 minutes had been scheduled for the section. Peterborough was passed in 60 minutes 39 seconds from

King's Cross, or 5 minutes 21 seconds early. The time taken by *Flying Scotsman* from Peterborough to Stoke summit – 23½ miles of adverse gradients – was 19 minutes 54 seconds at an average speed of 70.8mph; the last 10 miles from Little Bytham to Stoke were covered at an average of 82½mph on the 1 in 200. A high of 87mph was reached on the down gradient to Grantham, which was passed in 83 minutes 39 seconds, or 8 minutes 21 seconds early. The time from Peterborough to Grantham was 23 minutes for the 29.1 miles. C. J. Allen, who was recording the run, suggested that the engine was slightly eased after these exertions and *Flying Scotsman* went on to complete the journey of 185 miles from King's Cross to Leeds Central in 151 minutes 56 seconds, or 13 minutes 4 seconds early.

For the journey back to London, which departed at 2.00pm, two corridor thirds were added to the formation, taking the weight up to 207 tons gross. The train made good progress to Wakefield and at Doncaster the passing time was 30 minutes 58 seconds from Leeds. *Flying Scotsman* accelerated quickly from the slack at Doncaster to 77½mph at Black Carr Junction then 88mph at Scrooby. The speed remained high to Grantham, which was passed in 39 minutes for the 50 miles from Doncaster at an average speed of 75.6mph. Driver Sparshatt then pushed *Flying Scotsman* to the limit down Stoke Bank. Allen recorded the top speed as 97½mph for half a mile (he also repeated this figure later that evening when relaying details of the run to millions of British householders as part of a segment on the BBC's 9 O'clock News) but upon closer inspection of the dynamometer car record later the train had actually reached 100mph before passing Little Bytham, setting a world speed record for steam traction. The time from Grantham to Peterborough was 21 minutes 42 seconds while the average speed from Stoke to Werrington Junction was 87.2mph The train was now running 8 minutes early and only a few seconds were lost to arrival at King's Cross in 157 minutes 17 seconds from Leeds, or 7 minutes 43 seconds before schedule. Of the 371.4 miles travelled during the day, *Flying Scotsman* stayed above an 80mph average speed for 250 miles.

On 4 January 1935 a summary of the test was presented to the Board and authorisation was given for a further trial between King's Cross and Newcastle in preparation for the proposed new high-speed service to begin later in the year. Tests took place on 5 March 1935 with 'A3' class locomotive No 2570 *Papyrus*, which had run 7,719 miles from receiving a general repair. Driver Gutteridge and Fireman Wightman from King's Cross shed took the train out of the station, again at 9.08am. The train consisted of six carriages, weighing 217 tons gross, but the start was not as energetic as previously and in general Driver Gutteridge kept as far as possible to the section times. Hatfield, Hitchin and Huntingdon were all passed a few seconds

early, with 82.8mph averaged between the latter two places and a maximum speed of 88mph achieved. Peterborough was passed 2 minutes 16 seconds early and on to Stoke the climb was made at around 75mph; the time for the 10 miles between Little Bytham and Great Ponton was 7 minutes 47 seconds. Just less than 3 minutes were taken to Grantham from there, the train being 3 minutes 53 seconds early on the scheduled time of 10.40am and had taken 24 minutes 21 seconds from Peterborough. *Papyrus* was travelling at 78mph at Rossington, 4½ miles south of Doncaster, before fate intervened in the form of a derailed freight train at Arksey, just north of the town. Doncaster was passed 40 seconds early but the engine was brought to a stand at Moat Hills signal box for 24 seconds before setting off and negotiating the single-line working past the accident. Despite pressing the engine hard (83mph was reached between Arksey and Selby), Gutteridge could not prevent a loss of 2 minutes 33 seconds on the timing. Further hard running to York brought back over a minute and the city was passed at 11.53am after completing the section in 12 minutes 57 seconds on the scheduled 14 minutes for the 14 miles. On the level past York No 2750 attained 79mph by Beningbrough and maintained just over 80mph on the level track to Northallerton where the train was now 1 minute 57 seconds early. The engine remained in front to Newcastle and a total time of 237 minutes 10 seconds, or 2 minutes 50 seconds early, was recorded. The average speed was 67.9mph.

The locomotive was given a short rest before the return to London was made at 3.47pm. Driver Sparshatt and Fireman Webster were in charge of the up train, which was not altered in formation; they had travelled from King's Cross in the train especially for the duty. Sparshatt had a slow start from Newcastle but on to York the time for the section was 72 minutes 8 seconds, or 3 minutes 12 seconds early. This gain had almost been lost completely at Doncaster, which was passed at 5.33:47pm. The up line had been cleared from the morning's derailment but a restriction was still in force, leaving the train only 13 seconds early. Between Doncaster and Retford the average speed for the 17 miles was 75.6mph and a high of 85½ was achieved. The running was steady on to

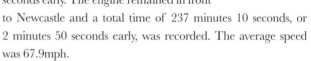

ABOVE No 10000's front-end design was an important step towards finding an adequate method of deflecting smoke away from the cab. The locomotive is seen at Leeds with an express.
Yorkshire Post Newspapers

Newark and Grantham, the times being 1 minute and 50 seconds early respectively. At Grantham 2 hours 28 minutes 40 seconds had elapsed. The speed was 68½mph, giving *Papyrus* a good start for Stoke summit. The 5½ miles of 1 in 200 were taken at roughly 70mph. Once over the top No 2750 was let go and at Little Bytham, 7¾ miles on, was travelling at 105mph and peaked at 108mph before Essendine. Between Corby and Essendine (12.3 miles) the time taken was 7 minutes 22 seconds and the average speed was 100.6mph At the record speed the cut-off was 32% with full regulator; the wheel revolutions were 453 per minute and the piston speed was 1,965 feet per minute. The train was 5 minutes 8 seconds early passing Peterborough but there was no more spectacular running and arrival was made at King's Cross at 2 seconds short of 7.39pm, or 8 minutes before due. The total time from Newcastle was 231 minutes 48 seconds at an average speed of 69.4mph. The coal consumption for the journey was 10 tons 15 cwt, or 44.93lb per mile.

Only a few days after the trial a preliminary drawing was handed to Sir Ralph Wedgwood for a new design of locomotive to haul the prospective train. Both this and the service were authorised by the LNER Board at the end of March 1935. In Gresley's Presidential Address of 1936 he also comments about why he chose a new design, when 'A3' No 2750 *Papyrus* had proved capable in the test. He said: 'I felt that to secure a sufficient margin of power it would be essential to streamline the engine and train as effectively as possible and at the same time to make sundry alterations to the design of the cylinders and boiler which would conduce to freer running and to securing an ample reserve of power for fast uphill running.' Gresley qualified this latter part by explaining that a 30mph increase in speed running downhill would only save 5 minutes, whereas if the same improvement in speed was made on the uphill section 15 minutes would be gained. He also noted the savings in horsepower that can be obtained from the use of streamlining to overcome air resistance. Although Gresley does not state when these tests between a normal Pacific model and a streamlined Pacific model took place (Eric Bannister, Draughtsman at Doncaster, recalls in his book that streamlining tests had been conducted before those for smoke deflection, suggesting a date around late 1934/early 1935); he recounts several savings of horsepower that were theoretically made by the streamlined design. At 60mph the saving figure was 40.82; at 80mph 96.90; 189.56 at 100mph; and 327.33 at 120mph. These figures do not take into account the wind or the varying angles of direction that this hits the train from which would have affected the outcome.

Gresley omits to mention the importance that was placed on the design of the streamlining for deflecting smoke and exhaust away from the cab. He had been concerned with this for several years and experiments had been undertaken on a variety of locomotives. The first LNER engine to feature a modified front was the high-pressure 'W1' class 4-6-4 (or 4-6-2-2) locomotive No 10000, which had been built at Darlington in late 1929. Earlier in the year wind tunnel tests on a model of the engine had been conducted by Professor W. E. Dalby of the City & Guilds Engineering College to determine a shape that would adequately deflect smoke away. The final arrangement saw the top of the smokebox slant at an angle of 18 degrees with the outer casing funnelling a stream of air to the chimney. Although there do not appear to be any details on how successful this was in service, there were no modifications made until after a Kylchap double blastpipe and chimney were fitted in 1935, when a cowl was placed between the sides of the chimney and the boiler casing.

On 22 March 1931 the LMSR's 'Royal Scot' train hauled by 'Royal Scot' class 4-6-0 No 6114 Coldstream Guardsman was derailed at high speed at Leighton Buzzard station. Three were killed, including the driver and fireman, and a further 15 were seriously injured. As the crew were victims of the crash, the cause was difficult to pinpoint. There was a possibility that exhaust steam had obscured the view forward from the footplate at the vital moment when a danger signal was passed prior to the train being diverted to a different line than normally used through the station. As a result the train went though the switch at high speed (no braking was noted until the last moment), causing the derailment. With this seeming the most likely scenario in an otherwise unexplained crash, the subject of smoke deflection came to the fore. On the LNER Gresley quickly instructed King's Cross Drawing Office to prepare a suitable arrangement for one of the Pacifics. No 2747 Coronach was the locomotive selected and the arrangement as fitted kept the circular shape of the smokebox but had the top section removed and a duct inserted, being at an angle of 13 degrees to direct air out of openings at the rear of the chimney. This did not work well enough for Gresley and soon afterwards trials were performed with No 2747 in October 1931. No 2751 Humorist was fitted with a similar arrangement, together with a double chimney. The rear portion of this allowed the air drawn through the vent to discharge immediately behind the exhaust. This was also found to be unsatisfactory as the air from the rear chimney just cut through the exhaust. After a few more unsuccessful alterations Gresley had Humorist's smokebox top cut away and vertical pieces of metal attached to the top of the smokebox. The angle of the slant was increased to 22 degrees but when under test in March 1933 eddy currents were experienced behind the chimney. Steps were taken to prevent these and the new arrangement proved to work well. However, no further action was taken and No 2751 went back to standard in 1934.

Gresley was quite concerned about the external appearance of his locomotives and this modification of the design after the fact probably did not sit too well with him. In May 1934 his 'P2' class 2-8-2 No 2001 Cock o' the North entered traffic with a front-end arrangement similar to No 10000. This was one of several unusual features present on the locomotive and added to the impressiveness of the engine, which was the largest and most powerful passenger engine in the country at the time. Cock o' the North was the culmination of several experiments Gresley had been conducting with feedwater heaters and poppet valves. Both of these appealed to Gresley as they offered increased efficiency of operation, especially the feedwater heater. While railway engineers on the Continent and America had found some success with these, this eluded Gresley to a certain extent and problems always seemed to accompany their application.

No 2001 also featured several modifications to the steam circuit in order to increase efficiency. These had been developed by Gresley's long-time acquaintance on the Paris-Orleans Railway in France, André Chapelon. He transformed several classes on the railway by taking a closer look at the design and applying thermodynamic theory to make improvements. The first change concerned the chimney and draughting. Chapelon developed a new type of double blastpipe and chimney incorporating a device invented by Finnish engineer Kyösti Kylälä, which mixed the exhaust gases and steam sufficiently to create an even draught through the boiler. Back pressure at the cylinders by the exhaust was also considerably improved, all contributing to an estimated 20% increase in the efficiency of the Pacifics concerned. Chapelon then turned his attention to

the steam circuit by increasing the diameter of the pipes, making them as straight and smooth as possible, thus reducing pressure losses through friction. On test the redesigned engine could produce 3,000 indicated horsepower very easily.

The next class to receive the modifications was the '4500' class Pacific compounds, which were also converted to 4-8-0s to create better adhesion for the mountainous terrain they were intended to work. On test one of the conversions, No 4521, produced indicated horsepower figures of 3,800 at 56mph and 4,000 at 70mph with a 575-ton train. All of this deeply impressed Gresley, as he commented to the Institution of Locomotive Engineers in his Presidential Address in September 1934: 'In preparing the designs of the new eight-wheel coupled express passenger engine recently constructed at Doncaster, I did not hesitate to incorporate some of the outstanding features of the Paris-Orleans engine, such as the provision of extra-large steam passages and a double blast-pipe.' He adds: 'There was no real novelty in these features, but the French engineers had worked at the designs scientifically and had proved them by results obtained in actual service.' Gresley also noted that the adoption of the double blastpipe reduced the back pressure at the cylinders from about 7/8lb to just 2lb when working hard.

Cock o' the North made quite an impression on the general public and British engineers at the time, being very well publicised in all arenas by the LNER. Shortly after entering service the locomotive underwent dynamometer car tests on 19 June 1934 from King's Cross to Barkston and back in order to demonstrate the haulage capacity of the engine. A total of 19 carriages weighing 649 tons were attached, but the engine had no trouble whatsoever in starting or maintaining speed up the banks, and on level track 70mph was a comfortable speed for the locomotive. The highlight of the run came on the rise to Stoke summit when close to Corby 2,090 drawbar horsepower was attained with 30% cut-off at 57½mph.

Despite this, and a generally satisfactory performance in service, *Cock o' the North*'s design was not perpetuated because of problems with the poppet valves and rotary cam valve gear as well as the feedwater heater.

The second 'P2' – No 2002 *Earl Marischal* – was fitted with conventional piston valves operated by the Gresley conjugated motion and exhaust steam injector. The engine performed as well as No 2001 but more economically, and a further four to this design were constructed; No 2001 was also rebuilt in 1938. A problem experienced with *Earl Marischal* was that the smoke deflectors would not lift the softer exhaust produced by the piston valves (the poppet valves produced quite a vigorous blast), and the exhaust had a tendency to drift and obscure the view from the cab. The result was that a second pair of deflectors were fitted in April 1935 at the edges of the running plate and curving inwards to follow the original profile. This improved the problem but, as with the 'A3s', was an addition to the original design and looked as such.

An improvement Gresley introduced on *Cock o' the North* and the final 'A3' engines also under construction at the time was the perforated steam collector. This was employed to remove any water particles that were left in the steam before entering the regulator and was achieved by passing the steam through 17 half-inch slots cut in the top of the boiler barrel. As a result the barrel was reinforced at this point by a large metal plate with holes that corresponded to those in the boiler top. There were also three support ribs of ¾-inch steel plate. The exterior casing was made from a steel pressing that was riveted to the boiler barrel; the steam dome was integral to this.

STYLE, COMFORT, PRESTIGE, 1935-1939

The first drawing for the new 'A4' class locomotive was produced in May 1934. This closely resembled 'P2' class No 2001 Cock o' the North, with an 'A3' diagram 94A boiler working at 220lb per sq in, a 50sq ft grate area, poppet valves with rotary cam valve gear, but with a single chimney and a 6,000-gallon tender providing space for 8 tons of coal. The following diagram created in March 1935 after No 2001 had been in France for tests shows the poppet valves discarded and the firebox with a 1-foot extension to the combustion chamber; the boiler tubes were correspondingly shortened. A means of deflecting smoke was present and the tender reverted to the corridor design with extensions to the side sheets. In the following month a new drawing appeared, featuring an increase in boiler pressure to 250lb per sq in and the size of the firebox was reduced to 41.25sq ft. The running plate also became curved and the front sloped at an angle.

Eric Bannister, Draughtsman at Doncaster during this period, recounts in his excellent book *Trained by Sir Nigel Gresley* some details of the wind tunnel tests performed for smoke deflection purposes. He says that he was asked by Bert Spencer to take the streamlined model of the 'A4' to the National Physical Laboratory for tests to be conducted in the wind tunnel by Professor Dalby. French chalk was used and when ejected from the chimney the particles took a route along the boiler. The model was lifted out for smoke deflector plates to be fitted to achieve an improvement. Before this was done, an impression – made by one of them when handling the model – was noticed behind the chimney. Professor Dalby suggested that they should try the model in that condition and surprisingly this caused the smoke to move clear of the cab on several tests and was applied to the final design.

Engine Order No 338 was placed at Doncaster in March 1935 and the frames of the first locomotive (works No 1818) were put down in the New Erecting Shop on 26 June. The main frame plates were made from steel $1\frac{1}{8}$ inches thick, then spaced 4ft $1\frac{1}{2}$in at the front, tapering inwards from the rear near the firebox to 3ft $2\frac{1}{2}$in. Parallel sections were fixed to the main frames just in front of the firebox end and were spaced 6ft $0\frac{1}{2}$in apart; these were also of a slightly reduced thickness. The total length of the frames was 42ft 3in. Only two lightening holes (1 foot in diameter) were provided between the rear and driving pairs of coupled wheels after the 'A1s' and 'A3s', which had a greater number, had been plagued by frame cracks. A new method of fixing the horn stays to the frames was also used to prevent this issue.

Gresley approved the design of the cylinders on 17 April, and on 6/7 June they were cast at Gorton (outside pair) and Doncaster (inside) respectively. The diameter of the cylinders was reduced to $18\frac{1}{2}$ inches (by 26 inches stroke) from the 19-inch diameter of the 'A3s' in order to allow the use of 9-inch-diameter piston valves. This change was made to improve the flow of steam in and out of the cylinders. Steam was brought to them via a 5-inch-diameter pipe from the superheater header and this pipe was made as straight and as smooth as possible to reduce friction losses.

The boiler was constructed under Boiler Order No 821 and was designated Diagram 107. As the boiler pressure was raised to 250lb per sq in, the boiler plates had to be made thicker than those used on the 'A3' type, being $^{13}/_{16}$ inch thick for the front parallel section, which was of 5ft 9$^5/_8$ in diameter, and $^5/_8$ inch thick for the rear conical section, which had a diameter of 6ft 5in. The firebox was made from copper plate $^9/_{16}$ inch thick for the sides and back plates while the tubeplate was 1$^1/_4$ inches thick. The grate area was 41.25sq ft with a new type of fire bar being used to provide a 56% air space (after experienced gained from No 2001), and the ashpan was fabricated through welding. The distance between the tubeplates was 17ft 11$^3/_4$in through the addition of the longer combustion chamber, and the smokebox tubeplate was made from steel $^3/_4$ inch thick. There were 121 small tubes 2$^1/_2$ inches in diameter, 10 IWG thick, 43 superheater flues 5$^1/_4$ inches in diameter, and 43 elements 1.244 inches in diameter. These provided heating surfaces, respectively, of 1,281.4, 1,063.7, and 748.9sq ft. The total evaporative heating surface was 2,576.3sq ft and the total heating surface was 3,325.2sq ft; the firebox heating surface was 231.2sq ft. The boiler was lagged with Alfol mattresses and 1$^1/_2$-inch wire mesh; the wrapper plates were $^9/_{16}$ inch thick.

Two Ross 'Pop' safety valves were used and these were 3$^1/_2$ inches in diameter. A perforated steam collector was also fitted and was the same as previously described. The regulator was of the balanced type, then only just introduced on the 'A3' and 'P2' classes, and the main steam pipe was of 7-inch diameter to allow greater freedom of movement for the steam from the 8-inch-diameter regulator valve. Two injectors fed the boiler: on the right-hand side was a Davies & Metcalfe No 10 exhaust steam injector and on the left a live steam injector. The centre line of the boiler was 9ft 4$^1/_2$in above rail level and the centre line of the locomotive was 5ft 11$^3/_4$in. 'A3' No 2598 *Blenheim* was tested to check this latter figure at Doncaster Works and the results showed only a slight discrepancy as the actual figure was 5ft 11$^3/_{16}$in.

For the first 'A4' class engine Gresley discarded the Kylchap exhaust system and used a 'jumper top' blastpipe, which was then in widespread use on the GWR after being introduced by Churchward. The fitting lifted when the engine was working hard, thereby providing extra area for the exhaust to escape; the blastpipe orifice was 5$^3/_8$ inches in diameter and the jumper top

TOP Riveters at work inside the Diagram 107 boiler for the new locomotive.

ABOVE Working on the smokebox end of the boiler.

FAR LEFT Streamlined corridor tender No 5589 outside the Paint Shop at Doncaster.

LEFT *Silver Link*'s cab as new. The Flamen speed recorder is yet to be fitted. In 1936 extra ventilators were also installed.

was $6^7/_8$ inches in diameter. The Kylchap type was omitted because of the difficulties experienced with the setting on *Cock o' the North* and the high costs involved in licensing the equipment from the British patent-holders.

The front end was wedge-shaped after Gresley noted the ease with which the Bugatti railcar cut through the air and deflected away steam from passing locomotives. With a radius of 12 feet, the wedge was horizontal rather than the more popular vertical type as the latter displaced air to the sides that could interfere with the stability of other trains travelling past the streamlined engine. A running plate was designed by Gresley with the shape of an aerofoil in mind and he drew this on the wooden model that had been mocked up for testing. The definite contour of this was interpreted differently by the Chief Draughtsman and Gresley was quite upset that this was being applied to the locomotive while under construction. The correct outline was hastily prepared and attached to the engine on wooden planks before a drawing was produced to stipulate the exact shape. Contained in the front casing was the smokebox and access was gained by two hinged doors opened by turning a mechanism located in front of the cylinders. A whistle was placed ahead of the chimney as there was no room in the traditional position at the cab end, following the lead of *Cock o' the North*; the whistle was of the Crosby Tri-Note type also used on that engine.

The bogie wheels were 3ft 2in in diameter and the axle journals were $6^1/_2$ inches in diameter by 9 inches long. Helical spring slide control was used, with the springs being $10^1/_2$ inches long (when uncompressed) and $5^1/_{16}$ inches in diameter. The minimum force of these was 2 tons and the maximum 4 tons, with a displacement on either side of the engine of $4^1/_2$ inches. The bogie had a 1-foot-wide dust shield to protect the springs and

axleboxes. The coupled wheels were of 6ft 8in diameter with journals $9^1/_2$ inches by 11 inches and laminated springs. These were formed from 16 plates, 5 inches wide and $^1/_2$ inch thick spaced at 4-foot centres; the deflection per ton was 0.26 inch. The trailing axle had 3ft 8in-diameter wheels with journals 6 inches by 11 inches. Laminated springs were also used, with 11 plates 5 inches wide and $^5/_8$ inch thick at 4ft 6in centres. The angle of the Cartazzi slides was 1 in 7.1. All engine wheels were balanced, with the coupled wheels being treated for 40% of the reciprocating weight, and for the inside cylinder the driving wheels only. The wheelbase was 35ft 9in and the axle load was 66 tons. The adhesion factor was 4.18 and the tractive effort 35,455lb.

Gresley employed Walschaerts valve gear and his conjugated motion for the centre cylinder. The maximum valve travel was $5^3/_4$ inches with outside steam lap of $1^5/_8$ inches, inside steam lap $1^{11}/_{16}$ inches, no exhaust lap and maximum cut-off set at 65%. The piston and rods were made in one forging from BSS Class C steel and the connecting and coupling rods were made from nickel-chrome steel. The outside crank pins were $5^1/_2$ inches by 6 inches and the inside crank pin was $8^1/_4$ inches by 6 inches. A Wakefield mechanical lubricator was used for the cylinders and valves and a six-feed mechanical lubricator from the same company fed oil to the Armstrong oil pads used in the coupled axlebox trays. The lubricators were driven from the right-hand-side trailing crank pin. The motion and wheels were covered by a skirting, which was a means of aiding the streamlined design.

Corridor tender No 5589, built under Tender Order No 64, was paired with the locomotive and was of a slightly modified design compared with the type produced for the 'A3s'. Small extensions were made to the height and width in order to make the tender conform more in shape to the engine – this caused a reduction in the coal capacity to 8 tons. A standard Pullman vestibule was fitted for connection between the corridor and first carriage; the couplers were of the standard buckeye type. A rubber sheet was fitted between the engine and tender to keep the weather at bay.

The cab was generally similar to that of the 'A3' but had straight side sheets, and back rests with the seats from new. The front of the cab was V-shaped in order to improve the front lookout as the angle of the glass reduced glare. This innovation had been picked up from the PLM Railway in France and had first been applied to No 2001. Another feature of French origin was the Flaman speed recorder, which was driven from the right rear coupled wheel and placed under the fireman's seat for the driver to see easily. A record of the speeds was made and was later looked at by the authorities in case any of the drivers broke the restrictions in place. The 'A4s' were fitted with vacuum brakes with two 21-inch-diameter cylinders employed, in addition to a 24-inch-diameter cylinder. This gave an increased stopping power of 93% of the adhesive weight compared to 66% of the 'A1s' and 'A3s'. The tender brakes were only slightly more powerful at 62% from 53%, as the lack of weight at the end of a journey could make a full brake application dangerous at high speed.

The most unusual feature of the locomotive, apart from the streamlining, was the livery. As the new high-speed service was to be called the 'Silver Jubilee' to honour the 25 years that King George V had spent on the throne, a colour scheme with this in mind was thought advisable. 'J55' class 0-6-0ST locomotive No 4800, which was working as a Doncaster Works shunter at the time, was given the honour of trying several different shades of the theme in order to see what looked the best. In the event a silver grey was chosen for the engine, tender and wheel centres,

black for the front of the wedge and battleship grey for the side skirting. Initially the silver grey was extended all the way along the boiler sides, but this was quickly modified so that the black extended a short distance along the smokebox and curved off towards the running plate. The locomotive was christened *Silver Link*, initially with straight nameplates that had curved edges, but these were soon removed and the name was painted in the centre of the boiler. This was done in silver with blue shading – a scheme also extending to the number, 2509, on the cab side and 'LNER' on the tender.

Silver Link was completed at Doncaster Works on 7 September 1935, some 73 days after assembly had begun. During the following day the engine was taken to Barkston (just north of Grantham) on trial and was photographed by signalman W. Morley passing Tuxford North box; the picture later appeared in the *LNER Magazine*. The locomotive headed south at the hands of Driver Hardiman and Fireman White on 13 September for running in from King's Cross shed. Several days were spent working the 7.10am King's Cross to Cambridge and the 11.40 return. Eric Neve notes that the engine was also rostered on the 7.45am to Peterborough and 11.38 return, then heading to Grantham on the 5.45pm King's Cross to Hull. No 2509 then came back with the 9.05pm meat train, which had originated in Aberdeen. Fortunately for the LNER, the locomotive had plenty of time to bed in before the new service started on 30 September, as the second locomotive was not ready for traffic at this time.

The 'Silver Jubilee' train was ordered slightly earlier than the locomotive in February 1935 under Doncaster Order No 646. The train was formed of seven carriages (two articulated pairs and one triplet) consisting of: third class brake, third class corridor (seating 30 and 42 respectively); third class restaurant car, kitchen, first class restaurant car (with 48 and 28 seats); semi-open first and first class brake (30 and 20 were accommodated). The total length of the train was 392 feet, the seating capacity was 122 (there were 76

BELOW 'A4' No 2509 *Silver Link* as finally completed with the black front extending on to the smokebox side.

TOP No 2509 between duties at an unidentified location in the first half of 1936. Note the holes for the nameplate.

ABOVE *Silver Link* has the full attention of staff at King's Cross shed in September 1935. *P. Ransome-Wallis*

reduce the noise level to just 60 decibels. Corrugated steel sheeting was used above the underframe and lined with asbestos insulation.

Three compartments were provided in first class and seated four each. Blue Rexine was used to cover the walls, and the ceiling had a lighter shade applied. The seats were upholstered in silver and blue broche with loose cushions of light blue silk. All fittings were of chromium. The third class compartments accommodated six passengers and the colour scheme was green, but still with chromium fittings. Similar decorations featured in the respective dining cars. The kitchen was equipped with all-electric cooking equipment.

The set appeared shortly after *Silver Link* and both underwent high-speed brake trials over the period 20-22 September when on several occasions 100mph was recorded, but the stopping distances were poor. After more duties on regular service trains, No 2509 was ready for the press demonstration run, which took place on 27th September. Sir Ralph Wedgwood made a speech at a special dinner held before the train left, commenting on the high level of speed that they were expected to attain and reassuring passengers that the train would be just as safe as the 'Flying Scotsman'. Wedgwood also said that the 'Silver Jubilee' was the fastest non-stop over a distance of 200 miles – regardless of power type – and that higher speeds had not been attempted before because of the heavy loads; this was the first train that was deliberately light for fast running.

The train was brought into Platform 6 at King's Cross at 2.00pm for the departure to Grantham at 2.25. The platforms were packed with passengers and excited onlookers. Driver A. Taylor and Fireman Luty took the train out with a hearty cheer from the assemblage. In

places in the dining cars) and the tare weight was 220 tons. The design departed from the LNER's traditional teak panels and instead used 16-gauge steel panels; these were covered with aluminium-coloured Rexine, an artificial leather. Teak was used for the body frames but the underframes were of steel and standard compound bolster bogies were employed. In an attempt to reduce noise as far as possible, asbestos acoustic blankets were fitted underneath the floor and between the ceiling and roof. Further, double glazing was employed and the panes were ¼ inch thick with ¼ inch of air between the two. These features were claimed to

nearly 5 miles *Silver Link* was up to 70mph at Wood Green and kept going to 75mph on the 1 in 200 to Potters Bar. On the falling gradients from there to Hatfield 95mph was reached and the time taken for the 17½ miles from King's Cross was 17 minutes 7 seconds. The engine kept the average speed in the high 80s/low 90s over the undulations to Stevenage before breaking the 100mph mark just before passing Hitchin in 26 minutes 14 seconds from the start; the average speed from Hatfield was 92.1mph. *Silver Link* continued the pace and on the slightly falling gradient to Arlesey reached 112½mph – setting the speed record for steam traction. The speed remained in the low 100s until No 2509 was pushed again to Sandy and 112½mph was attained for a second time at milepost 40. The last high of 109½mph was made a short distance from Offord where a necessary slowing was made for the curves there. This broke *Silver Link*'s stride as the engine completed 25 miles from Hitchin to Offord at an average speed of just over 100mph. The 76 miles to Peterborough had taken only 55 minutes 2 seconds. *Silver Link* made a quick recovery to 80mph from the 20mph restriction through the station before a series of signals broke what would have almost certainly been an impressive climb to Stoke summit. The signals were against the locomotive because the 1.40pm to Harrogate had been caught up. Grantham was reached in 88 minutes 15 seconds for King's Cross or just under schedule. Driver Taylor commented to the press upon the return to King's Cross (after no hard running was attempted) that *Silver Link* was 'the fastest engine we have ever had … we could have easily gone faster if we had wanted to – we were not all out by any means.' Gresley was quick to congratulate him for the effort as the CME had been keeping time in the train during the run with a rather large stopwatch. Driver Taylor was later awarded an MBE for his achievement.

The first 'Silver Jubilee' drew similar interest on 30 September and civic dignitaries and company officials were out in force to celebrate the inauguration of the service. The train

from Newcastle to King's Cross was the first of the day and was allowed 4 hours for the 268 miles, with an average speed of 67.07mph being necessary. A stop at Darlington was made at 10.40am to collect passengers – leaving at 10.42 – and completed the remaining 232¼ miles to King's Cross in 198 minutes at an average speed of 70.3mph. Several figures higher than this were required on individual sections, such as 82.7mph between Thirsk and Alne and four instances of 77mph; two were between Darlington and Thirsk and the other two were from Huntingdon to Hitchin, then to Hatfield.

Silver Link was at the head of the train with Driver Payne and Fireman Challis of King's Cross on the footplate. Present on board the train were the Lord Mayor of Newcastle; Lord and Lady Mayoress of Darlington; Deputy Chairman of the LNER Sir Murrough Wilson; C. M. Jenkin Jones, Superintendent of the NE Area; and CME H. N. Gresley. The remainder of the accommodation was taken up by members of the public – generally businessmen who were targeted to use the train. The 'Silver Jubilee' arrived at King's Cross 2 minutes 30 seconds early and on the platform to greet the train was Sir Stephen Killick, Lord Mayor of London, William Whitelaw and Sir Ralph Wedgwood. These distinguished gentlemen, and those who had travelled, then went to the cab to praise Driver Payne for the excellent manner in which he had handled the locomotive. To add to the spectacle the second 'A4' class engine – No 2510 *Quicksilver*, which had been completed at Doncaster on 21 September, then sent south for running-in on the 26th – was at the adjacent platform, providing the first view of two 'A4s' together in service.

BELOW All eyes are on No 2509 as the engine leaves King's Cross with the demonstration run on 27 September 1935.

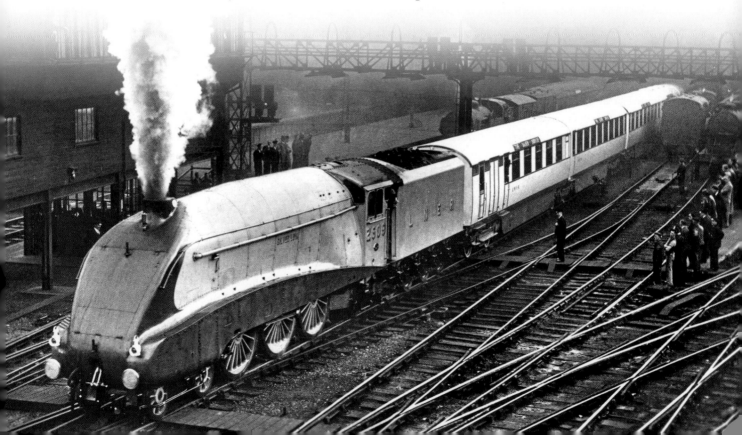

No 2509 was quickly serviced in readiness for the down train to Newcastle, which left King's Cross at 5.30pm. Arrival at Darlington for the first stop was booked for 8.48pm, the train leaving 2 minutes later for Newcastle where the service would terminate at 9.30. The section timings were generally similar to the up train, even though many gradients were against the engine – for example, 2 minutes more were allowed heading from King's Cross to Hatfield at 18 minutes. Also, 24½ minutes were given for the adverse gradients from Peterborough to Grantham, where Stoke had to be tackled, when in the opposite direction 24 minutes were scheduled. The highest average speed required was 80.8mph from Hitchin to Huntingdon and there were three at 77mph – the next highest was 71.3mph from Peterborough to Grantham. *Silver Link* was again cheered off by a large crowd and a description of the scene before departure was relayed via radio to America. The *LNER Magazine* reports what was said: 'The platform is full of people; there are actual passengers, who are clustered about the carriage doors with the pleased and sheepish air which record-breakers assume in public; there are the wedged-in or slowly cruising policeman; there are dignitaries, who may be recognised by their silk hats or (in extreme cases) by the hint of purple or scarlet in their robes. But the thickest of the press is collected around the engine.' Many people, both at the time and since, have commented on the stir that the shape and colour of the 'A4' caused. Many were immediately taken in, while others had to get over the 'shock of the new' before taking the class to heart; some remain steadfast in their opinion that the 'A1s' and 'A3s' were the best-looking of the Gresley Pacifics. The down train did not fare as well as the southbound service after a permanent way restriction was encountered at Aycliffe, just north of Darlington, and a late arrival was recorded.

There were some difficulties, as could be expected, with the introduction of the 'Silver Jubilee'. The main problem was that, despite an increase in the braking power, this was still inadequate for the speeds that the train was regularly attaining. This led to the streamliners requiring two signal block sections being reserved in order to provide a sufficient distance for them to stop. In the NE Area the new two-aspect colour light signalling system was also deemed inadequate and had to be upgraded to three aspects. Until this was performed the train was limited to 70mph in the NE Area, causing the GN section timings to be quite close to the limit of what was possible – without delays on the crowded line coming into the equation. In the latter half of 1936 Wedgwood recommended the Board authorise over £14,500 to be spent on the repositioning of distant signals all over the network, but many were between London and Edinburgh to give the 'A4s' more advance warning of a signal at danger, as, he noted, there had been several instances of over-running the home signal by some distance.

The Operating Department did quite a good job of finding a path for the train through the various other services running on the East Coast Main Line. Eric Neve notes that only two trains were delayed for the down train to go past, while the up train interfered with the same number. Also, the Newcastle train previously occupied the 5.30pm slot and this was moved to a slightly later time. The 'Silver Jubilee' also caused close attention to be paid to the track. The layout was improved in certain places for high speeds to be maintained and the use of longer rails was tried in order to improve the riding. The standard was 60-foot 95lb rails, but sections of 90 feet and 120 feet were laid at Thirsk and Holme respectively. Modifications were made to the train's suspension shortly after the trial in order to absorb more of the imperfections in the track. The locomotive's bogie was also altered so the minimum force was increased to 4 tons and the maximum became 7 tons – this was made standard for the following 'A4s'. Moreover, thoughts also turned to the superelevation of the track to permit increased speed round curves, even though the science was relatively obscure at the time. Some curves were only set up for speeds slightly lower than the required average from Darlington to King's Cross, leading to restrictions that forced the engine to work harder.

The 'Silver Jubilee' was rostered to King's Cross men from the start of the service, and they would travel north and lodge on Sunday night for the first up train on Monday (the service did not run at the weekend or Bank Holidays). Another crew would then take the first down train in the evening and return the following day. After the final service of the week the 'A4' would return to King's Cross on Saturday morning with the 'Flying Scotsman'. No 2509 was the only locomotive rostered for the first three weeks and No 2510 *Quicksilver* was not involved until 17 October, but was then replaced by No 2509. Prior to working the 'Silver Jubilee' *Quicksilver* was tested on a train to York and back and averaged just over 60mph for both journeys.

As mentioned, No 2509 appeared on the train for three weeks before being relieved – a feat that was perhaps unprecedented in terms of reliability and punctuality, especially with a high-speed train. In the nine days after 30 September, which is recorded by O. S. Nock in *The Gresley Pacifics of the LNER Part 2: 1935-1974*, six early arrivals were made at King's Cross by *Silver Link* and a further two were on time. There was one late arrival on 11 October and this was 5 minutes past 2.00pm as a points failure had stopped the streamliner. Travelling north to Newcastle all nine journeys resulted in an early appearance in the station. Of these one was 4 minutes early, three were 3 minutes, two came in 2 minutes before and another two were in front by a minute. The up train gained 5 minutes on the timetable on 1 October, 3 minutes on the 2nd and 2 minutes on the following two days. The next week saw the first two arrivals 3 minutes 30 seconds and 2 minutes 30 seconds

before time respectively, then two on-time entries were made to King's Cross. Drivers Payne and Taylor were rostered for the 30 September-4 October and Drivers Peachey and Samwells from the 7th to the 11th.

There are reports from several sources that the large gathering of people at King's Cross and Newcastle was not confined to the first service but continued right into the winter of 1935. Darlington station saw a threefold growth in the number of platform tickets sold to spectators, and along the route people would stand at the lineside to catch a glimpse of the locomotive and train. Michael Bonavia in *A History of the LNER 2: The Age of the Streamliners* remarks that people in York became accustomed to checking their watches when they heard the distinct 'A4' chime whistle to see how well the engine was keeping to schedule; a similar ritual has been claimed at various points along the line. The LNER was quick to cash in on this interest, producing jigsaws, cut-out models, postcards and box labels featuring both *Silver Link* and the 'Silver Jubilee'. Several distinguished people also visited the train, including General Karl Vaugoin, President of the Austrian Federal Railways.

Not all the publicity for the locomotive and train was glowing, as *The Engineer* commented in the issue of 4 October 1935 that the exploits of the trial run and subsequent reporting had been rather overblown. The article said: 'We may now safely assume that 50 million people know that on Friday last a speed of 112mph [sic] was attained by a steam locomotive run by a British company. Of these millions most must have learnt of the achievement through the sensationalised accounts of the run by the daily press and the B.B.C., which were rendered even more spectacular by the dramatic skill of the announcer, who contrived to make the journey more exciting than Captain Wakelam's running commentary on an international rugby match.' The feature goes on to make the point that the regular attainment and maintenance of high speeds was not an impossibility, especially with the standards of maintenance for both the rolling stock and permanent way being at a high level during the period. The use of streamlining is praised for being present but the ultimate judgement of this characteristic was reserved until greater experience in service was gained. The writer of the article suggests that the real feat worthy of mention was fast running accompanied by economies in coal and water consumption and low maintenance costs.

No 2509 was not without trouble during the first three weeks on the 'Silver Jubilee' as the brick arch in the firebox gave trouble on a couple of occasions. On one a brick fell out and a fitter from Gateshead shed went into the hot firebox to repair

ABOVE No 2510 *Quicksilver* **prepares to depart from Newcastle in 1935 or 1936.**

the problem – demonstrating to a degree the pride employees felt in keeping the locomotive on the train when an 'A3' would have proved a suitable replacement. Gresley was said to have been quite upset when informed of this and did not condone such an action. The first failure of an 'A4' prior to the departure of the 'Silver Jubilee' occurred on 4 November 1935 when *Silver Link* was declared unfit at Newcastle and 'A3' No 2503 *Firdaussi* was substituted; the locomotive was recorded as arriving on time at King's Cross with the train. The first failure when the service was under way was not documented until 4 September 1936. No 2510 *Quicksilver* was taken off the up train at York and 'C7/2' class Atlantic No 732, which was then fitted with poppet valves, was put on as far as Doncaster, where a new engine was requested. 'C1' Atlantic No 4452 was attached and completed the remaining mileage in the respectable time of 139 minutes at an average speed of 67.3mph.

The remaining two 'A4' class locomotives from the order were not completed until 5 November – No 2511 *Silver King* – and 18 December – No 2512 *Silver Fox*. At first the former was allocated to King's Cross, but on 18 November a transfer to Gateshead occurred and from there *Silver King* was assigned as the standby for the up 'Silver Jubilee'. If the engine was not needed, which was usually the case, employment was found on the Newcastle to Edinburgh portion of the Leeds to Glasgow train, then travelling south to York or Leeds before returning to Newcastle. *Silver King* had to wait to be used on the 'Silver Jubilee', the first occasion not being until 13 December. When No 2512 *Silver Fox* was put into traffic the engine was slightly different from the earlier three in that several embellishments were fitted. These were a silver fox on each side of the boiler, which had been presented by Samuel Fox & Co of Sheffield, and stainless steel boiler bands. The locomotive went new to King's Cross and was first rostered on the 'Silver Jubilee' on 3 January 1936. Between the two engines being completed 'A3' No 2503 was used on the train for coal consumption trials conducted on 19 November; the 'A4s' were tested earlier in the month. The results favoured neither design, as could have perhaps been expected; the 'A3' used 36.15lb of coal per mile compared to the 36.7lb of the 'A4'. Gresley later gave the average coal consumption on the 'Silver Jubilee' as 39lb per mile and suggested that a 4lb saving had been achieved through the use of streamlining; over a year this would account for 200 tons of coal.

From 4 May 1936 the seating arrangements in the 'Silver Jubilee' were slightly altered so that more passengers could be accommodated, the realisation having been made that in the open portions of the carriages meals could be served to passengers at their seats without the need for them to head to the respective dining car. With some rearrangement in carriage No 1582 and No 1585 eight more first class seats could be sold and as many as 24 extra in third class. In March 1938 further accommodation was provided in third class with the addition of another compartment carriage. The number of seats was then

ABOVE No 2511 *Silver King* at Gateshead shed in 1936.

BELOW No 2512 *Silver Fox* passes through Oakleigh Park station at speed with the up 'Silver Jubilee' during the first half of 1936.
F. R. Hebron

OPPOSITE After almost a year in service *Silver Link* has acquired extended drawgear and buffers after a fatal accident at King's Cross was caused by the original, shorter components; the engine's number was also applied to the front end at this time. No 2509 is seen on 26 September 1936 in Doncaster Works' Weigh House to illustrate the new 'Voiron' weighing equipment.

183 and the weight of the train was 248 tons tare with the same timetable in force.

After a year in service the 'Silver Jubilee' had completed nearly 500 journeys between King's Cross and Newcastle. A total of 67,885 passengers had been accommodated – 32,245 up, 35,640 down – at an average of 130 to London and 143 to the North East (Wedgwood said in October 1936 that the Newcastle to King's Cross traffic had increased 12% and the train had stimulated the use of other services). Of the 133,464 miles that had been run (100,000 was reached on 2 July when going past Hitchin at 85mph), in excess of 115,000 had been travelled at an average speed of 70.4mph and approximately 30,000 were run at 80mph and over. The train had made gross receipts of 13s 11d per mile and operating expenses were 2s 6d per mile. These figures are taken from Gresley's Presidential Address to the Institution of Mechanical Engineers in 1936 and he goes on to say that these exclude the profits from the dining car and interest on the engine and train's capital cost, which was £34,500. Assistant General Manager Robert Bell gave a variation of these figures to the Institute of Transport earlier in the year. Receipts were 16s 2d per train mile against working expenses of 4s 2d and he compares this to the receipts of all the LNER passenger services, which was 5 shillings per mile and the operating expenses 2s 6d per mile. Gresley goes on to record that the 5 shillings first class and 3 shillings third class supplementary fares had made £12,000 profit for the company.

A record of *Silver Link*'s performance on the train during the summer of 1936 was made by 'A Railway Engineer' and appeared in *The Meccano Magazine* for February 1937. Driver Haygreen and Fireman Fisher took charge for the northbound run and soon had the train up to 69mph after tackling the 1 in 200 to Potters Bar. The speed rose further to 82mph at Hatfield and was only lower by 3mph at Knebworth after approximately 5 miles of 1 in 200. The locomotive was then slowed to 55mph for the tender to pass over Langley water troughs; the author notes that this was nearly double the speed previously attempted by engines collecting water. On the 1 in 200 falling gradient to Hitchin an acceleration was made to 87mph and further momentum was gained to Three Counties where the speed was 92½mph; to Offord – 20 miles – 89mph was the average speed. After slowing to 73mph for the curves at Offord, the regulator was opened and No 2509 went up the 3½ miles of 1 in 200 to Abbots Ripton at a minimum of 77mph. The engine then moved to the 90mph maximum until slowing for Peterborough station. The time taken was 63 minutes, or 2 minutes early. Just 1½ miles on from the restriction 66mph was reached. At Tallington the speed was 91mph with 18% cut-off, but this dropped to 76mph at Little Bytham before an acceleration was made to 81mph up the 1 in 200 to Corby. Only 3mph was lost on the final 3 miles of 1 in 178 to Stoke summit; the time at this

point was 82 minutes 15 seconds, or 19 minutes 15 seconds from Peterborough at an average speed of 71.6mph.

The running was steadier on to Doncaster where the engine was brought to a stand because of a signal failure and Shaftholme Junction (just to the north) was passed 2 minutes late. *Silver Link* attained 90mph heading on to Selby and reduced the deficit slightly before a high of 86½mph at Naburn on the section to York. The city was passed a minute late before high speed was reached and sustained on the long stretch of straight and level track to the north, with 90mph at Raskelf, 3 miles from York, then through Thirsk at 91mph. A similar level was maintained on to Darlington where the stop was made 3 minutes early. The log ends here as the 'Railway Engineer' was travelling no further, but before the train left he had a chance to see Driver Haygreen and Fireman Fisher, whom he knew. The latter commented: 'What d'you think o' that for a bit of stuff?' – evidently quite satisfied with how the train had been handled.

Just as the LNER thought that steam could successfully haul lighter trains at higher speed than a more expensive, and relatively untested, diesel unit, many other railways also thought the same. In England the GWR linked the introduction of a high-speed train to the centenary of the opening of the Paddington to Bristol line, calling the service the 'Bristolian'. The train was of a similar formation to the 'Silver Jubilee' and was given a schedule of 105 minutes for the 117-mile down journey and 118-mile eastbound route. The average speed of the 'Bristolian' was just over 67mph and was handled at first by 'King' class 4-6-0s.

ABOVE LEFT Captured just south of York at Chaloner's Whin Junction, No 2510 *Quicksilver* is at the head of the up 'Silver Jubilee' on 16 August 1937. *IAL*

ABOVE RIGHT *Silver Link* passes 'K3' 2-6-0 No 4008 at New Southgate with an express to Harrogate in late 1935. *IAL*

ABOVE No 2511 *Silver King* travels eastward past Haymarket shed in the first half of 1936. *W. J. Reynolds*

RIGHT A larger style of numbering was applied to the front end of all but *Quicksilver* in 1937; No 2512 was so treated towards the end of the year. *Silver Fox* is pictured at Marshmoor on the up 'Silver Jubilee'. *IAL*

In America, the Chicago, Milwaukee, St Paul & Pacific Railroad inaugurated a steam-hauled high-speed train between Chicago and Minneapolis called the 'Hiawatha', completing the 410 miles in 6 hours 30 minutes with several stops en route. The average speed was 63mph but high average section times were required in some instances. The locomotives employed were specially designed Atlantics with streamlining, which was predicted to reduce the power required by 50%. The boiler was oil-fired and worked at 300lb per sq in. In service the engines were found to be capable of high speeds and those in excess of 100mph were not uncommon; claims were made of 112½mph sustained for several miles but not proven by evidence. The purpose-built 'Hiawatha' train weighed more than the 'Silver Jubilee' at 360 tons and provided seats for 265 passengers.

The *LNER Magazine* of June 1936 reported on the receipts of the 'Hiawatha' in relation to the 'Zephyr' diesel railcar. The latter had earnings of 5 shillings per mile, whereas the steam-hauled train received 14s 8d with expenses of 4s 9d. The article – on 'Transport Developments in 1935' – explained that the passenger traffic in America had increased by 2½% from the previous year, but revenue was falling because prices had been lowered in order to tempt passengers back and encourage travel. In Britain an increase in revenue of 3% was recorded for the 'Big Four' thanks in part to the new features offered by them.

Deutsche Reichsbahn also provided a steam alternative to the 'Flying Hamburger', as two streamlined 4-6-4 locomotives were built in 1935 and classified '05'. These were then tested extensively and speeds over 119 and 121mph were claimed, but those available for scrutiny were between 110 and 112mph with about 250 tons. DR organised special trials again the following year with No 05.002 taking part in May. With 197 tons the engine made several attempts at high speed on the line to Hamburg and recorded figures between 110 and 120mph before setting the world record for steam traction at 124.5mph.

In early May 1936 Wedgwood set the wheels in motion for the introduction of a second streamlined service. The initial plans, formulated in July, saw the train travel at 12.15pm from the English to the Scottish capital, taking 6 hours and running to Newcastle in 3 hours 55 minutes. There was then a connection on to Aberdeen, which would have been booked for 3 hours for the approximately 130 miles, arriving at 9.15pm. A similar schedule was set for the southbound train, which would leave Aberdeen at 9.15am. Wedgwood did not agree with the

ABOVE The CMStP&PR's Class A Atlantic locomotive No 1 was the first of four to be built for the 'Hiawatha' train by the American Locomotive Co in May 1935.

departure times and pushed for the train to be given a late-afternoon slot in order to suit the businessman traveller, and dropped the idea of a dedicated connection on to Aberdeen. The times were agreed to be 4.00pm from King's Cross and 4.30pm from Edinburgh Waverley, beginning in mid-1937.

On 27 August 1936 a special test was organised using the 'Silver Jubilee' set and the dynamometer car. The aim was to measure the coal and water consumption on the up and down journeys, but the authorities also wanted to raise the speed record. The engine chosen for the task was No 2512 *Silver Fox* and the Driver was G. Haygreen for the train to London. The load was 252 tons gross and the normal schedule was kept, although the Darlington stop was omitted. C. J. Allen noted that the running as far as Grantham was quite out of keeping with what would generally be encountered on the service. At this point the engine was finally given full regulator for the 5 miles of 1 in 200 to Stoke summit, but *Silver Fox* did not react well to the combination with 25% cut-off and the speed dropped from 71½mph to 68½mph. From the summit 15% was used before being gradually opened out to 35%, and 106mph was reached on the declivity before peaking at 113mph at Essendine, just over 11 miles from the summit. The journey returned to normal after this before matters took a turn for the worse after Hatfield, where the train was 4 minutes in front of schedule. Several loud noises came from the engine, but no stop was made and *Silver Fox* limped to King's Cross station, where arrival was made 7 minutes late, as steam liberally filled the atmosphere. The high-speed exploits (with a train full of passengers) had caused overheating of the big end of the connecting rod for the middle cylinder and the total disintegration of the component, with the result that the piston had forced off the cylinder cover. Partially because of this, the 'A4s', and other classes such as the 'A1s' and 'A3s', were fitted with a chemical that would exude a pungent odour detectable on the footplate when any overheating of the middle big end occurred; the part was particularly susceptible to this. A. J. Mullay in *Streamline Steam* quotes Driver Haygreen as saying that he did not know anything about the British record attempt prior to Corby, where he was informed to 'go all out'. This is surprising given that the record attempt was relayed to a great number of people that were not directly involved – several members of the press had been told to be at King's Cross for the arrival.

Despite this unfortunate incident, the 5.30pm was taken out as normal with the dynamometer car behind No 2509 *Silver Link*. Driver Sparshatt was at the regulator and ran the engine flawlessly, getting almost full pressure in the boiler and using full regulator with short cut-offs where possible. A highlight of the journey came between Peterborough and Grantham when Sparshatt had *Silver Link* up to 90mph 8 miles from the former station. The speed dropped off only gradually as progress was made: 86½ at Essendine; 78mph at Little Bytham; 80½mph at Corby. On the final stretch No 2509 was travelling at 75mph and had averaged 82mph from Tallington. In total 4 minutes would be gained upon completion of the journey. This was not quite the best performance recorded over this section with the 'Silver Jubilee', but *Silver Link* has the honour of holding the top spot with an average speed of over 84mph for the 15¼ miles.

The dynamometer car was again behind an 'A4' on Saturday 27 September when trails were conducted over the Newcastle to Edinburgh section for the proposed service. No 2511 *Silver King* was the engine (with Gresley on the footplate for at least part of the journey) and the 'Silver Jubilee' set was again used. The departure was booked for 11.05am and arrival at 1.00pm, which was a 32-minute reduction on the usual allowance between the two cities. Driver Dron was on both trips and completed the first in 118 minutes and the return to Newcastle in 114 minutes for the 124½ miles. The latter run saw the engine reach the summit of Cockburnspath bank, which comprises approximately 2 miles at 1 in 210 and over 4 miles at 1 in 96, at 68mph. Gresley, in his 1936 Presidential Address, records that the drawbar horsepower was recorded as 1,460, adding that to overcome gravity, air resistance and friction – amounting to around 1,000 horsepower – the indicated horsepower from the cylinders was in the region of 2,500 or 2,600. He postulates that such a figure had never been attained in Britain before.

Gresley was pleased to show off the works in which the 'A4' class were produced when the Institution of Mechanical

Engineers organised a week for members in Yorkshire, visiting several places important to the LNER. Gresley guided the party around Doncaster on 10 June and at this time *Silver Link* was present after undergoing light repairs, which allowed the group to have a photograph taken with the engine. Also present were No 4472 *Flying Scotsman*, Ivatt Atlantic No 4420, 'P2' class No 2003 *Lord President* and 'V2' 2-6-2 No 4771 *Green Arrow*. The 'P2' was the first of the second batch of four to be built. These engines were fitted with the 'A4' wedge-shaped front end from new as the arrangement had been found to be much better for smoke deflection than that fitted to *Earl Marischal*. There had originally been plans for the 'V2' to be modelled on the same lines as *Cock o' the North*, then the 'A4s', but the decision was ultimately made to revert to a conventional profile.

The appearance of *Silver Link* and the other engines at this event was perhaps not just a coincidence. The LNER often held public exhibitions of locomotives and rolling stock as a means of promoting a good image for the company and also for raising money to aid local charities, such as those benefitting railwaymen. The *LNER Magazine* throughout 1936 notes that the 'A4s' were present at several such events including: No 2509 at Sheffield and Aberdeen; No 2511 *Silver King* at Sunderland and Kirkcaldy; and No 2512 *Silver Fox* at Walthamstow, where 'B17' class 4-6-0 No 2870 *Tottenham Hotspur* was named in the presence of the club's Chairman and several directors and players. The same publication also reported on the case of a young boy who had enquired about the nearest place he could see the 'Silver Jubilee' train from Sheffield, where he was staying at the time. The LNER responded by having the station master greet him at Doncaster and showing the boy the best place to see the train pass through the station. A special tour of the station was also provided.

In January 1936 authorisation was given for a further 17 'A4s' to be used on both named and ordinary express passenger services under Doncaster Order Nos 340 and 341. The money for the order, which cost over £127,000, was obtained from the Railway Finance Corporation. Also placed at this time were boiler orders Nos 825 and 826 and tender orders Nos 66 (for ten non-corridor) and 67 (for seven corridor type). The first engine of this batch was No 4482 *Golden Eagle* and construction was completed at Doncaster on 22 December 1936. The engine was paired with 1928 corridor tender No 5323, which had briefly been allocated to *Flying Scotsman* when new. The 10 non-corridor tenders built with the first 10 locomotives were sent to 'A3s', which at the time were paired with the corridor type. There were some modifications to these in order to bring them closer to the design of the engine and the corridor tenders built for the earlier 'A4' locomotives. The wheels were changed from the spoke-type to the disc-type; additional metal plating was fitted to the front and rear; the side sheets were made wider by over 1ft

ABOVE No 4482 *Golden Eagle* wore Apple Green livery for 13 months, followed by Garter Blue. *IAL*

3in; and new longer handrails were attached. No 4482 also had a different livery from the silver theme of the first four and had the normal LNER Apple Green passenger livery with black and white lining; the wedge front remained black, but this colour replaced the battleship grey on the valances. Numbering and lettering were in gold with red shading and nameplates (straight with square corners and a black background) were fitted to the smokebox sides. The numbering scheme used by the new engines was initially to have filled several gaps in the list, so instead of being Nos 4482-4498, which the engines carried from new, they would have been Nos 2031, 2036, 2039, 2049, 2052, 2063, 2064, 2077, 2111-2115, 2515, 2516, 2519 and 2520 (although not in this order). The naming theme was birds that were either powerful or fast in flight, and this had been chosen by Gresley himself.

A large gathering of people occurred for the first departure of No 4482 from King's Cross on Wednesday 6 January 1937. The passenger service concerned was the 1.20pm to Newcastle, which was formed of 16 carriages weighing 500 tons gross, and under the guidance of Driver Ellis and Fireman Luty. LNER Director Andrew K. McCosh gave the train the 'right away' and Gresley was lineside at the station to see his latest Pacific in traffic. *Golden Eagle*, which was allocated to King's Cross when new, was soon called into exhibition service at Leeds on 22 February. Approximately 2,200 schoolchildren attended the event, which was opened by Lord Mayor Councillor Tom Coombes. He commented: 'In the whole of the world there has been no greater development of the railways than in the United Kingdom and the LNER are to be congratulated on the wonderful achievement of an engine like this [in reference to

Golden Eagle and the exploits of the 'silver' engines]'. No 4482 was in the works a short time later to be prepared for an exhibition at New Barnet on 5/6 June 1937. The new 'A4' was also incorporated into advertising material – in particular a poster for the 'Scarborough Flyer' – giving the impression to the general public that improvements and high speed were spreading to other parts of the system.

A steady stream of 'A4s' went into traffic during 1937 after No 4483 *Kingfisher* was completed in late December 1936. This engine and the following four (Nos 4484 *Falcon*, 4485 *Kestrel*, 4486 *Merlin* and 4487 *Sea Eagle*) had a slightly modified livery when new. The black front extended further back to the first boiler band due to concerns that the paint might not stand up to the heat produced in the smokebox. Nos 4483-4487 were the first 'A4s' to be allocated to Edinburgh Haymarket shed when new, but No 4487 were transferred away in March 1937 to Gateshead. The Haymarket engines were used on the principal expresses to Glasgow, Dundee, Aberdeen and southbound services such as the 'Flying Scotsman'. No 4488 entered Doncaster Works Paint Shop on 17 April with *Osprey* nameplates fitted. As the aforementioned livery was not particularly suited to the locomotives, a search began for an appropriate shade of blue, given that 1937 was the coronation year for King George VI. The locomotive remained in the Paint Shop for several weeks while this occurred, and in the meantime No 4489 *Woodcock* was built. As the scheme had not been decided upon, works grey livery with white lining was applied, while the wheel centres remained green. The engine left Doncaster on 4 May and was run in for a brief time before being recalled to have the new livery applied and to be renamed.

RIGHT At the end of 1937 No 4484 *Falcon* would have this experimental colour scheme removed. *IAL*

LEFT No 4487 *Sea Eagle* in Doncaster Works' Paint Shop prior to entering traffic.

BELOW At Potters Bar with the up 'Flying Scotsman' is No 4485 *Kestrel* in original livery.

P. Ransome-Wallis

Nos 4488, 4489, 4490, 4491 and 4492 were specially chosen to work the LNER's new high-speed streamlined express service between King's Cross and Edinburgh Waverley – the 'Coronation' – beginning on 5 July 1937. The livery finally settled on was Garter Blue with black on the front and red and white lining applied to the curve sweeping back from the front only, with no lining to the boiler or the tender. The wheel centres were painted dark red and the numbering and lettering were applied in stainless steel pieces, this material also being used for trim to the bottom of the valances and the tender. To combine with the theme of the coronation, the dominions of the British Empire were chosen to provide names for the locomotives: *Union of South Africa*, *Dominion of Canada*, *Empire of India*, *Commonwealth of Australia* and *Dominion of New Zealand*. The nameplates for these were chromium plated and had red backgrounds. The engines were also fitted with the countries' respective coat of arms on the cab sides.

The choice of names afforded the LNER an opportunity to publicise the service and locomotives by having them named by the respective High Commissioners. On 28 June at King's Cross station No 4488 *Union of South Africa* was christened by Mr C. T. te Water, No 4490 *Empire of India* by Sir Firoz Khan, and No 4492 *Dominion of New Zealand* by Mr W. J. Jordan. To further distinguish the engines the LNER either suggested, or were simply presented, with whistles belonging to railways operational in these territories: No 4488 received a South African Railways whistle and No 4492 a New Zealand Government Railways whistle, although not initially – the type was fitted in May 1939. *Dominion of Canada* had the honour two weeks earlier on Tuesday 15 June. The *LNER Magazine* carried a description of the event,

ABOVE The Canadian Pacific Railway donated No 4489 *Dominion of Canada*'s bell and whistle, which are seen with the locomotive at King's Cross shed on 20 March 1938. *IAL*

which saw the naming ceremony officiated by William Whitelaw, Sir Murrough Wilson and Sir Ralph Wedgwood. The High Commissioner of Canada, Mr Vincent Massey, unveiled No 4489's nameplates and was then invited on the footplate with Gresley to drive the locomotive to the end of Platform 6 and back. A special lunch was held afterwards and Mr Massey congratulated the LNER on the enterprise the company had demonstrated by introducing the service and highlighted this as being one of the many important developments made in Britain that the dominions were sure to adopt. Only two days later No 4489 had the honour of being selected to haul the 'Night Scotsman' as far as Grantham because the Prime Minister of Canada, Mackenzie King, was using the train to reach Dundee. On 18 June No 4491 *Commonwealth of Australia* was named by Mr J. M. Bruce.

The train set for the 'Coronation' service was to follow the 'Silver Jubilee', but after careful consideration Gresley decided to make some alterations. The capacity swelled to 48 first class passengers and 168 in third class. No restaurant car was provided as meals were to be served at the passengers' seats. The formation consisted of four twin articulated carriages: brake third (24), open third (42); kitchen third (15), open third (42); two open firsts seating 24 each; and kitchen third (15), open brake third (30). Additionally, there was a 'beaver-tail' observation car that could seat 16 passengers for 1 hour at a time for a charge of 1 shilling.

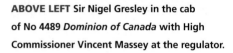

ABOVE LEFT Sir Nigel Gresley in the cab of No 4489 *Dominion of Canada* with High Commissioner Vincent Massey at the regulator.

ABOVE RIGHT No 4491 at King's Cross shed with nameplates covered.

RIGHT The two 'Coronation' beaver-tail observation cars under construction at Doncaster Works.

This was initially meant to run all year but experience soon found that there was not much of a view in the winter months and during this period the carriage was stored. The shape of the observation car had been developed in the wind tunnel to aid the movement of the train through the air. The general construction of the set was the same as the 'Silver Jubilee' but more soundproofing was used. The tare weight of the nine carriages was 312 tons, but when reduced to eight was 278 tons. The total length was 513ft 2¼in, or 584ft 1¾in with the locomotive. The bodies were 56ft 2½in long by 9 feet wide; the observation car was 51ft 9in long. Three sets were built; two for the 'Coronation' and one as a spare should a failure occur or when maintenance needed to be carried out.

Externally the carriages were only slightly different from the 'Silver Jubilee' as the set retained fairings between the bodies and skirting extending down to within a short distance of rail level. The steel panels were left uncovered after the Rexine used on the 'Silver Jubilee' proved to be unsuitable through absorbing a certain amount of water, which caused the metal underneath to corrode. The colour scheme was Garter Blue for the lower body and Marlborough Blue for above the waistline. Lettering and coach numbers were in stainless steel. At the two ends of the train there were originally three lions representing England and a single lion for Scotland, but these only remained for a short period as a joke was made in Doncaster Drawing Office

suggesting that the train belonged to a circus with a similar logo and the decoration was swiftly removed. Internally the carriages were open with a centre aisle but were partitioned into sections. In first class there were four seats facing each other in a section with one on each side of the gangway, and in third class there were two seats on one side and just one on the other. There were generally 12 seats per section, but there were 15 in the kitchen third and six in the end of the open thirds. Rexine was used on the interior and was a green colour, which, in the main, was the scheme used throughout; the carpets were also green and the upholstery was fawn. Fittings were in aluminium and air conditioning was again provided.

Supplementary charges were made, but as stops were present these varied from 6 shillings first class and 4 shillings third class from King's Cross to Edinburgh, 3 and 2 shillings from Edinburgh to Newcastle, and 4 and 2 shillings between London and York. The average speeds of the 'Coronation' were higher than the 'Silver Jubilee' over certain sections, but the overall average was slightly lower at 65.5mph in both directions. Between King's Cross and the first stop at York (188 miles in

ABOVE Interior of the observation saloon.

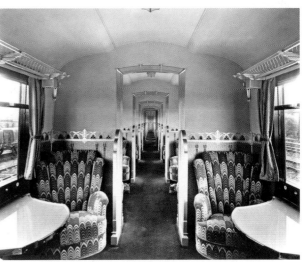

ABOVE Accommodation in first class.

157 minutes) an average speed of 71.9mph was required, making this section the fastest in the country. From Hitchin to Huntingdon the highest point-to-point speed was raised to 85.1mph and the second fastest was Hatfield to Hitchin, which demanded 77.7mph from the 'A4'. The averages remained in the 70s until past Selby, when section speeds fell to the high 60s at best. The maximum from Newcastle to Edinburgh was 72.6mph for the 11 miles between Dunbar and Drem Junction. The up train slightly bettered the average speed of the 'Silver Jubilee' from Newcastle to King's Cross at 68mph, but there were no high point-to-point times booked over 80mph The greatest was 77.7mph for the 14 miles from Hitchin to Hatfield and the time allocated 11 minutes. Again the southern section was the harder task for the locomotive.

Three sheds – King's Cross, Gateshead and Edinburgh Haymarket – were involved in working the train, leading to quite complicated arrangements. The King's Cross crews would travel to Newcastle on Sunday and work the up train on Monday, Wednesday and Friday, taking the down train to York on Tuesdays and Thursdays, travelling as passengers to Newcastle. Gateshead men ran the service from King's Cross to York on Monday, Wednesday and Friday, returning to King's Cross from Newcastle on the other days. A second set of men from Gateshead would relieve their shedmates at York on Monday, Wednesday and Friday and carry on the journey to Edinburgh, returning to Newcastle on the days in between with the up train as far as Newcastle. The Scottish crew would take the up train as far as Newcastle three days a week and would stay in York to take the down train to Waverley on Tuesday and Thursday.

The LNER organised a press run for 30 June 1937 from King's Cross to Barkston and back. Prior to the journey Sir Ralph Wedgwood gave a short speech and again attempted to quash any thoughts that the train was solely trying to accomplish high speeds. He said: 'You are not going to break records today. Our drivers are confident they can do 120mph with these engines, but we do not encourage them to try. We want to show you that we can travel at a cruising speed of 90mph in perfect comfort and that it will feel like 40mph. If we can achieve that with our new train we shall please our customers and we shall have carried rail travel one stage forward on the road of progress.'

No 4489 *Dominion of Canada* was the engine chosen for the journey and Driver Burfoot was at the regulator with Fireman Middleton assisting. The running conformed to Wedgwood's statement and no high speeds in the manner of the 'Silver Jubilee's' press outing were attempted with the down run. The train was actually 1 minute late at Hatfield but No 4489 made this up to Peterborough, and Grantham was passed in 87 minutes 34 seconds for the 105½ miles; an additional 5 minutes 55 seconds were taken for the 6 miles to Barkston. There, the locomotive and train stood for a time before heading back to King's Cross, and Burfoot soon had the engine up to 66mph at Grantham station, maintaining 69mph up the 1 in 200 to Stoke summit. In the 3 miles to Corby No 4489 gained 20mph and in the 7 miles to milepost 90 went to 100mph at milepost 93, jumped from 102.9mph at 92 to 107.5mph at 91, then peaked at 109.1mph. *Dominion of Canada* then trailed off and no further fast running was attempted. The time from Grantham to Peterborough was 20 minutes 53 seconds, or just over 2 minutes 30 seconds ahead of schedule, the average speed being 84mph for the 29¼ miles. Arrival at King's Cross was made in 86 minutes 3 seconds from Grantham, which was slightly early.

This attempt at high speed was a disappointing riposte to the LMSR, which had only the day before run a press train to introduce the company's own streamlined service – the

'Coronation Scot' – and on this 114mph had been achieved. The company had not made an immediate response to the 'Silver Jubilee', requiring sufficient time to develop such a service, including the new 'Coronation' class Pacifics, which were streamlined. High-speed tests had been conducted with the 'Royal Scot' and 'Princess Royal' class Pacific No 6201 *Princess Elizabeth* in November 1936 and the results were favourable. Averages of 68.2mph and 70mph were achieved on the down and up trains respectively, but the engine required mechanical attention between the two journeys. The LMSR announced the train in early 1937 (after the LNER) and the timings were later disclosed as 6 hours 30 minutes both ways for the 401 miles from departure at 1.30pm with a stop at Carlisle. The average speed necessary was 61.7mph.

On the press trip for the 'Coronation Scot', which weighed 263 tons with one carriage less than usual, an attempt was made for the British record down from Whitmore summit to Crewe – this being only 8 miles or so from the crest to the station. The journey between Euston and Whitmore was steady and speed was maintained in the high 80s, being 85mph going over the top of the hill. This quickly rose to over 100mph in 3½ miles and peaked in the final 2 miles before the brakes were applied. Unfortunately the engine had been diverted into an unscheduled platform, which featured a reverse curve entry with a 20mph restriction. No 6220 *Coronation* took the curve at close to 60mph and the passengers were very fortunate that the train was not derailed. The top speed reached, from the speed indicator in the cab of the engine, was claimed to be 114mph, but C. J. Allen and several other recorders timing the train had noted the speed for the 2 miles at the end as 112½mph, therefore they claimed a maximum of 113mph. On the return high average speeds were attained, with the 158 miles from Crewe being completed in 120 minutes at an average speed of 79.7mph, including over 70 miles at nearly 89mph.

The first 'Coronation' trains left their respective stations on 5 July with the down train behind No 4491 *Commonwealth of Australia* and Driver T. Dron and Fireman C. Charlton of Gateshead on the footplate. They were relieved at York by Driver H. Hutchinson and Fireman S. Jobling. At King's Cross for the departure were 2,000 people (estimated by the *LNER Magazine*) and Sir Ralph Wedgwood saw away the passengers, which included William Whitelaw and Gresley. When the train moved off for the first time there were cheers and shouts of 'Hurrah!' and 'Good Luck!' Also reported was the fact that the train was the first to be televised by the BBC via a long-range camera placed at Alexandra Palace. No 4491 made good progress, with highs of 94 and 98mph between Hitchin and Huntingdon, and Peterborough was passed 2 minutes early. The gains reached 3 minutes 30 seconds at Shaftholme Junction but were slightly down at York for the first stop. Arrival was made at Waverley 1 minute early and a warm reception was afforded to the train and the passengers. No 4489 *Dominion of Canada* ran from Waverley with Driver Maguire and Fireman Wilson, with Driver Burfoot and Fireman Middleton relieving. The Lord Provost of Edinburgh was on hand to see the train away and the journey was concluded on time.

In the first week of the 'Coronation' the patronage was quite poor, averaging about 55 people leaving the train at Waverley station. Alighting at York were about 25 people, and they were not replaced be a meaningful number from there. The up train was more successful and half the seating capacity was occupied upon arrival at King's Cross; the stop at Newcastle was also taken advantage of. Heading through the summer and into the winter months the position of both trains saw little improvement and the number of passengers barely reached half full for the train north and just over half for the southbound service.

There were no late arrivals during the first five days that the train ran and in general this was the norm during the first two months when only 14 of 76 journeys failed to be completed in time. No 4491 *Commonwealth of Australia* monopolised the journeys made during this period, with 48 of the first 51 headed by the locomotive; No 4490 *Empire of India* was also prolific in the first few months. The first failure, on 16 September, was No 4491, when the engine was taken off the up train at Newcastle and replaced by 'A3' No 2597 *Cicero*, which managed to complete the service with only 1 minute lost. A further six failures would be recorded to the end of the year, two of these being trains to London and the remainder to Waverley. No 4488 recorded one, Nos 4489 and 4490 two, and No 4497 *Golden Plover* (built in October 1937) accounted for the final one of the year. In two instances 'A1s' Nos 2577 *Night Hawk* and 2658 *Sceptre* took the train forward, but were unable to catch up time; 'A3' No 2505 *Cameronian* and classmate No 2597 *Gainsborough* also headed the streamliner. 'N1' 0-6-2T No 4582 had to take the train from Potters Bar to King's Cross when No 4488 *Union of South Africa* failed, and arrival was made 1 hour 23 minutes late.

An unusual problem befell the 'A4s' working the 'Coronation' during the final months of 1937. On several occasions the engine arrived back on shed with very little or no coal left in the tender, and on 2 December No 4490 *Empire of India* exhausted the supply at Hitchin. Even though the coal consumption was relatively low at approximately 40lb per mile, which would equate to about 7 tons over the 392 miles, inclement weather or delays encountered en route in the form of signal checks or speed restrictions would cause the consumption to increase. The solution was to have the streamlining plates at the top of the tender removed so that 9 tons could be accommodated, but shed staff at King's Cross and Haymarket found that this could be increased by a ton or so if the coal was packed in by hand. This was not only experienced by the LNER but also by the LMSR's 'Coronation Scot'.

A log of a run behind No 4491 *Commonwealth of Australia* was made by 'A Railway Engineer' for *The Meccano Magazine* shortly after the 'Coronation' began. At Waverley station, before the train departed at the hands of Driver Ferguson of Gateshead, a large number of people were inspecting the train and engine. After leaving Edinburgh the speed was soon up to 80mph, but on the coast mist was coming inland and the locomotive was necessarily slowed to 55mph. This lost the impetus for the climb up Cockburnspath bank and the speed fell to 39mph at the top of the hill. On the falling gradient to Berwick 84mph was achieved and No 4491 was running on time. The author makes an interesting remark concerning the observation car, where the riding was said to be good. The exhaust from the engine

BELOW No 4490 *Empire of India* in King's Cross shed yard with 'A3' Pacific No 4480 *Enterprise* on 17 July 1937. The 'A4' was transferred to Haymarket in March 1938. *E. R. Wethersett/IAL*

TOP LEFT Ready to leave King's Cross with the 'Coronation' on 19 April 1938 is No 4492 *Dominion of New Zealand*. *L. Hanson*

BELOW LEFT An early view of No 4495 as *Great Snipe* in Apple Green livery at Doncaster.

Grantham station the locomotive was doing no less than 70mph and only lost about 6mph running up to Stoke. At Corby the speed rose to 85mph, and 95mph 5 miles on at Little Bytham, then climaxing at 106mph. This was then sustained through Essendine and Tallington stations to Werrington Junction where the engine was slowed for the Peterborough restriction. From Little Bytham to Werrington the time taken was 7 minutes 22 seconds for the 12 miles with an average speed of 103.5mph. Some more good work was produced to Stevenage with 69½mph when breasting the 1 in 200 and 96mph passing Hatfield. At the top of the 1¾ miles of 1 in 330 to Potters Bar 85½mph was reached, but a signal was encountered at Finsbury Park and arrival was made at King's Cross 3 minutes late.

O. S. Nock, in *The Gresley Pacifics 1935-1974*, documents a journey on the down train from the same period behind No 4490 *Empire of India*. Driver Auger of King's Cross lost some time out to Hatfield, which was passed at 86½mph. The arrears were 1 minute 48 seconds at Hitchin despite the speed being 87mph on the downward gradient from Stevenage. A peak of 94mph was made at Arlesey and at Huntingdon *Empire of India* had averaged 83.4mph from Hitchin. A top speed of 95mph was achieved at Holme before Peterborough where the total time was 64 minutes 21 seconds, now only 51 seconds late. Three miles on at Werrington Junction No 4490 was up to 69½mph. At the foot of Stoke bank *Empire of India* was recorded at 90mph and 7½ miles on had only dropped to 83½mph. At Corby the reading was 76mph and at the summit was 74mph. The 20½ miles from Werrington to Stoke took 16 minutes 28 seconds at an average speed of 74.7mph, while the 15 miles from Tallington took 11 minutes 19 seconds and the average was 80.8mph. The time at Grantham was 87 minutes 52 seconds – 22 seconds late – but on to Newark 1 minute 30 seconds had been gained on the section and this was just about carried over to Doncaster. A signal was caught before Selby, yet arrival was made at York on time.

followed a path along the train and swept down the beaver tail in a smooth stream, demonstrating that the air was being pierced without much disturbance.

The journey on to Newcastle was quite routine but some time was gained leading to adverse signals on the way into the station. The train was 1 minute early coming to a stand at the platform, then Driver Walker took over. The restrictions for colliery subsidence halted progress south of the city and moderate speeds were recorded to York and Selby where the engine was just over time and this persisted to Doncaster. Driver Walker pressed No 4491 south of the town, having just over 2 hours to travel the 156 miles to King's Cross – the average speed necessary was 74.8mph. The engine was soon at 86mph at Scrooby (10 miles south of Doncaster). From 64mph at Markham summit *Commonwealth of Australia* went into the mid-90s – with a peak of 96mph at Crow Park, 8 miles from the top. Passing through

On 7 March 1938 the 'Coronation' began to make a stop at Newcastle for passengers on the down train in order to increase the number of patrons, which worked to a degree, but no change was made to the schedule. The first train was hauled by No 4497 *Golden Plover* and arrival at Waverley was made 2 minutes 25 seconds late. Also at this time the crews' diagrams were altered so Gateshead men did not have to relieve the crew at York and return to Newcastle the following day. Haymarket men went instead to Newcastle on the up train and the down crew also changed at Newcastle. Furthermore, the schedule south of York was given 3 minutes extra after the resignalling was completed north of the city.

ABOVE The interior of the 'West Riding Limited' first class carriage.

ABOVE Seats 62 and 63 in first class aboard the 'West Riding Limited'.

Following the introduction of the 'Coronation', the stream of 'A4s' from Doncaster continued with No 4493 *Woodcock* being dispatched to Gateshead in July 1937. No 4494 *Osprey* was sent a short distance away to Heaton in mid-August and was then followed by No 4495 *Great Snipe* at the end of the month. No 4496 *Golden Shuttle* entered traffic at the beginning of September. The last two locomotives mentioned were chosen to work a third streamlined service between King's Cross, Leeds and Bradford named the 'West Riding Limited'. This was ordered in partnership with the 'Coronation' but went into traffic at the end of the summer season on 27 September 1937 and was virtually the same as the former, but with a different interior colour scheme. No 4495 was returned to Doncaster Works in early September in order to be prepared for the start of the service, while No 4496 was chosen while under construction. Nos 4493-95 had been given Apple Green livery so the latter had to be repainted in Garter Blue and was also renamed *Golden Fleece* to connect with the West Riding's rich heritage in the textile industry.

The 'West Riding Limited' was scheduled to run the Leeds-King's Cross section non-stop in 2 hours 45 minutes at an average speed of 68mph. The departure time at Bradford was 11.10am, but the train headed from there behind specially prepared 'N2' class 0-6-2T engines before being attached to an 'A4' to leave Leeds at 11.33am. The return service was a late departure with a slot booked out of King's Cross for 7.10pm, heading north with an expected average speed of 68.5mph. In the event this was difficult to achieve as the train's path was in the midst of the late expresses and the early evening freight trains, also being in close proximity to the 5.50pm to Leeds, which was a heavy and slowly timed train stopping on the

LEFT At Leeds prior to departure with the demonstration run of the 'West Riding Limited' is No 4495 *Golden Fleece*. *Yorkshire Post Newspapers*

ABOVE The two 'West Riding Limited' engines – No 4495 *Golden Fleece* and No 4496 *Golden Shuttle* – pose in this scene at King's Cross. *IAL*

way north. Supplements were again charged to passengers, these being 4 shillings for first class and 2 shillings for third class. A new link was created at King's Cross for the service, No 1A, consisting of six sets of men, and unhappily for Leeds-based enginemen they were not involved. For the 'West Riding Limited' to be able to work into Leeds behind 'A4s' or other Pacifics, Bridge No 60 over the River Calder at Wakefield had to be strengthened and would be replaced by the end of the decade.

The press demonstration train took place on Thursday 23 September, leaving Bradford at 2.18pm and Leeds at 2.45pm to travel to Barkston in 77 minutes for the 75½ miles from Leeds. No 4495 was at the head of the train with Driver J. Sherriff at the controls and Fireman Schofield with the shovel; both men were from Doncaster shed. No extraordinarily high speeds were attempted, but the crew had the train running at 93mph past Crow Park on the first leg. At Barkston the Lord Mayor of Leeds, Alderman Tom Coombs, was taken to the footplate by Mr R. A. Thom, Mechanical Engineer, Doncaster.

The service began the following Monday, but No 4495 had to be substituted from the first up train as a hot bearing developed while working from King's Cross the day before. No 4492 *Dominion of New Zealand* was hastily dispatched north and

was ready for work with Driver W. Beach and Fireman C. Kerton the next morning. The train, which had Gresley on board, arrived 2 minutes early, but the first down train did not fare well and was badly held up by signals, arriving in Leeds over 14 minutes late, despite some impressive running to Doncaster. No 4492 remained on the service for another two days before being relieved by No 4491 *Commonwealth of Australia*. No 4492 set a high watermark for the locomotive as on the second day two 100mph top speeds were recorded and over 90mph was maintained for 23½ miles between Biggleswade and Hatfield.

The 'West Riding Limited' appears to have worked in relative obscurity in comparison to the 'Silver Jubilee' and the 'Coronation' streamlined services. A similar number of recorded performances are not to be found, despite the train promising an eventful journey given that the timing between Leeds and London was one of the toughest on the LNER. Of some of the runs that were recorded and presented by C. J. Allen in his 'British Locomotive Practice and Performance' article in *The Railway Magazine* of November 1940, gains of nearly 10 minutes could be made in both directions. No 4493 *Woodcock* took the up train the 185 miles in 155 minutes 30 seconds net at an average speed of 71mph, while the down journey was completed by No 4498 in 156 minutes 45 seconds net. The failure rate was also very low, with the available information showing that No 4489's breakdown north of Doncaster in 1938, when a 'K3' took the train forward, was the only such occurrence on the 'West Riding

BELOW The men behind the LNER Pacifics celebrate the naming of No 4498 with Sir Nigel Gresley.

RIGHT Sir Nigel Gresley poses with No 4498 at King's Cross shed.

Limited'. There are instances of the rostered engine being failed before the train departed and several non-'A4s' stood in, including 'A1s' (No 4472 *Flying Scotsman*) and 'V2s' (No 4789, which acquitted itself well by only dropping 4 minutes on the schedule). Nos 4495 and 4496 worked roughly half of all of the 'West Riding Limited' services and, appropriately, worked the final trains in 1939.

During October 1937 the final two 'A4s' of the order were sent into traffic – No 4497 *Golden Plover* and No 4498 *Sir Nigel Gresley* (he had been knighted in 1936). The latter was the 100th of Gresley's Pacific designs to be constructed and in order to honour this momentous occasion the name chosen was that of the CME, as a result of a suggestion made by a member of the Railway Correspondence & Travel Society, Mr K. Risdon Prentice. An official, but private naming ceremony was organised for 26 November 1937 at Marylebone station. Mr William Whitelaw unveiled the nameplate, commenting that the LNER was very grateful for all the work Gresley had undertaken during his tenure and noted the high esteem in which he was held by both his colleagues in the LNER and the engineering fraternity. Whitelaw added that he was very pleased to perform this duty and that he hoped Gresley's association with the company would continue for many more years. Gresley replied to these kind words, after receiving a silver model of No 4498, by saying that he was thankful to the members of staff who had assisted him in the production of all his engines, then, in relation to the Pacifics, Mr F. Wintour (Works Manager at Doncaster when the first Pacific was built) and Mr R. A. Thom, who had overseen the construction of the streamlined Pacifics. Gresley then gave thanks to the drivers and firemen that worked his engines and highlighted the excellent manner in which this

was done regardless of the conditions. Finally, Gresley mentioned how indebted he was to the practices in America and on the Continent and the research into locomotive design that had been conducted by the railways there. The CME then took to the footplate and drove the engine to the end of the platform and back.

With two orders of four and 17 engines completed by October 1937, the allocations were: King's Cross, Nos 2509, 2510, 2512, 4482, 4483, 4489, 4490, 4495, 4496 and 4498; Gateshead, Nos 2511, 4485, 4487 and 4493; Heaton, No 4494; and Haymarket, Nos 4484, 4486, 4488, 4491, 4492 and 4497. Joining these engines in service before the end of the year were three of Order No 341A placed in November 1936, together with two other orders, Nos 342 and 343, for ten and one locomotives respectively. Nos 4462 *Great Snipe*, 4463 *Sparrow Hawk* and 4464 *Bittern* were built in November and December 1937 and added to the ranks at King's Cross, Gateshead and Heaton respectively. For the final two engines of order No 341 and the subsequent 'A4' class locomotives the livery was standardised as Garter Blue but with shaded gold transfer numbers and lettering. The 'green' and 'silver' locomotives followed suit in late 1937 and during 1938; the first four also received nameplates at this time. The new locomotives came out with streamlined non-corridor tenders, the majority of which were new, while five for Nos 4464, 4468, 4901, 4902 and 4903 were from 'A1s' and 'A3s' that had the type.

During late 1936 and for much of 1937 'W1' class 4-6-4 No 10000 was in Doncaster Works for rebuilding after Gresley called a halt to his high-pressure experiment. For the engine's new guise Gresley employed two of his latest developments: the streamlined casing of the 'A4' class and a boiler based on that

fitted to the last 'P2' class engine, No 2006 *Wolf of Badenoch*. This had the longer combustion chamber used in the 'A4s' and the working pressure of 250lb per sq in, but with the 'P2' 50sq ft grate area. 'A1'-type 20-inch-diameter cylinders with 8-inch piston valves were fitted and the Walschaerts/Gresley motion was employed. For the exhaust system Gresley went back to the Kylchap double blastpipe and chimney. Later experience would prove the engine to be about equal in terms of performance with the 'A4' class, despite a higher tractive effort, but was somewhat hamstrung by the small piston valves.

There was more streamlining on the LNER during 1937 as two 'B17' class 4-6-0s were fitted with the 'A4'-type casing for the inauguration of the 'East Anglian' express service from Liverpool Street to Norwich, which began on 27 September 1937. The schedule of 2 hours 15 minutes for the approximately 114 miles called for an average speed of 50.6mph, perhaps giving some indication as to how necessary the streamlining was to the operation of the train. The two engines concerned were No 2859 *Norwich City* – renamed *East Anglian* – and No 2870 *Tottenham Hotspur*, which became *City of London*.

The use of Kylchap blastpipes and chimney on an 'A4' class engine was authorised in early 1938 after experience gained with the 'W1' and also 'A3' No 2751 *Humorist*. The 'A4' arrangement was modelled on these rather than the larger 'P2' design. The orifice diameter was 5 inches with No 3 taper

blocks. The top of the chimney was 1ft 5³⁄₈in in diameter, the choke was 1ft 3in in diameter, and the bottom was of 1ft 4¹³⁄₁₆in diameter. Nos 4465 *Guillemot*, 4466 *Herring Gull* and 4467 *Wild Swan* were not considered for the exhaust system to be fitted, and the first was therefore No 4468 *Mallard*. The first three went to King's Cross, Gateshead and King's Cross respectively while the latter was allocated to Doncaster so a close analysis of the engine's performance could be made. While still quite new *Mallard* worked for the first and last time on a streamlined train – the 'West Riding Limited' – after the failure of No 4489 mentioned earlier required the engine to deputise on the up train. No 4468 was regularly used on the 'Yorkshire Pullman', which, at nine carriages, was one of the longest Pullman trains in operation on the LNER and had a timing of 155 minutes from Doncaster to King's Cross. The train had required rescheduling following the introduction of the 'West Riding Limited' and had 15 minutes stripped from the 4-hour running time. A diversion was also made so the train omitted Leeds and Bradford, travelling via York to Harrogate, with a portion from Wakefield and Hull travelling independently to Doncaster.

After the poor results with the increased braking power Gresley contacted the Westinghouse Brake & Signal Co to task them with producing an improved means of getting the brakes of the train to apply more quickly and reduce the stopping distance. The company came up with the Quick Service

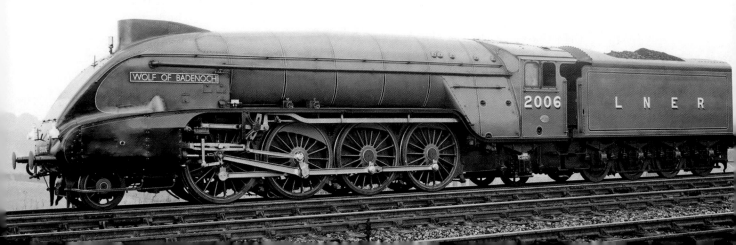

Application (QSA) valve, which was fitted to each carriage as part of the existing system. Whereas the air was admitted through the driver's valve first before heading down the train, the new valve admitted air to the brakes almost as soon as the application was made, therefore reducing the lag between each carriage considerably. The first trials were conducted in late 1936 with old suburban stock before matters progressed to the 'Coronation' set. Every Sunday for some time brake tests would be conducted on the ECML at certain points to measure the stopping distances, then improvements would be made in order to reduce the lengths still further. Gresley's Technical Assistant for Carriage & Wagon matters, Norman Newsome, oversaw these trials and was going over the results with the CME one day when the latter enquired if Newsome thought that the train could go faster than the current British record. The reply was in the affirmative and a high-speed test was arranged – in much secrecy – for Sunday 3 July 1938. To make sure that there would be no doubt as to any records set up, the dynamometer car was sent south from Darlington the day before, replacing one of the twin sets from the 'Coronation' train and making the load 240 tons gross. The measuring apparatus in the dynamometer car was altered so that 2 feet of paper would run through the recorder instead of the usual 1 foot to ensure greater accuracy.

The locomotive specially chosen for the task was No 4468 *Mallard*, as the fitting of the Kylchap blastpipe and chimney was known to be important for producing a good draught and steaming rate for the attempt and for removing the steam efficiently from the cylinders, which would absorb a good deal of the power if not dealt with. Equally as crucial was the choice of crew for the run. Driver Joe Duddington and Fireman

Tommy Bray had been allocated *Mallard* at Doncaster from new and were quite familiar with the individualities of the engine. Driver Duddington was also known to be a man who would push an engine to the limit if necessary.

On 3 July the train left a siding at Wood Green station and headed north to Barkston. On the train were four men from Westinghouse, five from the LNER in the dynamometer car, with Assistant to the CME D. R. Edge in charge of the test. Several men were also in the first class carriages including Newsome and Eric Bannister, while the crew were joined on the footplate by Inspector J. Jenkins. After making several brake tests on the way, the train did not arrive at Barkston until 2.49pm. Bannister, in *Trained by Sir Nigel Gresley*, recalls that he and Inspector Jenkins went underneath the locomotive prior to departure in order to apply a large amount of superheater oil to the inside big end in order to ward off any possibility of the component failing. Apparently D. R. Edge offered the Westinghouse team the chance to leave if they had any misgivings about what was about to happen, but all elected to remain aboard.

At 4.15pm Duddington turned his cap back to front and opened the regulator full to begin the attempt. There was a snag early on as permanent way works were being undertaken just north of Grantham station, leaving the speed at 20mph when much higher would have been expected normally. Thus *Mallard* had a harder task to gain speed on the 5 miles from the station to Stoke summit.

ABOVE *Mallard* prepares to begin the record-breaking run with the dynamometer car behind the engine.

This was demonstrated, as recollected by P. T. W. Remnant of the Westinghouse team, when the engine passed through Stoke tunnel: '…there was a slight delay before the guard switched on the lights and the passengers were treated to a thrilling display as the whole car was lit up by a torrent of red-hot cinders streaming back on both sides from the locomotive's twin chimneys.' On the bank the speed was 60mph with 40% cut-off and full boiler pressure. Duddington tried to continue from halfway up with 30% cut-off, but had to revert back to 40% before the top, where *Mallard* recorded 74mph. Before Corby 96½mph had been reached and in the next mile the speed had jumped to 104mph. Just before the train flew through the station at 116mph the record was broken around milepost 94. The run did not stop here and Duddington and Bray kept working. At milepost 93, after Duddington returned to 40% cut-off following a brief spell at 45%, the speed was 119mph and crept slowly up to 122½mph at milepost 92, 124¼ at milepost 91. A peak of 125 was maintained for 306 yards close to milepost 90. The boiler had been steaming at about three times the normal rate at this point and the wheels were turning at 8½ revolutions per second. *Mallard* had exceeded 120mph for 3 miles and for 5 miles had averaged 120.4mph.

RIGHT Fireman Bray, Driver Duddington and Inspector Jenkins pose for the camera at Peterborough station after 125mph had been reached.

The train was now just a mile away from Essendine where there was slight curvature of the track and Edge gave the order for Duddington to slow down. A few moments later the unmistakable smell of the 'stink bomb' permeated the air, indicating that the middle big end bearing was running hot and further orders were given to stop the train at Peterborough. After examination No 4468 was deemed unfit to continue to King's Cross and an Ivatt Atlantic was requisitioned to take the train on. While at Peterborough Edge telephoned Gresley with the news and, while his reaction has gone unrecorded, one can perhaps guess how pleased he must have been. At King's Cross the press were out in force and even though the engine concerned was not present (the official statement was that the locomotive had duties to perform elsewhere) they were ushered into the dynamometer car to see the evidence that a speed of 125mph had been reached. This figure was the one given by the LNER and Gresley and not 126mph, as later declared by British Railways on the commemorative plaques fitted to the boiler. The figure of 126mph was a possible maximum for 1 second, but Gresley would not claim this because the time period was too short.

When *Mallard* was subsequently examined at Doncaster the bearing was found to need no more attention than remetalling and the engine returned to work after 10 days out of service. There has been the suggestion – in several publications – that the overheating was the result of the regulator being closed at such a high speed, with the consequent loss of load on the piston and connecting rod. In Germany the '05' class locomotives had suffered a similar failure in the same circumstances and the drivers were instructed to not fully close the regulator at over 100mph.

LEFT Pictured in September 1938 at Grantham, No 4466 *Herring Gull* had only transferred there in April from King's Cross and would remain until August 1944.

double blastpipe and chimney from new. These engines were allocated to Gateshead, King's Cross and Doncaster respectively.

The difference between the standard blastpipe and the Kylchap type extended not only to high speeds with light loads but to heavy trains as recorded by 'A Railway Engineer' in *The Meccano Magazine* of July 1939. No 4902 was observed with the 1.20pm to Edinburgh, weighing 480 tons, and was said to be 'playing' with the train for long distances. On the 1 in 200 to Potters Bar *Seagull* maintained 56mph up the bank when other engines with the same load were expected to be travelling 10mph slower. At Stevenage 70mph was steadily achieved with just 16% cut-off. Then, on the relatively easy section from there, the locomotive had the regulator shut to just one-third open to keep the speed below the 90mph limit after a high of 95mph at Three Counties. The writer then cites a previous trip on the same train behind No 4499 *Pochard* when the 5½ miles from Peterborough station to Helpston took 8 minutes to complete, while *Seagull* was timed at 6 minutes 30 seconds.

A total of 35 'A4' class Pacifics were in traffic for the summer of 1938 and these were working the LNER's principal expresses, having ousted the 'A1s' and 'A3s' as the main motive power. This was manifested most prominently with the 'Flying Scotsman', which began to see more 'A4'

ABOVE *Kestrel* – now in Garter Blue – is seen at Newcastle Central station with an express for the north in 1938. *R. E. Kirkbright*

Another important achievement was made only a few days after No 4468's exploits when, on 6 July, 'A1' No 4476 *Royal Lancer* was the first Pacific to accumulate 1 million miles in service, while travelling north of Knebworth.

Following *Mallard* into traffic at the end of March was No 4469 *Gadwall*, then No 4499 *Pochard* and No 4500 *Garganey* in April. No 4900 *Gannet* was the only 'A4' built in May before June and July saw the final three class members enter traffic. No 4468 had obviously pleased Gresley up to this point as Nos 4901 *Capercaillie*, 4902 *Seagull* and 4903 *Peregrine* also had the Kylchap

haulage after the introduction of the second batch, and 1937 would prove to be the last year the non-stop would feature 'A1s' and 'A3s'. The first trains of this year had two 'A4s' on them; No 4484 *Falcon* took the northbound train with a new 7-hour schedule in force, and No 4485 *Kestrel* was on the up service. The average speed of the 'Flying Scotsman' was 56.1mph but had some exacting portions such as the 110 minutes for King's Cross to Grantham and 105 minutes heading to London, with the weight of the train being over 450 tons. The last 'A3' used was No 2750 *Papyrus* on 6 August when travelling to Waverley, and back the next day. The corridor tender used – No 5329 – was removed on 6 September to be fitted to No 4498 and was carried by this engine for the next six years. The standout performer over the season was 'A4' No 4492 *Dominion of New Zealand*, which worked

incline to Potters Bar in fine fashion, breasting the summit at 49mph. The speed was then 56mph at Brookman's Park, and Hatfield was passed in 25 minutes from King's Cross, or 3 minutes ahead of time. Further gains could have been made by the veteran engine had the train preceding the special not been dawdling and the schedule had to be kept to Stevenage. There a fine contrast was made with the 'A4' and the new stock. The volume of photographers documenting the event caused a late departure, but Driver W. Sheen, Fireman S. Findlay and Inspector J. Jenkins soon had No 4498 up to 80mph. At Biggleswade 90mph was reached and it was still near that figure with 88mph 6¼ miles on at Tempsford. The time from Hitchin to Fletton Junction (just south of Peterborough) was 33 minutes 6 seconds for the 43 miles and the average speed was 77.9mph. From Peterborough to Stoke summit 25 minutes 45 seconds were taken and at the top of the acclivity the speed was 53mph. To cap the event No 4472 *Flying Scotsman* travelled past the train while at Barkston. On the return the only part of the performance of note was the 10 miles from Stoke summit, which were travelled at an average speed of just less than 90mph.

E. H. Livesay recorded a return trip on the 'Flying Scotsman' with No 4491 *Commonwealth of Australia* in *The Engineer* for 31 March 1939, but does not give too many details as he lost his notebook while riding on 'Coronation' class Pacific *Princess Alice*! Nevertheless, the article offers an interesting insight to the working of a typical train. The weight was 470 tons gross and Livesay notes that this was not a particularly taxing proposition

ABOVE No 4492 *Dominion of New Zealand* departs from Edinburgh Waverley with the 'Flying Scotsman' on 20 August 1937. *IAL*

52 trains without a break and accumulated 20,436 miles in the process. The winter timetable for the 'Flying Scotsman' allocated 7 hours 20 minutes for the 392¾ miles, with four stops by the down service and five by the southbound train.

For the summer of 1938 Gresley designed a new set of carriages to be used on the 'Flying Scotsman' comprising 12 vehicles (14 in the summer), including a buffet lounge and a restaurant triplet set. The seating for the summer was 36 first class and 213 third class, while in the winter these were 60 and 258 respectively; the tare weight was 426 tons for the former and 503 the latter. The LNER made quite a spectacle of unveiling these new carriages on 30 June 1938 as GNR Stirling 'Single' No 1 was restored and paired with carriages replicating the 1888 'Flying Scotsman' formation. This train took specially invited guests to Stevenage where No 4498 *Sir Nigel Gresley* was waiting to take the passengers to Barkston in the new set. GNR No 1 left King's Cross promptly at 2.00pm and went up the

RIGHT The use of Stirling 'Single' No 1 to publicise the new 'Flying Scotsman' train was an impressive idea from the LNER's Publicity Department. *Yorkshire Post Newspapers*

ABOVE The up 'Flying Scotsman' is headed by No 4482 *Golden Eagle* over Berwick-upon-Tweed's Royal Border Bridge on 22 August 1939. *IAL*

for the locomotive, nor was the timing. After the train was started, cut-off was 25% and would be taken down to 15% when more speed was gained. At Potters Bar the train was travelling at 60mph and to Stevenage 75mph was averaged. The fireman kept the boiler pressure at 240lb per sq in and generally filled the firebox, not using the 'little and often' method. The quality of the coal was quite good and did not affect the fire. The deflection of smoke away from the cab was also noted as not being a hindrance to the sighting of signals. The speed was kept to 65mph and the boiler pressure never fell below 225lb per sq in. No 4491 brought the train into Waverley station 3 minutes early. The up train the next day was run in much the same way and the coal consumption was said to be approximately 40-45lb per mile.

The trains were not always as easy even though the 'A4' class could make this appear to be the case. No 4490 *Empire of India* was

handed a 17-carriage 'Flying Scotsman' weighing 635 tons gross at King's Cross, and north of Hitchin the speed was up to 90mph. At Stoke summit the speed was just below 50mph and Grantham was passed in 108 minutes from the start, which was a 2-minute saving on the schedule with a normal load. Four minutes were lost to York thanks to a signal check, but at Newcastle the locomotive had completed the 80¼ miles in 86 minutes – 4 minutes ahead of the timetable. However, the arrival time there was late as there had been problems manoeuvring carriages off the train at York.

The 1938 summer season was deemed a success by *The Meccano Magazine* of February 1939, as some of the figures from the workings are presented. The down train was punctual at Newcastle for 49 of the 69 journeys, with a similar figure being true for the up service, and the average load was approximately 460 tons. No 4491 *Commonwealth of Australia* was the star performer with a total of 36 trips made, while No 4489 *Dominion of Canada* was in second place with 33. In the following summer the latter was again a regular on the train, bettering the figure by one journey, and some work was also done on the 'Coronation' and 'West Riding

LEFT At Ganwick (just south of Potters Bar) No 4463 *Sparrow Hawk* speeds by with an express to the capital during 1938. *IAL*

Pacific Locomotives taking the 5.30pm Leeds to King's Cross, weighing 500 tons, from Peterborough. No 4500 *Garganey* had handled the first portion but had lost a considerable amount of time at Doncaster through a stubborn coupling refusing to allow a coach to be detached. The engine made up some time travelling south and completed the section to Grantham nearly 5 minutes early, and just over 3 minutes were gained to Peterborough. Ten minutes had to be found on the remainder of the journey by Driver Ovenden and *Osprey*, but another minute was lost before departure due to a lengthy switchover of locomotives. At Holme – 7 miles from the station – the speed was 71½mph, then dropped to 57mph while climbing the 1 in 200 to Abbots Ripton. On the falling gradient to Huntingdon 76½mph was attained and No 4494 went through Offord at 71mph. A peak of 77½mph was achieved at Sandy before Hitchin was passed at 64½mph in 41 minutes 38 seconds for the 44 miles from Peterborough. The time from Huntingdon was 20 minutes 21 seconds for the 27 miles at an average speed of 79.6mph. A final high of 79mph was made at Hatfield before arrival was made at King's Cross in 73 minutes 44 seconds for the 76 miles; the average speed had been 62mph. Incredibly, over 11 minutes had been regained, so a punctual arrival was realised.

In the December 1939 issue of *The Meccano Magazine* R. A. H. Weight was reporting another instance of time being gained by an 'A4' during the summer workings. No 4488 *Union of South Africa* was hauling the 5.20pm Newcastle to King's Cross with Driver Ferguson of Gateshead at the regulator. The train weighed 425 tons as far as Doncaster where a number of carriages were added from various other places in Yorkshire, taking the weight to 630 tons. Six miles to the south, on the 1 in 198 rise before Bawtry, the speed was 50mph, then reached 70mph through the town, and the 17½ miles to Retford were completed in 20 minutes 30 seconds. A delay was experienced there and 15 minutes were lost before the train could continue. Despite the presence of 3 miles

ABOVE Emerging from Welwyn South Tunnel with an Edinburgh to King's Cross express is No 4484 *Falcon* on 8 June 1939. *IAL*

Limited'. No 4484 *Falcon* was on the first train in the summer of 1939 on 3 July.

The 'Flying Scotsman' was just one of the many expresses the 'A4s' worked. No 4494 *Osprey* was recorded by C. J. Allen in *British*

of 1 in 178 a short distance away from the station, No 4488 had the train up to 43mph on the bank. Travelling from the peak into the Trent valley 77mph was achieved and the speed was just under 70mph through Newark station. At Grantham 58mph was recorded as *Union of South Africa* swept through, and this rate of travel only fell to 45mph at Stoke. Down from the top a high of 89½mph was reached before Peterborough, where the time was 62 minutes 30 seconds with an average speed of 59.7mph. The train was now 8 minutes 30 seconds better off, but experienced interrupted running through signals at Holme and Tempsford. Despite these an average speed of 72.2mph was made from Huntingdon to Arlesey and a maximum of 78mph was achieved near New Southgate before arrival was made at King's Cross in 150 minutes from Retford – 5 minutes ahead of the schedule.

In early 1939 No 4498 was noted as hauling the Royal Train when King George VI and Queen Elizabeth visited Newcastle and returned via Bishop Auckland to King's Cross. The *LNER Magazine* also recorded *Sir Nigel Gresley* as the engine used to haul a special for the Crusaders' Union (a religious group for young people now known as Urban Saints) from King's Cross to Grantham in April 1938. There the party went on to RAF Cranwell where Hurricanes were witnessed before returning to Barkston where the group waited to see the down 'Coronation' pass at 90mph. No 4498 then conveyed the expedition (consisting of 14 carriages weighing 500 tons) back to London in 108 minutes 45 seconds from Grantham.

No 4492 *Dominion of New Zealand* was chosen for a special on 27 July 1938 when taking 170 passengers, including the High Commissioners of New Zealand, Canada and South Africa, to Wallsend for the launch of *Dominion Monarch*. The spare 'Coronation' set was used and a schedule of 4 hours 30 minutes was set, the arrival being made 2 minutes early. The return was allocated 4 hours 36 minutes, including a stop at Wood Green to allow the Managing Director of the Shaw, Savill & Albion Line, which ordered the vessel, to alight, and the average speed was 62mph.

Also around this time No 4489 was involved in a special occasion that saw Mr J. C. Patteson, European Manager of the Canadian Pacific Railway, present the engine with a bell of the type used on the company's locomotives. He was travelling on the up 'Coronation' on 5 May 1938 subsequent to visiting the Empire Exhibition in Glasgow. *Dominion of Canada* was chosen to head the train for the bell to be rung for the first time upon departure and again on arrival at King's Cross. Operation of the bell was performed via steam and coil springs from a cable in the cab. Unfortunately the feature was taken out of use before the end of the 1930s after an incident where the driver rang the bell for a small boy at King's Cross upon starting with the 'Coronation'. The driver then found that the mechanism had jammed and the bell continued to ring until York!

From 1 March 1939 No 4469 *Gadwall* became *Sir Ralph Wedgwood* to honour the Chief General Manager who was retiring after 16 years in the role. On 3 March a ceremony was conducted

BELOW *Dominion of New Zealand* exits Welwyn South Tunnel with an up express from Harrogate and Leeds on 17 September 1938; note the white background to the signals to aid sighting. *IAL*

at Marylebone station and the nameplates were unveiled by Sir Ronald Matthews, LNER Chairman. He commented that the naming was particularly appropriate given that the high-speed trains for which the engines were intended were first suggested by Sir Ralph. In his speech, Wedgwood stated that his ambition since the age of five was to have his name grace a 'railway engine' and he was extremely glad that this dream had been fulfilled. The renaming was the first of three for the 'A4s' in two months as No 4500 *Garganey* became *Sir Ronald Matthews* a couple of weeks later and in April No 4499 *Pochard* was rechristened *Sir Murrough Wilson* after the Deputy Chairman of the LNER. The three engines were further distinguished by having their transfer numbers and lettering replaced by the steel variety.

On 31 August 1939 the last streamlined trains were run, as 1 September saw Germany invade Poland and mobilisation of the British Army began in preparation for war being declared on Germany two days later. A total of 1,952 'Silver Jubilee' trains had run between 1935 and 1939, and according to *Locomotives of the LNER Part 2A* the 'silver' engines managed to work the service 1,509 times. The most

ABOVE No 4500 *Sir Ronald Matthews* is pictured in Doncaster Works' West Yard shortly after renaming.

BELOW At New Southgate with a down express in 1938 is No 4462 *Great Snipe*. *IAL*

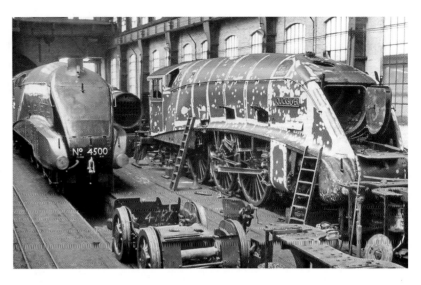

RIGHT In early 1939 No 2510 *Quicksilver* is in Doncaster Crimpsall Repair Shop for a General repair, while No 4500 *Sir Ronald Matthews* is in for just light attention; both are standing in 4-bay.

active was No 2509 *Silver Link* with 564 journeys completed (with a further 44 appearances on the other streamlined services), second was No 2510 *Quicksilver* with 456, third was No 2512 *Silver Fox*, having run 409 trains, while No 2511 *Silver King* only worked 80. The failure rate of the 'Silver Jubilee' was better than the 'Coronation' as 32,726½ miles were run between each of the 16 failures that occurred during the four years of operation. Of these No 2510 recorded the highest with nine and No 2509 had five, while Nos 2512 and 4495 *Golden Fleece* had one each. 'A1s' worked the 'Silver Jubilee' seven times, 'A3s' twice and 'C1' Atlantics on five occasions. Two failures had occurred in 1936, five in 1937, six in 1938 and three in 1939.

The punctuality rate of the train was about 70% in both directions for the first two years with an average late arrival being 2 minutes. The coaching stock was very reliable, only failing once on 13 April 1937 when a hot axlebox forced a replacement set to be sent north from Wood Green to allow the train to continue from just south of Grantham. Comprehensive figures for punctuality are not available, but generally the 'Silver Jubilee' appears to have been on time or slightly early. A sample made from October to November 1938, when 30 arrivals at King's Cross were recorded, shows that 26 were right time or early and the other four were not late to a significant degree, with two instances being the result of heavy fog. Unfortunately, out of three 'silver' 'A4s' available – No 2510 *Quicksilver* was in Doncaster Works – the last 'Silver Jubilee' trains were hauled by Nos 4489 *Dominion of Canada* and 4499 *Sir Murrough Wilson*.

The 'Coronation' ran 1,084 times between July 1937 and August 1939, with 39 failures recorded from a total of 425,741 miles travelled, which equated to a failure rate of one every 10,916 miles. Twenty occurred in 1938 and 12 in 1939. During the former year, the northbound train was more prone to the engine being unable to continue, while in the latter year there was an even split in the failures experienced. The most common causes of these were an inability to produce sufficient steam to work the train and hot bearings, which had seven instances each; there were four separate cases of hot inside big ends. R. A. H. Weight made a record of the punctuality of the 'Coronation' between Edinburgh and Newcastle for the months March to November 1938 and, of the trains arriving, 43 were early while only three were not on time. From

June to September the train was only late once, and for this the arrears upon leaving were 8 minutes, but No 4493 *Woodcock* managed to arrive on time at King's Cross. Of the engines entering Newcastle with the northbound 'Coronation' from the start of the summer season, 42 of 76 recorded were early by 1-3 minutes and 77 were on time, while 16 were on average 5 minutes behind the timetable. There was one failure causing an excessively late arrival; this casualty was perhaps No 4486 *Merlin*, which was taken off at Newcastle and replaced by No 2746 *Fairway*, which arrived at Waverley 48 minutes late.

Despite the failures a number of engines managed spells of uninterrupted service, one being No 4497 in 1939 when 39 'Coronation' services were handled by the locomotive with a high level of punctuality. For the final two months 58 services ran on time while 16 were late. No 4488 was on the last up train and No 4487 took the last 'Coronation' into Waverley. *Locomotives of the LNER Part 2A* again names the star performers for the service, with No 4490 *Empire of India* accumulating 125 appearances and No 4497 *Golden Plover* 104.

A surprising fact from the 'Coronation' service is that of all the recorded locomotive performances, the best appears to have been made by 'A3' class Pacifics. No 2595 *Trigo* replaced No 4491 at Newcastle on 22 March 1939 and went on to complete the 268 miles to King's Cross in 230 minutes, or 225 minutes net if the delays are removed from the time, saving over 10 minutes from the schedule. On 24 March No 2507 *Singapore* completed the same section in 228 minutes 30 seconds with three signal checks worth 6 minutes of time. On both of these occasions Driver Nash and Fireman Gilbey were on the footplate.

Overall financial figures for the three streamliners do not appear to have been compiled, but a four-week sample was given to the LNER Board in 1938 showing that the 'Coronation' earned £12,748 in gross receipts, which was the highest. The net receipts were £2,018, and this was £734 more than the 'Silver Jubilee' and £1,079 more than the 'West Riding Limited'.

WARTIME INTERLUDE, 1939-1947

The declaration of war against Germany came on 3 September 1939 after the international situation had been escalating for several months. The LNER and the other railways had been obliged to prepare for this eventuality, which would immediately mean the nationalisation of the 'Big Four' companies under the Railway Executive Committee. This body was formed in September 1938 from the top railway officials, and representing the LNER was Sir Ralph Wedgwood, who was also Chairman, and he remained active in this role until 1941. The REC liaised with the Railway Control Officer from the Ministry of Transport, which directed the overall operation of the network under the power of the Emergency (Railway Control) Order 1939.

The plans produced in the months leading up to the war led to the serious curtailment of passenger trains. The first sign of this occurred on 1 September when the streamliners and other services were cancelled so that children could be evacuated from urban areas and transported to places not under threat of immediate enemy action. They would be followed into relative safety by many different government departments and private companies; the LNER moved personnel to a country house near Welwyn and to Gresley's residence near Watton. Afterwards the timetabled passenger services were affected by a reduction in their frequency and an increase was made in the number of carriages in the formations to make up for those lost. The journeys also became much longer as a maximum speed of 60mph was applied to all trains. They were required to limit their speed further during air raid warnings to just 15mph, as well as stopping at the nearest station to let off those passengers who wanted to take shelter. From 2 October a new timetable was introduced and the 'Flying Scotsman' was given 9 hours 30 minutes to complete both northbound and southbound journeys. Other services were similarly affected such as the 10.30am from King's Cross to Leeds, arriving there at 4.15pm, and the midday train to Newcastle was given a schedule of 7 hours 5 minutes. The 'A4' class at King's

Cross were put into store for a time as soon as war was declared, but they were back in traffic by the end of 1939 since they could not be left on the sidelines any longer when the loads were heavier than ever. The class members allocated to other sheds were kept at work as more than 5,500 special trains were run in the first three months of the war.

December 1939 witnessed further revisions to the timetable as the expected waves of bombing did not materialise. The number of passenger trains was increased and the times were slightly faster than they had been in October and November, but the amount was still 30% lower than the pre-war figure. Restaurant and sleeping carriages, which had been withdrawn in September, were almost completely reinstated, although the dining cars soon became employed as normal carriages due to the numbers being carried. There was no relaxation of train weights and these continued to be much heavier than what had previously been considered normal. Despite an initial drop in passenger numbers from 1,239 million in 1939 to 989 million in 1940 there would be a steady increase to a peak of 1,377 million in 1945. While some of these were the general public, who had to rely more and more on rail travel as petrol became rationed, troop movements accounted for a good portion of this figure.

The performances of locomotives working the principal services still created headlines. However, these now told of the extreme loads that were frequently being faced by the 'A4' class and the 'A1s', 'A3s' and 'V2s' that often assisted. Where possible the trains would be split into two portions, but on occasions this could not be done and the weights became very high. Prior to the war one of the heaviest recorded passenger trains was 661 tons, which was brought into King's Cross one Sunday by 'A1' class Pacific No 2551 *Prince Palatine*. This was soundly beaten early in the conflict when No 2509 *Silver Link* was attached to the 1.00pm to Edinburgh, which consisted of 23 carriages weighing 734 tons tare, 790 tons gross. On 5 April 1940 No 2509 went further by taking the 1.00pm to Newcastle out of King's Cross with no less than 850 tons gross behind the tender. The engine took some time to progress, but Grantham was eventually reached in 139 minutes, or some 11 minutes late. This would only rise to 15 minutes overdue at Newcastle, with *Silver Link* completing the whole run at an average speed of 45.9mph. Not to be left out, 'V2' class No 4800 also handled a similar load with the 10.45am from Newcastle on 31 March 1940. From Peterborough to King's Cross (76¼ miles) the time was 102 minutes with the average speed of 44.8mph.

Some further good running was noted in 1941 when No 4497 *Golden Plover* gained 10 minutes between Newcastle and Edinburgh with 19 carriages. No 4468 *Mallard* and Driver Duddington were also keeping up their performance levels with a run from Peterborough to King's Cross in 78 minutes. The train concerned was the express from Hull weighing a moderate 400 tons, but the departure was 18 minutes late and was only 2 minutes behind when entering King's Cross station. The average speed for the journey was 58.6mph. C. J. Allen, in *The*

ABOVE No 4901 *Capercaillie* was always a strong performer, but the engine's wartime exploits are perhaps the most impressive.

BELOW A pre-war view of No 4903 *Peregrine* heading the 4.00pm from King's Cross to Leeds at New Southgate on 10 September 1938. *IAL*

Gresley Pacifics of the LNER, notes a particularly impressive performance that was recorded by Rev G. C. Stead involving No 4901 *Capercaillie* on the Plain of York. The engine was on the 8.00am from Newcastle and had 730 tons behind the tender. For nearly 25 miles from Otterington to Poppleton Junction an average speed of 75mph was maintained and a peak of 78mph was achieved. The time for this section was 3 seconds under 20 minutes. The use of the 'A4s' for prestigious occasions was not dampened by the conflict. No 4903 *Peregrine* hauled a special

train for Prime Minister Winston Churchill and his staff after meeting President Roosevelt to sign the Atlantic Charter in August 1941. Driver Hirst and Fireman Quince of Doncaster were on the footplate. However, the indiscriminate allocation of engines to whichever duty had priority is well illustrated by *Silver Link* working a coal train, while *Mallard* was spotted on a goods service during this period.

O. S. Nock reproduces several accounts of working with heavy loads in *The Gresley Pacifics 1935-1974*. In these the lightest load was 590 tons by No 4902 *Seagull* and a good time would have been made if not for several signals. The service was progressing satisfactorily to New Barnet when the first was against *Seagull*, bringing the train to a stand, and the 3 miles to Potters Bar took over 10 minutes to complete. The second signal was 'on' just a short distance ahead and the 5 miles to Hatfield took a further 10 minutes, with a similar period being taken to reach Knebworth after another slowing. At Hitchin the time was 53 minutes 38 seconds for the 32 miles from King's Cross, and to Huntingdon a further 24 minutes 8 seconds elapsed with an average speed of 67.1mph; a high of 71mph was recorded past Arlesey. Going past Tallington No 4901 was up to 70mph and to Stoke summit the time was 15 minutes 24 seconds with just over 45mph at the peak. The average speed was 59.4mph. Arrival at Grantham was made just under the 130-minute schedule in force, but if the delays were removed as much as 16 minutes could have been taken off the time.

No 2510 *Quicksilver* had 90 tons more than No 4902 but still performed respectably after an uninterrupted run. The 13 miles to Potters Bar took just over 23 minutes and another 19 minutes 51 seconds were added to the time after the 19.2 miles to Hitchin; the average speed was 58.1mph. The 27 miles to Huntingdon required 26 minutes 12 seconds and the rate of travel over the section was 61.8mph. From Tallington, where the speed was around 60mph, to Stoke summit, at which point the train was running at 41mph, the time was 18 minutes 51 seconds with an average of 48.5mph. The engine entered Grantham station just over 6 minutes early.

Travelling to London from Grantham No 4466 *Herring Gull* had a train of 740 tons gross. The time to Stoke was 11 minutes 41 seconds, then down to Tallington 13 minutes 24 seconds were added for the 15.3 miles; the average speed was 68.2mph, with a high of just over 70mph. *Herring Gull* completed the 1 mile of level track and 5½ miles of 1 in 200 to Abbots Ripton at 58.4mph, while Arlesey to Stevenage – 9½ miles of 1 in 264 and 1 in 200 – took 11 minutes 30 seconds at an average speed of 49.5mph. The overall time to King's Cross was 127 minutes 25 seconds and the 105½ miles had been completed at 49.7mph.

In February 1941 Gresley introduced a mixed-traffic 2-6-2 – classified 'V4' – for use on all but 1,414 miles of the LNER's 6,000 route miles. The two engines built were powerful, but light in weight through the use of fabrication and welding, which were relatively unused techniques at the time. No 3401 *Bantam Cock* was the first in traffic, while No 3402 was unnamed. The latter made up for this omission through possessing the unique features of a steel firebox fabricated by welding and two Nicholson thermic syphons to improve the flow of water around the firebox and the transfer of heat. At this time Gresley was also working on two possible improvements to the 'A4' class. One was a Pacific with a boiler pressure of 275lb per sq in and the other was a 4-8-2 locomotive with 21-inch-diameter cylinders and a boiler working at 250lb per sq in. Unfortunately the 'V4s' would prove to be the only two built and these schemes would remain on the drawing board as Gresley died on 5 April 1941 after a short illness – he was 64 years old.

This tragic event came as quite a shock to those who knew him and the LNER Board, which had expected Gresley to continue in his position for the immediate future, despite approaching retirement age. There have been suggestions that O. V. S. Bulleid, who had left the LNER for the Southern Railway, was approached about returning, and enquiries were made as to the availability of R. C. Bond, Stanier's assistant on the LMSR. In the event

LEFT No 4466 *Herring Gull* is seen here at Newcastle in 1938 with a southbound express.
R. E. Kirkbright

ABOVE 'V4' 2-6-2 No 3401 *Bantam Cock* was Gresley's last design and was to have formed the basis of a ubiquitous class. In the event the role was taken by Thompson's 'B1' 4-6-0.

Edward Thompson, Mechanical Engineer of the Southern Area, was given the job at the end of April. He had been with the LNER since Grouping and the NER and GNR prior to that. Thompson was the most senior mechanical engineer with the company, making him the LNER's most qualified candidate.

Thompson's design principles were quite different from Gresley's, as he favoured the use of two cylinders instead of three for any locomotive operating below an express train's power requirements. When three cylinders were to be used he preferred to employ three independent sets of Walschaerts valve gear instead of the Gresley conjugated motion. Thompson did not have a fondness for this on account of the wear that could develop if the components were not strictly maintained (although he had attempted to improve the construction of the gear while Mechanical Engineer, North Eastern Area, in an effort to reduce wear), and in the most serious cases this would lead to badly uneven valve events. Two of Thompson's other beliefs were the need for simplicity of construction and ease of maintenance for staff. The deterioration of the conjugated motion was kept in check through very high levels of attention from skilled workers during the 1920s and 1930s. During the war years such maintenance was difficult to provide and, when coupled to the hard work and long distances that the Gresley engines were travelling, matters quickly deteriorated. Throughout the conflict the LNER lost around 24,500 men to the armed forces and nearly 1,000 women were also redeployed. There were problems replacing these people, not just through a shortage of suitable applicants but also through the railways not providing an appealing employment opportunity, whether in sheds, workshops, or

on the footplate. The rate of pay was below other jobs helping the war effort, such as munitions manufacture and aircraft construction, leaving a void and putting a strain on employees still at work. The position only got worse as the war dragged on, even though efforts had been made to stop more workers being called up unless absolutely necessary. The maintenance of the company's locomotives was not the only area affected, as attention to the track was curtailed to only the absolutely necessary level. The rate of renewal was about 70% of the pre-war rate. The quality of coal also deteriorated, with consequent problems in locomotive performance.

To maintain the 'A4' motion shed staff would have to remove the valances and, as quick turnarounds became the order of the day, these would be left off to get the engine back in traffic. This practice was given official approval when No

RIGHT Women filled the gaps left by men on the railways during the Second World War. A group are seen here giving some close attention to No 4900 *Gannet* at Doncaster Carr locomotive shed.

LEFT There appears to have been some hesitation at Doncaster before all the skirting was removed. No 4462 *Great Snipe* is pictured in this condition, then, after being renamed *William Whitelaw*, the valances in front of the cylinders were restored. The engine ran for over a year in this condition before removal took place.

CENTRE LEFT The renamed No 4462 *William Whitelaw*. Note the hinged cover for access to the front of the cylinders.

BELOW LEFT The most recognisable guise of the 'A4s' – with no valances and the wheels exposed – was the result of wartime maintenance requirements. No 4487 *Sea Eagle* was one of the pioneers.

the skirting removed, as did No 4487 *Sea Eagle*. The process of changing the rest of the class continued into the late summer of 1942. The 'A4s' were not the only engines to receive this alteration as 'W1' class No 10000 and the two 'B17s' lost their valances as well.

Thompson next turned his attention to the conjugated motion and compiled a list of failures that were attributable to the bearing of the middle big end. He then presented this information to the LNER Board together with a report on the motion that was compiled by E. S. Cox of the LMSR and endorsed by Stanier. This document described that in the event of extreme wear the over travel of the middle valve would occur, causing strain on the middle big end, which was highlighted as being the main weak point in the system. At low speed the power would also be reduced due to poor port openings. Thompson used these issues to get the Board to authorise the rebuilding of several locomotives that were to be the prototypes for a small number of standard classes that would eventually replace the existing LNER fleet.

The new CME had a lot of previous experience of rebuilding a number of classes (while working at Stratford and Darlington), and the 'Q4s' and 'J11s' were the first designs to be modified. The most successful engine produced during Thompson's tenure was arguably the two-cylinder 'B1' 4-6-0 for mixed traffic, which took the place of Gresley's 'V4' and featured many standard components. The controversial reconstruction of the 'P2' class 2-8-2s as Pacifics followed, but a notable feature retained was the Kylchap double blastpipe

4462 *Great Snipe* was sent to Doncaster Works in mid-1941 for a General repair and emerged minus the side skirting behind the cylinders, but that in front remained with an access plate to the conjugated motion lever. No 4462 returned to service in July and was also renamed at this time to *William Whitelaw* in honour of the LNER Chairman who had left the company in 1938 after 15 years' service. His name had previously adorned 'A1' No 2563 from new in August 1924, and the alteration was confirmed at a naming ceremony that took place at York on 24 July (No 2563 became *Tagalie*). No 4462 was reallocated to Haymarket shed to recognise Whitelaw's Scottish heritage and received corridor tender No 5323 from No 4482 *Golden Eagle* at this time; the two engines also swapped places and the latter went to Heaton depot. No 4482 was undergoing a General repair in June 1941 and emerged from Doncaster with all of

and chimney, which Thompson would employ on his subsequent 4-6-2 designs. The final four 'V2s' were on order at this time and the decision was made to swap the pony truck for a bogie and they were also provided with the Kylchap exhaust. In Thompson's standardisation plans the 'A3' and 'A4' Pacifics were deemed 'non-standard' types but would be kept in service until the end of their useful lives.

At the end of 1941 Garter Blue was no longer available and black had to be used for the livery of the 'A4s'. From November several class members were sent into traffic after repairs with the new colour scheme: Nos 2512, 4484, 4487, 4492 and 4464. These were followed in December by Nos 2509, 4486, 4495 and 4500. Initially, 'LNER' remained on the tender sides but from mid-1942 this was abbreviated to 'NE'. All of the class were not repainted black until late 1943.

No 4469 *Sir Ralph Wedgwood* had only been in traffic for 12 days after a General repair in April 1942 and was being held at York shed overnight while being run in. On 29 April York was targeted in a bombing attack in retaliation by the Germans for the destruction of Lübeck on 28 March. The enemy raids were concentrated on places of historical and cultural importance rather than military targets, giving rise to the nickname 'Baedeker raids', which arose from a German travel guide that ranked areas of interest in Britain. Many places were hit in York during the raid, including the railway station and the locomotive depot, where No 4469 was resting. The right-hand side of the engine took the force of a high-explosive bomb, causing irreparable damage. No 4469 was returned to Doncaster during mid-May and was officially withdrawn on 6 June. The tender was salvaged and, after a number of years languishing around

ABOVE No 4469 *Sir Ralph Wedgwood* amongst the devastation at York shed after the air raid.

BELOW The remains of the locomotive after being towed to Doncaster Works.

the works, was paired with Thompson 'A2/1' Pacific No 3696 (later named *Highland Chieftain*).

Further renaming occurred during 1942 with Sir Ralph Wedgwood's successor Charles H. Newton having his name replace No 4901's *Capercaillie*. The plates were unveiled at an informal ceremony before the engine took the 'Flying Scotsman' out of King's Cross on 25 September. Following closely in October was No 4494 *Osprey*, which became *Andrew K. McCosh* after the Chairman of the LNER Locomotive Committee. In June 1943 No 4901 saw a slight alteration as Newton was knighted

and the nameplates became *Sir Charles Newton*. No 4466 *Herring Gull* was later chosen to carry the name *Sir Ralph Wedgwood* after No 4469's destruction, but the nameplates were cast new and fitted in January 1944.

As a direct result of the heavy wartime loads, the decision was made to increase the maximum cut-off to 75% in order to give the 'A4' class engines a bit more power when starting. The maximum valve travel became $6^5/_8$ inches and the first locomotive to be changed was No 4499 *Sir Murrough Wilson*. With positive results obtained, Nos 4487 *Sea Eagle* and 4466 *Sir Ralph Wedgwood* were given the new setting in January 1944, followed by No 4462 *William Whitelaw* in April, No 4496 *Golden Shuttle* in June, and No 2511 *Silver King* in July.

The 'Flying Scotsman' was allowed 8 hours 35 minutes to travel from Waverley to King's Cross from January 1943, with four stops made on the way south. No 2578 *Bayardo* worked the train – 17 carriages, 580 tons – from Edinburgh to Newcastle during this period and managed to keep time, even with a stop being made at Dunbar where the following gradients are against the engine. At Newcastle another carriage and two vans were added taking the weight to 700 tons, and 'V2' No 4886 came

on. The engine handled the load steadily travelling south, gaining nearly 10 minutes in the process. The locomotive was 5 minutes late away from York but 2 minutes were regained to Grantham where No 2512 *Silver Fox* took over. The train was so long that the carriages had to be taken into the platform in two stages. Departure was 2 minutes 15 seconds late but at Hitchin 6 minutes 45 seconds had been gained by the locomotive. The 27 miles from Huntingdon had taken 28 minutes 15 seconds with an average speed of 57.3mph. *Silver Fox* was 4 minutes early at Finsbury Park but was brought to a stand by signals before reaching King's Cross, making the arrival late.

A sample of a summer evening's arrivals at King's Cross in 1942 highlights the overloading and the effect this had on punctuality: No 4467 *Wild Swan* with 440 tons; No 4498 *Sir Nigel Gresley* on the 6.20pm from Newcastle loaded to 20 carriages; the 7.08pm from Leeds weighing 645 tons with No 4485 *Kestrel*; and the 7.26pm from Edinburgh loaded to 620 tons behind No 4484 *Falcon*. Interestingly, the 'Flying Scotsman' was split into two portions weighing 660 and 658 tons, being handled by 'V2s' Nos 4892 and 4821 respectively. The 7.26pm was over 30 minutes late while the others were between 5 and 15 minutes

LEFT The LNER Board could not let Sir Ralph Wedgwood's name lapse, and No 4466 was honoured with the rechristening.

LEFT Charles H. Newton (later knighted) stands alongside the former *Capercaillie* after the first renaming in September 1942.

ABOVE No 4484 *Falcon* has wandered off the main line and is seen at Shepreth near Cambridge with empty coaches bound for London on 31 July 1943. *IAL*

LEFT Premium Apprentices at Doncaster Works: D. Sandiland (on locomotive), P. N. Townend, B. Taylor, J. Taylor, H. Steel, A. Coggon and R. H. N. Hardy pose with *Mallard* during August 1943.

behind schedule. There was difficulty at the station manoeuvring all these long trains. A system later had to be devised, being used at King's Cross, York, Darlington and Newcastle, whereby engines assisting heavy trains from the rear when starting did not have to communicate with the lead engine using the whistle while in the confines of the station.

In early 1943 No 4483 *Kingfisher* ran 1,488 miles in 96 hours with four Grantham to London round trips and two Doncaster to King's Cross services. At this time the engine had gone approximately 13 months from the last General repair and would wait until June for the next works visit. In July 1943 the Pacifics and 'V2s' were noted by *The Meccano Magazine* as being under repair or temporarily failed, necessitating a number of Atlantics to be used on the principal trains such as the 'Flying Scotsman' and 'Aberdonian'. Of the 34 class members, five were undergoing a General repair at Doncaster (Nos 2512, 4484, 4488, 4463 and 4465), while three would enter at the end of the month (Nos 4482, 4491 and 4902) and No 4494 was in for a Light repair; No 10000 was also present at the end of July.

There was no wholesale reorganisation of the allocations of the 'A4' class during the war, but a number of small changes did take place from time to time. At Heaton and Gateshead several of the sheds' 'A4s' were transferred between them over the six years, while Grantham saw a steady influx of streamlined Pacifics over this period. No 4466 *Herring Gull* was the only one on the books at the outbreak of the conflict but was joined by Nos 4495 *Golden Fleece* and 4496 *Golden Shuttle* in December 1939, as both were released from King's Cross depot. Grantham required the Pacifics to relieve King's Cross locomotives working trains northwards. No 4494 was loaned to the shed for a week or so in early 1941, but the next new arrival did not occur until October 1942 with No 4903 *Peregrine* leaving 'Top shed'. During mid-October 1943 Nos 4467 *Wild Swan* and 4468 *Mallard* were transferred from the capital, while No 4900 *Gannet* was sent south from Doncaster earlier in the month. Several star performers then went to Grantham in 1944, the first two being Nos 4902 *Seagull* and 4498 *Sir Nigel Gresley* in April, then Nos 2509 *Silver Link* and 2510 *Quicksilver* in August. As 'A3' No 2570 *Papyrus* was also at Grantham for the first half of the 1940s, the shed could boast an impressive stud by the mid-point of the decade.

At the end of 1944 Thompson had two types of 'A2' class Pacifics in traffic and he authorised assessments between them and a representative of the 'A4' class, which in the event was No 2512 *Silver Fox*. 'A2/1' No 3697 and 'A2/2' No 2003 *Lord President* were the Thompson engines chosen. The tests were scheduled for 15-30 January 1945 on the King's Cross to Leeds train, returning the following day. The trains were well over 500

LEFT A new breed of LNER Pacific – No 500
of Edward Thompson's 'A2' class.

tons, approaching 600 tons in some instances, although this load was reduced at Doncaster. *Silver Fox* began on 22 January with the 10.30am service weighing 582 tons, reduced to 293 from Doncaster. *Locomotives of the LNER Part 2A* reveals that the coal consumption for the journey was 52.3lb per mile, which was due to the heaviness of the train, the many signal checks encountered and difficult weather conditions. On the up 7.50am service the tests had to be abandoned due to a broken water scoop. The 'A2/2' had worked a slightly heavier train a few days before and consumed 70.5lb of coal per mile, and the 'A2/1' just less with a figure of 69lb per mile with a lighter load. The latter also had a mechanical issue travelling back to London and the trials were stopped, with many factors contributing to making these unrepresentative of true performance capabilities. New tests were therefore set for the late spring, with Grantham replacing Leeds as the destination, and goods trains also being worked to Peterborough. The same crews were kept with the three engines for the week, making the performances slightly more reliable. The passenger services were the 10.30am northbound train and the 3.17pm back to King's Cross, which were handled by No 2512 between 30 April and 4 May. Generally, the loads were around 550 tons and the crew managed to reduce the coal consumption from 41.79lb on the first day to 38lb per mile on the last test. The second best figure was recorded by No 3697 with 41.69lb per mile, and last was No 2003 with 42.73lb. The overall averages for the locomotives were, respectively, 40.5lb, 43.3lb and 46.1lb per mile. From 14 to 18 May *Silver Fox* was working the 12.25am King's Cross to Peterborough New England goods service, heading back south with the 4.50am. The trains were mostly in the order of 50-60 wagons and weighed 500-700 tons. No 2512's most economical performance came on 17 May with an average fuel consumption of 45.7lb per mile. This was a good deal more than the other two engines, as No 3697 returned a figure of 36.75lb and No 2003 40.89lb. The final results were grouped closer together: No 3697, 41.4lb; No 2003, 45.2lb; and *Silver Fox* 45.4lb.

'A1' Pacific No 4470 *Great Northern* was rebuilt in September 1945 and the design was intended to be the first of a new express passenger class to replace the 'A4s' and 'A3s'. No 4470 had an

'A4'-type boiler, 19-inch-diameter cylinders with 10-inch-diameter piston valves and three sets of Walschaerts valve gear. A Kylchap double blastpipe and chimney was fitted with, initially, smoke deflectors of the 'wing' type before being changed to the larger plate type. Again tests were carried out between the engine and an 'A4', in this instance No 4466 *Sir Ralph Wedgwood*. The trains were the King's Cross to Grantham and return, leaving the capital at 10.30am and coming back at 3.25pm. The average load for both locomotives was 475 tons northbound and 479 tons southbound. No 4466 went first on 5 November and returned a figure of 39.9lb for the week; the finest run gave a result of 38.4lb per mile on Thursday 8 November. Following, No 4470 consumed 39.8lb of fuel on average for the week, with a best of 38.1lb per mile. Despite these close results the 'A4' was deemed slightly better for having a reduced chance of slipping through a higher factor of adhesion than the Thompson Pacific.

Following victory in the Second World War, Britain began the task of reconstruction and renewal after just under six long years of conflict. The railways in particular had been 'flogged' for the duration and were in desperate need of attention to both the rolling stock and the track. Prior to the end of the war the LNER had produced ambitious plans for new infrastructure and improvements to existing facilities totalling £25 million, but as the Government control continued and plans for the nationalisation of the railways were voiced, many of these did not come to fruition. Some immediately implementable changes were reductions in journey times and large cuts were made for the winter timetable of 1945. However, an overall speed limit of 75mph remained in force for some time due to the condition of the track. There were special trains run on 21 and 22 May 1946 to see how the permanent way would react to high-speed running at pre-war levels as a guide to reintroducing a streamlined service. No 2512 *Silver Fox*, fresh from a General repair, headed a modest train of 205 tons from King's Cross to Waverley with an average speed of 59mph for the 392 miles and a timing of 6 hours 39 minutes; a further 2 minutes were allocated for the return. Both schedules were easily kept and there were two instances of over 100mph on 22 May, but the Civil Engineer was not satisfied with measurements he made of the quality of the track and a return to the streamlined glory days of the pre-war years was ruled out.

In spite of such restrictions to speed, impressive recoveries were still feasible. In 1945 O. S. Nock recorded a decidedly run-down No 4482 *Golden Eagle* between York and Newcastle with

ABOVE On 22 May 1946 No 2512 *Silver Fox* passes Brookmans Park with the return leg of the high-speed test train. *Ken Nunn*

RIGHT Edward Thompson, Colonel Bingham and A. H. Peppercorn with General Eisenhower's armour-plated carriage – codenamed 'Bayonet' – at Doncaster on 12 March 1945.

BELOW RIGHT No 4496 *Golden Shuttle* was transformed into *Dwight D. Eisenhower* during 1945.

over 600 tons recovering 6 minutes of arrears. At Newcastle No 4483 *Kingfisher* was a good deal fresher and took the train forward to Edinburgh and reached 84mph on the downwards slope south of Beal. Mr K. Hoole also wrote to the *LNER Magazine* in 1946 reporting an excellent recovery on his trip to York. 'A3' No 2570 *Papyrus* – then renumbered 96 – lost nearly 13 minutes between King's Cross and Grantham. No 2511 *Silver King* was then attached and started to regain time with a sprint from Retford to Doncaster in 15 minutes 30 seconds at an average speed of 67.3mph. The time made up to York was approximately 9 minutes.

No 4496 was taken into Doncaster Works for a General repair on 4 July 1945. After undergoing mechanical refurbishment and replacement of worn parts, the locomotive was taken to the paint shop and, according to Premium Apprentice at the time Doug Brown, was painted in gloss black with red lining on either side of the boiler bands. This livery did not last for long as *Golden Shuttle* was chosen for a name change in honour of the Supreme Commander of the Allied Forces, 1944-45, Dwight D. Eisenhower.

As a result the engine was the first 'A4' to return to the full Garter Blue livery. However, the nameplates remained covered for a period as the company hoped that General Eisenhower would come to England and be present for an unveiling, but he was evidently too busy with his role as Governor of the US Occupation Zone in Southern Germany.

In a general push for the reapplication of the livery, *Silver Link* was the next engine to have the scheme applied. This was performed at a light repair for an appearance at Edinburgh as

LEFT No 14 *Silver Link*
**(formerly No 2509) stands
resplendent after Garter Blue
was reapplied at Doncaster
Works during June 1946,
in addition to stainless steel
numbers and lettering.**

part of a special exhibition on 19 and 20 June 1946 to celebrate the centenary of the North British Railway opening the Edinburgh to Berwick line. The event attempted to demonstrate how much progress had been made by the railways in those 100 years, and *Silver Link* was chosen as being a good example of the improvements in steam technology. Also present were No 2001 *Cock o' the North* and No 4470 *Great Northern*.

Doug Brown also related to the author that *Silver Link* received new nameplates for this occasion as the old pair were 'looking very weather worn and dishevelled', being dumped on a bench in 4-bay of the Crimpsall Repair Shop. An enquiry was made for their purchase but unfortunately they were either

scrapped or snaffled by persons unknown before a transaction could be completed. A further reminiscence concerned No 4491 *Commonwealth of Australia*, which was also in for a General repair in mid-1946. The nameplates belonging to the locomotive were the longest fitted at 10ft 3in, but these were cast in two sections and joined between the 'H' and the 'O'. The plates had to be attached to the engine as one piece and the task of getting them up to the right height took the strength of three people. Unfortunately, the fitter at the 'Australia' end could not support the weight and Doug tried to take the strain but was unable to and the plate dropped with a thud on the Crimpsall floor. The result was a kink in the plate near the 'S', but he recalls that a few well-placed blows with the right-size hammer was enough to restore the plate, and a second attempt yielded a successful fitting. The plates were difficult to get into position, especially the longer ones. The front end was secured through the smokebox with nuts, washers and split pins. At the rear end access was made difficult by the splashers for the leading coupled wheels and had to be gained from the inside of the frames over the slidebars.

The end of 1946 saw the first sign of a return to normality with the reintroduction of two named trains. On 7 October the 'East Anglian' recommenced from Liverpool Street, then from 4 November the 'Yorkshire Pullman' began to run between King's Cross and Doncaster in 2 hours 44 minutes at an average speed of 57mph. The train was split at Doncaster, with a portion going on to Hull and the remainder to Harrogate via Wakefield and Leeds. For this service and the 'Flying Scotsman' the reservation of seats was possible for the first time since 1939.

Thompson's renumbering scheme (which brought a more ordered approach to the gap-filling method then in use) was

ABOVE LEFT Return to prestige: No 27 *Merlin* **has the finishing touches put to the Garter Blue livery by Jack Ellis (left) and Doug Monday (right), while Thompson 'A2/3' No 519** *Honeyway* **prepares to enter traffic in early 1947.**

LEFT No 3 *Andrew K. McCosh* **is 'wheeled' in 4-bay of the Crimpsall Repair Shop during a General repair on 7 June 1947.**

LEFT No 6 *Sir Ralph Wedgwood* leaves
Copenhagen Tunnel with an up express
on 7 June 1947. *IAL*

BELOW LEFT Travelling south out of Doncaster
with the 'Flying Scotsman' on 17 June 1947 is
No 16 *Silver King*.

numbers of the previous scheme, these being
Kingfisher (585), *Kestrel* (587), *Merlin* (588) and *Sir
Ralph Wedgwood* (605) – this engine was the first
changed in January 1946. *Falcon* was supposed
to be altered to No 586 in March 1946, but was
undergoing a General repair at this time and,
when sent back into traffic on 4 May, the
number 25 was applied, which was the first
instance of the new scheme being used on an
'A4'. On the following day *Kingfisher* and *Merlin* became No 24
and No 27 respectively, while 10 May saw *Dominion of Canada*
take the number 10. There was then a gap until the end of the
month when *Wild Swan, Kestrel, Woodcock, Sir Ralph Wedgwood*
and *Golden Plover* were given Nos 21, 26, 29, 6 and 31 respectively.
The last alterations were *Union of South Africa, Commonwealth of
Australia* and *Sir Nigel Gresley* on 12 January.

In 1947 a fresh attempt was made to solve the problem of
hot inside big end bearings. The middle cylinder of the 'A3'
was known to produce more horsepower compared to the
outside pair when working at higher speeds after indicator tests
had been performed with No 2751 *Humorist* in 1931. At 43mph
and 30% cut-off 1,504 indicated horsepower was produced,
with the left-hand cylinder giving 463hp, the inside cylinder
513hp and the right hand side 527hp. At 75mph and 20% cut-
off there was 1,467 horsepower produced, 402 in the left
cylinder, 585 in the middle and 480 on the right. Even though
the 'A4' was not indicated because of the streamlined front end,
a similar disparity was thought to be occurring and, in addition
to the wear in the joints caused by poor maintenance, the
overstress of the bearing caused failures. The scheme
implemented saw the inside cylinder lined up to a diameter of
17 inches in order to limit the power output. Five engines
received this change during the year and were classified 'A4/1':
No 3 in June, Nos 12, 14 and 31 in August, and No 20 in October.

Shortly after modification No 31 *Golden Plover* was tested
against No 113 *Great Northern* in September between Edinburgh
and Dundee on the 10.00am down train and the 2.43pm up. The
loads averaged, respectively, 400 tons and 350 tons, and the results
for the two days worked on the services were a 47.2lb average for
Golden Plover and 39.3lb for *Great Northern*. A further day of readings
was taken working from Edinburgh to Newcastle and back with

implemented in early 1946. Initially the 'A4s' were to occupy
Nos 580-613 of 1-1000 allocated to express passenger engines,
and some of these were applied before a wholesale change was
made. From April the 'A4' class were given the sequence 1-34,
but thought was given to the names of the locomotives,
especially those of the company officials. Nos 1 and 2 were
occupied by the Chairman and Deputy Chairman of the LNER,
Sir Ronald Matthews and Sir Murrough Wilson respectively.
The Chairman of the Locomotive Committee, Andrew K.
McCosh, came third, and No 4 was given to former Chairman
William Whitelaw. The present and former Chief General
Managers came next before former CME Sir Nigel Gresley at
No 7 and No 8 with Dwight D. Eisenhower. The 'Coronation'
engines took precedence over the 'Silver Jubilee' locomotives,
but following them came the last batch from 1937/38 before the
second order started to fill up the list. The last three numbers
were taken by the locomotives fitted with the Kylchap double
blastpipe and chimney.

The task was a slow process and was enforced between May
1946 and January 1947. Only four of the class carried the

RIGHT The change from *Sea Eagle* to *Walter K. Whigham* was the penultimate renaming for the LNER after 10 had occurred in the 13 years since the class had been introduced.

the 10.15am and 3.22pm, the loads being about 480 tons. The results were closer in this instance as No 31 burned 39.2lb of coal per mile and No 113 consumed 40.9lb. Certain disadvantages were noted in the working of the locomotives, such as No 31 struggling at moderate speeds on adverse gradients, while *Great Northern* had problems with slipping.

As 1947 drew to a close more officials of the LNER were honoured by having an 'A4' bestowed with their name. The first occasion occurred in October when No 28 *Sea Eagle* became *Walter K. Whigham*, after the Deputy Chairman of the LNER from 1946 following the death of Sir Murrough Wilson. Then in November No 26 *Kestrel* was rechristened *Miles Beevor* after the Chief General Manager who succeeded Sir Charles Newton

upon his retirement. With the partition of India taking place in 1947 there were also plans to change the name of No 11 *Empire of India* to *Dominion of India* and No 20 *Guillemot* was to receive *Dominion of Pakistan*, but in the event neither change took effect.

Arthur Henry Peppercorn succeeded Thompson on 1 July 1946 as the latter retired from his position. Peppercorn had a similar background, having held various positions in the mechanical engineering department before taking the CME's role. Thompson's standardisation programme was only partially completed when Peppercorn took office and there had also been little improvement in the maintenance situation (although in 1946 579 miles of track were renewed and £250,000 was spent on improving stations). With the election of a socialist Labour Government after the end of the Second World War giving rise to the possible nationalisation of many industries, the railways were left in a certain limbo about the future and had to plan their requirements accordingly. While Peppercorn continued the standardisation policy to a degree, there was an immediate reorganisation of the CME's department and many of the men who had been transferred by Thompson were brought back into the fold. The result of this was that only 15 of the 30 Thompson 'A2/3' Pacifics authorised were constructed and the remaining 15 on order had a new design prepared for them. The perforated steam collector replaced the steam dome; the cab had a V-shaped front; the cylinders were placed between the bogie wheels (as the Thompson classes experienced several problems as a result of the elongated front end). Retained were the three sets of valve gear and the divided drive. Surprisingly, a return was made to the use of a single blastpipe and chimney, but towards the end of construction sense prevailed and six received the Kylchap

ABOVE LEFT A rare colour image of an 'A4' from 1947: No 11 *Empire of India* is impatient to depart from Newcastle with an express. *Colour-Rail*

LEFT *Empire of India* narrowly missed out on an alteration to the name after the independence of the country. Here, the engine leaves Newcastle with the 3.53pm express to Glasgow. *H. Gordon Tidey*

apparatus. The new 'A1' class also went through a number of modifications as several designs were attempted – a few even featuring streamlining. The final one chosen was almost the same as the 'A2' class, and the 'A4'-type boiler was not used, with the 'A2' type substituted; the Kylchap exhaust was used from the engines being new. A total of 49 locomotives would be constructed between August 1948 and December 1949.

Even with all these Pacifics on order and in service, the LNER was seriously considering the introduction of diesel locomotives for express passenger services, with associated repair and maintenance facilities also being provided. Michael R. Bonavia, who was employed by the LNER at this time, recounts some of the details of these scheme in his book *A History of the LNER, 3: The Last Years 1939-1948*. During the fuel crisis of 1947 – when the Government instructed the railways to convert some steam locomotives to be fired by oil – the savings possible by a change of fuel type became apparent. The fact was related to Bonavia that '…a ton of fuel oil burnt in a locomotive firebox would save 1½ tons of coal, the same quantity of diesel oil used in a modern diesel locomotive would save five tons of coal.' This information

BELOW No 10 *Dominion of Canada* is in a truly dishevelled state near Brookmans Park signal box with a van train. *M. W. Earley*

was then conveyed to the Assistant General Manager, who had a scheme devised for introducing diesel-electric locomotives on the LNER. The Joint Locomotive and Traffic Committee considered and approved the introduction of 25 such locomotives to replace 32 Pacific engines at a cost of £45,100 each, or £1,127,500 (the cost for the 32 Pacifics is given as £16,000, or a total of £512,000); there was an additional £260,000 for facilities. The reasons given in the report for action to be taken were: the average age of the express locomotives was quite high; a large number were unavailable because of repairs being necessary; and shortage of coal and its deteriorating quality. The diesel-electric was seen as being suitable for use on the ECML because of the expected ability to run long distances without the need to refuel and a higher average yearly mileage than steam. Further advantages were said to be the cheaper cost of fuel per ton (£16 of diesel for a journey between King's Cross and Edinburgh compared to over £20 for coal), and overall operating costs of 28.3d per mile against steam's 30.7d; the annual saving was 2.75% of the difference in construction costs. There was also the relative cleanliness of the diesel-electrics and the publicity and prestige value to be gained from their introduction. Inspiration was taken from America, where further development had taken place during the late 1930s and 1940s, and similar units to those proposed by the LNER were in operation. These locomotives were rated at 2,000 horsepower and were often coupled together to take much longer and heavier trains than the streamlined 'Zephyrs'. The *LNER Magazine* for December 1946 observed that nearly three-quarters of America's streamlined passenger service miles were in the hands of diesel traction. Of the nearly 5,500 miles run at 70mph, some 80% was done behind these powerful units.

REACHING THE PEAK, 1948-1966

The Labour Government formed in 1945 swept to power because the people of Britain demanded a better standard of living following the hardships of the Second World War. Swathes of the population believed that the Conservatives – under Winston Churchill – could not offer this. Therefore, a Labour Government under Clement Attlee was appointed after promises of a Welfare State, National Health Service, full employment and better conditions for workers. The two former policies were enacted in 1946 and were then followed by the nationalisation of the Bank of England and civil aviation. In 1947 the coal industry and the railways came under public control, and before the end of Labour's term of office the utilities and steel industry would be similarly treated.

The Transport Act was given Royal Assent in August 1947 and took effect on 1 January 1948. This created the British Transport Commission to oversee the provision of 'an effective, adequate, economical and properly integrated system of public inland transport and port facilities for passengers and goods.' The 'Big Four' railway companies became part of the new British Railways, which was organised into six regions: Eastern, Southern, London Midland, North Eastern, and Scottish. In total 20,000 route miles were managed and the Railway Executive had responsibility for 650,000 male and female employees. There were over 20,000 steam locomotives, 40,000 carriages and around 100 diesel locomotives (mostly shunters), but just prior to nationalisation the LMS introduced two 1,600-horsepower diesel-electric units. The steam locomotive stock inherited by the Railway Executive was of an idiosyncratic character and this was coupled with different working methods used by the employees of the former 'Big Four' companies. The task faced by BR of integrating the system into a whole that functioned efficiently and cheaply was difficult to say the least.

LEFT Grantham-allocated and renumbered 'A4' No 60030 *Golden Fleece* is seen on King's Cross turntable after working an express in September 1948. *W. J. Reynolds*

The LNER handed over 6,454 locomotives in 1948 and many of these also varied in power, performance and reliability. The Peppercorn 'A2' and 'A1' Pacifics were both constructed during the first year of BR's existence, in addition to the Thompson 'B1' and 'L1' class 2-6-4T. The 'K4' 2-6-0 rebuild with two cylinders was also perpetuated, becoming Peppercorn Class K1. A total of 396 engines (also encompassing the 'J72' for shunting) would be erected to these designs up to 1952; this number was relatively modest compared with the GWR and LMS figure of 452 and 640 respectively. The Eastern and North Eastern Regions – headed until 1949 by A. H. Peppercorn – were thus left in a relatively healthy position in the motive power department, meeting the projected traffic requirements for the immediate future.

The first noticeable effect of nationalisation on the 'A4' class was the addition of an 'E' prefix to the numbers in use. No 4 *William Whitelaw* was the first to receive this alteration, which was painted above the cabside number – in some instances the 'E' was placed on the left-hand side – on 20 January 1948. The locomotive also has the distinction of being the first of the class to receive the 'British Railways' identity on the tender. Following with the 'E' prefix on 5 February was No 21 *Wild Swan*, and the final two engines were Nos 22 *Mallard* and 27 *Merlin* in March. That month saw the first alterations to the new BR numbering scheme, which added 60,000 to the existing system; No 10000 was exempted from this and was allocated the number 60700. No 60007 *Sir Nigel Gresley* was the joint first 'A4' to receive the BR number after a General repair on 24 March, sharing the accolade with No 60034. The latter was at Doncaster for Non-Classified attention and was also

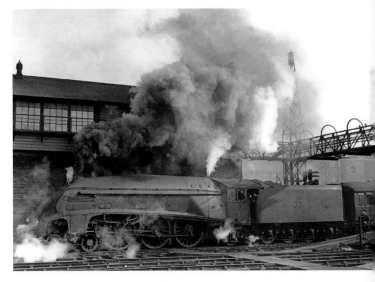

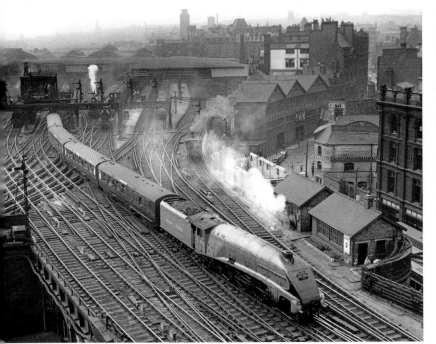

TOP No 16 *Silver King* travels through Prestonpans on the final leg of the 8.40am down express from Leeds on 23 April 1948. *IAL*

ABOVE Making a fine display while leaving Platform 10 at King's Cross with the 1.10pm express to Leeds is No 29 *Woodcock* on 12 February 1948. *C. C. B. Herbert*

LEFT Viewed from the castle on 28 July 1948, No 60012 *Commonwealth of Australia* is seen passing through Newcastle Central station with the 'Flying Scotsman' to Edinburgh. *Kenneth C. Footer*

renamed *Lord Faringdon* at the same time after the GCR-built 'B3' class 4-6-0 engine that had originally carried the name was condemned for scrap. Lord Faringdon had been the Chairman of the GCR and the Deputy Chairman of the LNER from the Grouping until his death in the mid-1930s. No 60023 *Golden Eagle* was next on the 25th, but there was not a strong impetus to change the locomotives quickly (perhaps given the size of the task); however, 25 were dealt with in nine months from the first implementation, including the four

with the 'E' prefix. The final engine was No 60025 *Falcon*, which had received a General repair on the eve of nationalisation and another visit to Doncaster did not occur until 16 December 1949 – almost two years later.

The number change was not the only one afoot after BR was formed. There was no firm decision in place as to what livery should be applied, so several locomotives from many classes were volunteered to try a number of schemes. Four engines from the 'A4' class – Nos 60024 *Kingfisher*, 60027 *Merlin*, 60028 *Walter K. Whigham* and 60029 *Woodcock* – had a purple applied, with red, cream and grey lining. *Woodcock* was altered in time for an exhibition of rolling stock at Doncaster Works on 17 and 18 July, with the last LNER Pacific to be built, 'A2' No 60525 *A. H. Peppercorn*, also in attendance. The colour scheme did not find favour and in mid-1949 BR chose a blue livery with black and white lining for all express passenger engines. No 60013 *Dominion of New Zealand* was the pioneer in May, while *Seagull* and *Silver Link* followed in June; the purple persisted on the affected engines until the end of 1950. A further change would be made in mid-1951 as BR green became the standard with black and orange lining. Nos 60001 and 60026 were the first and last, in mid-1951 and early 1953 respectively.

R. A. Riddles was the man appointed as Member of the Railway Executive and Mechanical & Electrical Engineer for BR and had perhaps the unenviable task of moving the organisation forward at the behest of the politicians in charge. There was little money available at the time for wholesale changes such as electrification, which would have been the preferred move forward for many, nor any appetite to adopt diesel locomotives on a large scale – the LNER scheme recommended by the Board to BR was virtually ignored. Many of the absorbed railways had gaps in their motive power requirements or had designs that were becoming life-expired and would have been replaced sooner if the war had not made

this impossible. Therefore, the decision was taken to produce a series of steam locomotives for use either on specific parts or all over the system. These new locomotives were to be highly standardised and were to use the best features then favoured by the 'Big Four'. Riddles's background was at Crewe and Derby, subsequently taking a position as Principal Assistant to W. A. Stanier, and he was closely involved with the standardisation policy set in motion by the latter on the LMSR. Later, Riddles would be behind the War Department's standard 2-8-0s and 2-10-0s. Upon his appointment to BR, Riddles gave the top two positions under him to former colleagues on the LMSR, as R. C. Bond became Chief Officer (Locomotive Construction and Maintenance) while E. S. Cox was made Executive Officer (Design). The decision to make standard steam engines was agreed upon quite early, but their features were not. This resulted in a series of trials being set up involving express passenger engines, mixed-traffic types and freight locomotives.

Designs from all four constituent 'Big Four' companies were involved in the tests, which took place on all regions apart from the North Eastern. To try and make the results more reliable, the same crews were used for the week of the test after the previous week had been spent learning the road. The same type of Yorkshire hard coal was also supplied to all engines, although the WR authorities chose to repeat the tests on their route with Welsh coal later in the year. The dynamometer car ran behind all of the trains to give further scientific validity to the trials. There was one stipulation to the selection of the engines to take part, which was that they had to possess a mileage of more than 15,000 since their last General repair, and no special attention would be made to prepare them. This instruction evidently did not reach the SR, as the Bulleid Pacifics were given a thorough fettle when fitted with LMSR tenders with water scoops for the tests early in 1948. The committee formed to arrange and oversee proceedings featured Bert Spencer of the ER, R. G. Jarvis from the LMR, S. O. Ell of the SR, and C. S. Cocks of the WR.

The locomotives in the express passenger category were an LMR 'Royal Scot' 4-6-0 and 'Coronation' class Pacific, WR 'King' class 4-6-0, SR 'Merchant Navy' Pacifics and ER 'A4' class. At first the three selected to take part were Nos E21 *Wild Swan*, 25 *Falcon* and 26 *Miles Beevor*. This choice was soon overruled – by all accounts Bert Spencer intervened – and three engines fitted with Kylchap double blastpipes and chimneys were chosen: Nos E22 *Mallard*, 60033 *Seagull* and 60034 *Lord Faringdon*. F. A. S. Brown, in his authoritative *Nigel Gresley: Locomotive Engineer*, suggests that one of these engines was not quite on top form when selected, as attention was required to the middle big end and bearing, but this was not carried out beforehand.

The first test of an 'A4' took place on 20 April when No 60034 *Lord Faringdon* left King's Cross at the head of the 1.10pm to Leeds. The 185 miles were given a schedule of 236 minutes, which required the leisurely average speed of 47.2mph. The up train worked the next day was the 7.50am and this was allowed the slightly longer time of 241 minutes as there were stops at Wakefield, Doncaster and Grantham for the addition of carriages. The average speed therefore was just lower at 46.2mph. On the 20th *Lord Faringdon* was coupled to 500½ tons and

headed north to Wakefield where 127 tons were removed and arrival was made at Leeds 3 minutes 30 seconds late. A total of 40.12lb of coal per mile had been used, or 2.97lb per drawbar horsepower, with the water figure being 28.1 gallons per mile and 20.82 gallons per drawbar horsepower hour. Returning the following day the load began at 298½ tons and saw almost 200 tons progressively added to Grantham. At King's Cross No 60034's arrival was recorded as being 3 minutes early and the coal consumption was 40.35lb, and 2.93lb per drawbar horsepower hour. The numbers for water consumption were, respectively, 33.1 gallons and 24.1 gallons. The second run saw an improvement on the first with a train 1 ton lighter, and an on-time arrival was made in Leeds. The crew had managed to reduce the coal consumption by 2.32lb per mile and 0.13lb per drawbar horsepower; water consumption was also down fractionally. The final test on 23 April witnessed an arrival at King's Cross 2 minutes late after transporting 497 tons tare from Grantham. The figures were the second best of the week: 38lb, 2.92lb, 32.5 gallons and 24.92 gallons. Over the four days the average drawbar horsepower figures were 750, 759, 737 and 728.

These services were just one set of two that had all the engines in the express category take part, as the 'King' class

BELOW No 60034 *Lord Faringdon* waits to depart from King's Cross with an express to Leeds during the 1948 Exchanges.

The tests moved over to the WR for 'A4' No E22 *Mallard* on 27 April. The engine was on a preliminary run back to London on the 28th when the inside big end bearing ran hot forcing the substitution of the world-record-holder with No 60033 *Seagull*, which completed the remainder of the familiarisation runs and the tests beginning on 4 May. The train was the 1.30pm to Plymouth, timed at 287 minutes for the 225.1 miles. The average speed necessary to maintain this was 47mph, again due to the quality of the permanent way and the timetable being not as rigorous as had been the case before the war. C. J. Allen was on hand to record the first westbound test and the return the next day. *Seagull* left Paddington with a train weighing 482 tons and Driver Burgess made a leisurely start, being nearly 2 minutes 30 seconds late when passing Slough at 66mph. On to Reading a minute was regained and the time taken for the 36 miles was 46 minutes 6 seconds. The next section to Westbury passed quite steadily – a high of 69mph was reached at Lavington – and was completed 1 minute ahead of the 70 minutes allocated. A total of 53 minutes were given to the next section of 47 miles to Taunton and after being slightly down at Castle Cary No 60033 made up the time to arrive 1 second early. Between Taunton and Exeter (30.8 miles, schedule 38 minutes) the obstacle of Whiteball summit had to be tackled. This feature was made up of gradients from 1 in 369 to 1 in 174 and 1 in 90, plus a stretch at 1 in 80, for a total of 9 miles. A low speed of just over 40mph was noted at the foot of the climb at Norton Fitzwarren and this gradually fell off to 22mph at the summit with a time of 21 minutes. Over 70mph was achieved down the opposite side and this was sustained for several miles on to Taunton, but this could not prevent the engine being overdue by 13 minutes. At Newton Abbot over 5 minutes were dropped due to cautious driving coupled with the nature of the line, and the load was also reduced to 324.5 tons.

The final section comprised two formidable banks – Dainton and Rattery. On the former a relatively gentle gradient starts off proceedings, before quickly deteriorating to 1 in 98 1½ miles out, then 1 in 57 and 1 in 43 and finally 1 in 36. Driver Burgess managed to get the engine to speed up to 39mph in 2 miles before beginning to slow on the 1 in 57; the engine began to slip just before reaching the top but managed to recover to 18mph and post a time of 9 minutes 44 seconds, which was over time by 1 minute 45 seconds. After a brief respite through Totnes came the 9 miles of Rattery bank. The gradients started at 1 in 86 and 1 in 52 before easing a little to 1 in 80 and finally 1 in 240. From 49mph at the start the speed fell to 27mph after 2 miles but the

ABOVE An embarrassed No E22 *Mallard* leaves Reading shed to be repaired after failing with the return preliminary run to Paddington on 28 April 1948. *M. W. Earley*

locomotive was out of gauge on the LMR and SR. All the engines had the loads set at approximately 500 tons tare for the down train, giving rise to coal figures between 45.16lb per mile for 'Coronation' class Pacific No 46236 *City of Bradford* and 46.1lb for rebuilt 'Royal Scot' No 46146 *Queen's Westminster Rifleman* to 53.93lb for 'King' No 6018 *King Henry VI* and 57.92lb for 'Merchant Navy' Pacific No 35017 *Belgian Marine*. Travelling up to the capital the coal consumption was significantly improved upon and the best figures were 40.12lb and 40.74lb per mile recorded by the 'King' and 'Coronation' class engines respectively. The 'Royal Scot' achieved a best of 42.8lb per mile and No 35017's lowest number was 44.14lb per mile. The performances of the 'foreign' engines were generally characterised by signal checks, good running over certain sections, then cruising to keep to the schedule. Several arrivals at King's Cross were made on or before time.

next 1½ miles saw an acceleration to 38mph and nearly a minute was gained at this point. Thirty seconds were dropped on the last 4-mile section with the speed around 40mph. The final time at Plymouth was 52 minutes 38 seconds for the 32 miles, including two permanent way restrictions near the end of the journey. The total time was over 296 minutes with an average speed of 45.6mph. The coal consumption per mile was 39.76lb, or 2.98lb per drawbar horsepower hour. On the other down train on 6 May *Seagull* slightly bettered the time but had an increased coal consumption with the same load. Despite the fact that the 'King' class engine was using Yorkshire coal, the figures for the 'A4' were better by nearly 6lb on the best runs of the two engines.

Returning from Plymouth on 5 May with 328 tons as far as Newton Abbot, where the train weight was increased to 490 tons, *Seagull* almost immediately had to traverse Hamerdon bank. This was formed of 2 miles at 1 in 41 amongst other steep gradients. This task was made harder through the introduction of a permanent way restriction quite close to the start, leaving the engine with little momentum for the climb. No 60033 was travelling at 20mph at Plympton – 4 miles from the start and the location of a speed limit – but did manage to accelerate to more than 24mph when the climb began half a mile on. Driver Burgess selected full regulator and 50% cut-off for the task and succeeded in losing only 6mph along the length

ABOVE Repaired and being run in, No E22 *Mallard* is seen in King's Cross locomotive yard from the York Road platform on 5 May 1948. *B. W. L. Brooksbank*

BELOW After the excitement of the trials *Mallard* went back to work and is seen at Marshmoor with the down 'Yorkshire Pullman' on 19 April 1949. *IAL*

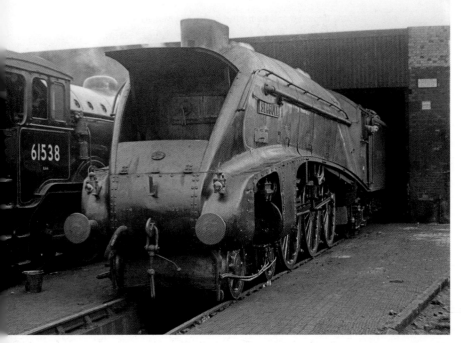

On to Newton Abbot No 60033 was still behind schedule and arrived 5 minutes 48 seconds late; if not for the track restrictions an early arrival would have been achieved.

At Newton Abbot the tare weight became 489 tons (525 tons gross) and the locomotive managed to press on to Exeter in just under the allotted time of 26 minutes for the 20 miles. From Exeter there was more uphill work to Cullompton, which was passed in 16 minutes 55 seconds for the 12.6 miles and the engine was travelling at 60mph A short distance further on there was 2 miles at 1 in 115 to Whiteball summit and *Seagull* was recorded travelling at 47mph near the top of this climb, but later slowed down for track maintenance at Whiteball Tunnel. The time at Taunton was just right with 38 minutes 48 seconds elapsing for the 30.8 miles.

From Taunton Driver Burgess had No 60033 up to a high speed for a reasonable distance. At Creech Junction 51mph was reached 2½ miles on from the station and this rose to 71mph at Athelney – 8 miles – and 75mph at Curry Rivell Junction – 11 miles out. At Somerton the speed fell on an acclivity of 1 in 264 to 61mph but soon recovered to 70mph and peaked at 75 passing Alford. The slack at Castle Cary was too carefully observed, although the speed stuck in the mid-60s for the remainder and *Seagull* arrived at Westbury 4 minutes 36 seconds early. The average speed for the 27½ miles to Castle Cary was 60.1mph and for the 20 miles to Westbury was 52.3mph. Of the first section C. J. Allen comments in *The Locomotive Exchanges*: 'If ever a Western Region "King" has made as brief a time out of Taunton with a corresponding load I have no recollection of having seen such a record.'

As Driver Burgess had gained time he was content to continue just in front of the schedule after leaving Westbury. From the start a high of 64mph was attained at Lavington and

of the acclivity, taking 7 minutes 37 seconds to complete the nearly 3 miles from Plympton to Hamerdon. Another restriction for track maintenance awaited No 60033 before Brent and the engine passed there nearly 7 minutes late, and this was only down slightly at Totnes, 7 miles on. Then came the 5 miles up Dainton Bank, which began with 1 in 70, easing off to 1 in 120 and 1 in 125 (separated by a level stretch) before increasing to 1 in 57 and 1 in 40 for the last mile. *Seagull* began this ascent at 45mph and was at 39mph on the 1 in 120. An acceleration was made on the level to 48½mph but a fall to 38½mph was registered along the 1 in 57, then 25mph on the 1 in 40. The time taken for this was 6 minutes 58 seconds and would prove to be one of the best climbs made by all the engines on the stretch.

the passing time at Patney was over a minute early at 18 minutes 12 seconds for the 14½ miles. At Savernake the gains had risen to 3 minutes 2 seconds, but some of this was lost to track work being carried out past Hungerford. To Newbury – 42½ miles – the section was completed in 48 minutes 44 seconds, which was under the 50 minutes 30 seconds allowed. No 60033 attained 69mph at Slough after slowing near Reading. and at the former the engine was just under 3 minutes early. Travelling into London a steady pace was made and from Westbury the time to Paddington was 110 minutes 50 seconds for the 95.6 miles – 2 minutes 10 seconds in front – but the overall time was just behind the 257 minutes booked. The coal consumption was 43lb per mile, or 3.33lb per drawbar horsepower hour. The first two journeys were the best of the week as a higher fuel consumption occurred on the next down and up journeys. The 'Coronation' Pacific – No 46236 *City of Bradford*, which was the only engine to run on all the regions – had the lowest coal consumption on one down run with a figure of 38.34lb, but per drawbar horsepower hour the figure was higher at 3.21lb. 'Royal Scot' No 46162 *Queen's Westminster Rifleman* produced two better figures to Plymouth with 37.68lb and 36.06lb per mile, but the coal used per drawbar horsepower hour was high at 3.60lb and 3.33lb.

The 'A4s' were given a brief break to the next tests on the LMR's Euston to Carlisle route, which were carried out between 25 and 28 May. From the 18th to the 21st the locomotive – No 60034 *Lord Faringdon* – worked familiarisation journeys on the 10.00am 'Royal Scot', then returning the next day with the 12.55pm. However, on both this and the test week numerous

restrictions and signals stopped performance capabilities being demonstrated to the full. As a result the schedule was extended to feature generous recovery margins, so the booked times were rarely kept to. With such conditions an overall performance of a satisfactory nature was difficult to create, but several of the engines produced noteworthy work on certain sections. On 27 May *Lord Faringdon* was nearly 6 minutes late at Rugby but recovered sufficient time on the 75½ miles to Crewe to be only just 1 minute late into the station despite two speed restrictions experienced, averaging 53.3mph. During the preliminary week No 60034 also managed to generate a good run up to Shap summit even though the LMR threw signals in the way, in addition to the restrictions. The load was 500 tons gross and from a speed limit at Preston the locomotive was up to 55mph at Barton 5 miles away. The speed remained steadily at that figure for the next few miles but caused nearly 2 minutes to be dropped at Garstang. On the following 5 miles the speed was 62mph but at Bay Horse there was a 30mph limit and at Lancaster the losses had gown to over 3 minutes, persisting to Carnforth. On the 12.7 miles to Oxenholme a recovery of sorts was made with an average speed of 50.6mph and the locomotive was now only 1 minute 24 seconds late. On the following 7 miles to Grayrigg, which consisted of gradients of 1 in 178 and 1 in 106, only a drop from 41 to 33mph occurred and the time taken was 11

BELOW No 60034 *Lord Faringdon* is captured near Bushey working the down 'Royal Scot' on 18 May 1948. *IAL*

minutes 1 second. The speed jumped to 53½mph at Low Gill before a restriction prior to reaching Tebay dropped the rate of travel to 21mph, hampering the start of the ascent to Shap summit. Only 55mph was recorded at Tebay and this had fallen by 20mph at Scout Green and went down by a further 10mph on the remaining 2 miles of 1 in 75 to the peak. The time for this difficult 5 miles was 9 minutes 23 seconds or just under 2 minutes in front of the allowance. *Lord Faringdon* went on to complete the last 30 miles to Carlisle with 4 minutes gained on the 39-minute allowance from Shap to Carlisle.

A total of 366 minutes were allowed for the 299½ miles from Euston to Carlisle and a further 7 minutes were given for the return. On the first test on 15 May – with a train of 504 tons tare – No 60034 lost over 12 minutes, and on the 27th (503 tons tare) this increased to 20 minutes. Such a delay obviously increased the use of coal from 40.05lb on the first day (water 33.4 gallons) to 43.74lb per mile (36.6 gallons) on the last down train, but the consumption per drawbar horsepower hour fell from 2.92lb to 2.90lb. The first up train on 26 May weighed 503 tons tare and was reduced to 477 tons at Crewe; on the 28th the trains were slightly lighter. On both occasions the timetable could not be adhered to and the losses amounted to over 10 minutes and 15 minutes respectively. Nevertheless, the coal consumed was 40.89lb per mile (32.7 gallons of water) and 39.92lb (32.1 gallons). The LMR 'Coronation' Pacific consumed slightly more coal than the 'A4' for much of the trials but achieved a low of 42.3lb per mile on the final train from Carlisle to Euston. No 46162 produced the best figure of 39.5lb when working the first train to Carlisle and the amount remained quite low for the duration. 'Merchant Navy' class 35017 *Belgian Marine*'s use of fuel was quite liberal as the engine produced some of the better performances to Shap summit in early May.

Only a few days after the exertions on the LMR were concluded No E22 *Mallard* was dispatched to the SR for the final set from Waterloo to Exeter on the 10.50am, which comprised 171½ miles and a timing of 209 minutes, or 218 for the return with the 12.37pm. No 60033 *Seagull* had been on the first preliminary attempt on 1 June but had to be removed after the inside big end bearing was found to be running warm. This allowed the world-record-holder the chance to shine after the problems earlier and R. E. Charlewood recorded one of the workings, which was reproduced in *The Locomotive Exchanges* by C. J. Allen. On the first test on 8 June Driver Marrable started quickly with 482 tons tare, taking just under 7 minutes for the 4 miles out to Clapham Junction and Woking (20 miles) in 28 minutes 47 seconds. A short distance to the west signals stopped the train and a good deal of time was lost, then before reaching Hurstbourne *Mallard* attained 70mph. This dropped to 47mph at Grateley and subsequently increased to 75mph at Porton before reaching Salisbury in 108 minutes 28 seconds.

No E22 was late departing and immediately jumped to work, attaining 51mph in 2½ miles from the restart, despite an adverse gradient awaiting out of the station. On the rising land through Semley this rate was kept up and the time was 21 minutes 13 seconds for the 17½ miles. After a high of 73mph *Mallard* passed Templecombe at just under 60mph. With a 1 in 80 following, a drop to 42½mph was experienced but 5 miles on at Sherborne No E22 was back at 75mph, dipping to just under 70mph through Yeovil Junction; the time from Salisbury was 41 minutes 39 seconds, or 5 minutes 21 seconds early. The next 10 miles featured Hewish bank and the rate of travel only fell to 36mph before rising again to 76½mph at Chard Junction. A peak of 82mph was recorded at Axminster before passing Seaton Junction where the 6-mile climb of Honiton incline started. This featured a prolonged stretch of 1 in 80, which caused *Mallard*'s speed to drop from 52 to 30mph at the summit. With a high of 70mph down the bank the time at Sidmouth Junction was 79 minutes 24 seconds for the 75.8 miles from Salisbury – this was 9 minutes 36 seconds quicker than the booked time.

The concluding 12 miles to Exeter featured a restriction down to 20mph just past Sidmouth but a recovery could not be made, meaning that arrival was 2 minutes 11 seconds down on the 16 minutes allowed. The time for the journey was a little over 197 minutes while the coal consumption was 41.57lb per mile (32.3 gallons of water), or 3.10lb per drawbar horsepower hour (24.74 gallons). Taking the up train on 9 June *Mallard* only ran to Salisbury before the trial was abandoned because the middle big end bearing had run hot. No 60033 *Seagull* had recovered sufficiently to return for the down train on 10 June and gained 7 minutes on the schedule, improving *Mallard*'s coal consumption figure to 38.31lb in the process. The final test on the 11th saw a late arrival by 1 minute at Waterloo and the fuel used per train mile reached 44.2lb. This was higher than the two runs by the 'Coronation' Pacific but lower than the 'Royal Scot' and 'Merchant Navy' class engines.

The overall results for the 1948 exchanges saw the 'A4s' come out on top in the ER and LMR with overall average coal consumption figures of 39.08lb and 41.25lb per mile – 2.92lb and 3.00lb per drawbar horsepower hour – and second best in the WR in terms of coal per mile, but top in terms of fuel used per drawbar horsepower hour. The 'A4s' were firmly in second place in the SR trials as the 'Coronation' Pacific consumed considerably less coal. For the entire tests the 'A4s' were again top of the list with 3.06lb of coal burned per drawbar horsepower hour with a corresponding water figure of 24.32 gallons; the next best express passenger engine was the 'Coronation' class Pacific (3.12lb). The only category where the 'A4s' were found wanting was the evaporation rate, which was 7.92lb of water per lb of coal; *City of Bradford*'s figure was 8.67lb and the 'Merchant Navy' 8.45lb. The figures for the 'A4s' were undoubtedly hollow victories given that three failures had taken place. Also, because the schedules were not at their most taxing and the driving styles were not uniform; some sought to make up time while others tried to keep the fuel consumption low. One constant in the driving of the 'A4s' was the use of full regulator and 15% cut-off on suitable stretches, which led to very little power being lost between the boiler and the cylinders, promoting good efficiency.

In the end there was no appreciable influence of the interchanges on the design of the standard steam locomotives, which BR would produce between 1951 and 1960. E. S. Cox, in his book *British Railways Standard Steam Locomotives*, comments: '[the tests] did confirm what had already been gathered from experience on the LMS that a properly designed steam locomotive would work satisfactorily anywhere from Land's End to John o' Groats on appropriate duties. They showed that the simplest and most straightforward designs were at no disadvantage compared with the more complex.' A number of features did find their way to the Standard classes from other railways, but more came from GWR and SR designs than the LNER. Two Gresley features used were the three-bar slide bar and the chime whistle for the most powerful types.

By the end of 1948 Rugby testing plant was operational, allowing BR to run locomotives on rollers under uniform conditions in order to evaluate their performance. This facility had been championed by Gresley for many years as he appreciated the benefits to be gained, both for the railway

companies and private contractors, from a place to test new features or the merits of existing designs. He had come close to having the Government provide the money for construction in the early 1930s, as this had been the case for plants erected in both France and Germany, but the scheme fell victim to the Depression. Gresley was not deterred and was even more determined after No 2001 *Cock o' the North*'s visit to Vitry in 1934/35. An agreement to construct a testing station jointly with the LMSR was made in 1937. The project was well under way when war broke out and the task could not be completed until after the end of hostilities. The official opening ceremony was carried out on 19 October by Alfred Barnes, Minister of Transport, and appropriately No 60007 *Sir Nigel Gresley* was the first locomotive to run on the rollers; Driver F. Moore of King's Cross was at the regulator and Fireman L. H. Goode of Rugby had the shovel. 'Coronation' class Pacific No 46256 *Sir William A. Stanier F.R.S.* was also present to acknowledge his role in the facility, along with the engine's namesake and members of Gresley's family, O. V. S. Bulleid, Edward Thompson, J. F. Harrison, A. H. Peppercorn, H. G. Ivatt and R. A. Riddles.

While the passenger services on the ECML gradually improved and increased throughout 1946 there was a step backward during the following year. The fuel crisis was coupled with difficulties in keeping the motive power maintained and in traffic, making the situation increasingly desperate. The coal supplied further aggravated matters as the quality was often poor leading to steaming troubles; the number of failures

BELOW As time progressed a return to the luxury of the pre-war years was made. One of the new trains was the 'Tees-Tyne Pullman', seen here behind No 60030 *Golden Fleece*. *IAL*

ABOVE No 60009 *Union of South Africa* is admired at Newcastle station before leaving with the 'Flying Scotsman'. *Eric Treacy*

attributed to this increased threefold during the period compared with the late 1930s. Therefore cuts were made to services and the 1947 summer timetable contained 10% fewer miles than the previous year. This only proved to be a small bump in the road and in 1948 there were some improvements in the express passenger services on offer, while BR attempted to reduce the backlog of track work for further advancements. The 'Flying Scotsman' summer non-stop returned for the first time after the war on 31 May, leaving King's Cross at 10.05am and taking 7 hours 50 minutes to complete the journey to Edinburgh Waverley. No 60034 *Lord Faringdon* was at the head of the first northbound train, which was seen off by the Lord Mayor of London, Sir Frederick Wells; Driver Moore and Fireman Hardiman were on the footplate. Heading up from Scotland was No 60009 *Union of South Africa*. The 'Queen of Scots' Pullman was also reintroduced on 5 July with departures from King's Cross and Glasgow at 11.30am and 10.15am respectively. The train ran non-stop to Leeds – although crews were changed outside Grantham station – with further pauses at

Harrogate, Darlington, Newcastle and Edinburgh. For the winter timetable a new Pullman train was introduced – the 'Tees-Tyne Pullman' – which left Newcastle at 9.00am, stopped at Darlington, then ran non-stop to King's Cross for an arrival scheduled at 2.16pm. The down train left London at 5.30pm and was to stop at Darlington at 9.57pm, terminating at Newcastle at 10.50pm. The average speeds were, respectively, 51 and 50.3mph. This was the 'Silver Jubilee' in Pullman form, with a similar number of carriages and standard of accommodation, but running an hour slower. Although the 'Silver Jubilee' stock had been stored during the war with a view to reinstating the carriages with the service after the conflict, the decision was made to split them up for integration into new sets. Some went into service between Newcastle and King's Cross while others were sent to Scotland.

For the 'Flying Scotsman' in the summer of 1948 two of the Kylchap-fitted 'A4s' allocated to King's Cross – *Seagull* and *Lord Faringdon* – were entrusted with running the train while Haymarket allocated the task to perennial favourites No 60004 *William Whitelaw* and No 60009 *Union of South Africa*. In late July/early August the weather was unseasonably wet and several days' worth or precipitation swelled river levels to dangerous proportions. Then on 12 August a downpour of a Biblical scale dumped an inordinate amount of water on the Border region causing widespread flooding. The first area of the ECML to be blocked was between Goswick and Scremerston (south of

RIGHT A workman suspended from the electricity cables over the ECML near Coxhoe Junction, Ferryhill, has a good view of No 60020 *Guillemot* passing underneath with an excursion train on 29 July 1951. *Sidney Teasdale*

ABOVE Grantham-allocated 'A4' No 60026 *Miles Beevor* leaves York with the down 'Flying Scotsman'. The engine was based at the shed between April 1948 and September 1951. *IAL*

Tweedmouth) in the afternoon, and into the night a total of 11 bridges between Dunbar and Berwick were rendered unusable due to the water. There were also landslips and the permanent way was washed out. The 'Flying Scotsman' travelled 35 miles north of Newcastle before having to turn back, along with the relief. This latter was diverted via the Waverley route but got stuck in water. The 'Flying Scotsman' was then stopped and turned back to take the West Coast Main Line and arrived some 10 hours late at Waverley. Over the next four days the trains between Edinburgh and King's Cross had to be diverted to Leeds and on to the LMR before the Waverley route was made passable late on 15 August.

The new path (from Carlisle to St Boswells, then heading east to the main line via the Kelso branch) totalled 408.6 miles, with much more difficult terrain to now cover including many speed restraints because of the work done and still necessary for the track. Therefore there was a further strain in hauling trains along the route and a stop had to be scheduled at Hardengreen and Galashiels to take on water and obtain banking assistance if required. This was taken up for several days before 24 August when Driver Stevenson of Haymarket with No 60029 *Woodcock*

declined both chances to stop and completed the 90 miles between Waverley and Lucker troughs without taking any water. This was an excellent demonstration of the economy of the 'A4s' and the driver's knowledge of the engine's ability. As the train continued on to King's Cross without stopping, this was claimed to be a record for the longest non-stop distance by steam traction. Driver Stevenson was not pleased to rest on this achievement and repeated the feat on the 'Flying Scotsman' for the remainder of the week with No 60028 *Walter K. Whigham* on the 25th and 26th, before taking No 60029 *Woodcock* for the 27th and 28th, then finishing off with the engine on the down train on 2 September. Stevenson's shed mates were not content to let him take all the glory and Driver McLeod and No 60027 *Merlin* achieved the down run non-stop on 26 August. Between 6 and 9 September all of the 'Flying Scotsman' services from King's Cross ran without stopping, these being No 60029 and Driver Swan, No 60012

Commonwealth of Australia and Driver McLeod, *Woodcock* with Driver Swan again, and Driver Prinkley with No 60031 *Golden Plover*. The southbound journey only saw two occasions that were non-stop over the same period, on the 7th and 9th. These were at the hands of Driver Swan with No 60029 on both occasions. On the 11th, 15th and 17th he would do this yet again with No 60012, No 60022 *Mallard* and No 60029 respectively. Rounding proceedings off on the 18th (when the summer season came to an end) Driver McLeod had No 60012. The diversion would remain in place until 1 November when the ECML was finally reopened, but about an hour extra was needed in the timetables because of the speed restrictions on the new parts of the line.

Illustrating how difficult the Waverley to Galashiels route was, O. S. Nock, in part of an article of his that appeared in *The Engineer* of 2 July 1954, detailed No 60027 *Merlin* travelling from Hardengreen Junction to Falahill summit – approximately 10 miles at 1 in 70. The journey was made shortly after the winter timetable was put in force and the load increased to 515 tons. A 'Glen' class 4-4-0 was attached and the train set off for the top with *Merlin* being given full regulator and 45% cut-off for part of the climb, reducing to 42%. The speed did not fall too far on the bank but the pressure went from 240lb per sq in to 180lb per sq in. The average speed for the climb, which was also performed in poor conditions, was 24.4mph.

The 1948 summer 'Flying Scotsman' would prove to be the last one run non-stop for several years. On 23 May 1949 a new service was introduced for the summer traffic – the 'Capitals Limited' – which was given 8 hours to travel between King's Cross and Edinburgh Waverley, departing at 9.30am with a rake of 13 Thompson carriages. There were also a number of other trains introduced at this time. The 'White Rose' began to run from King's Cross to Leeds in 4 hours 1 minute, then on to Bradford, while the 'West Riding' (no relation to the 'West Riding Limited') left the latter at 7.30am and Leeds at 7.50am to reach King's Cross at 11.55am. The 'Capitals Limited' was given a glamorous send-off for the first trip as actress Anne Crawford cut a ribbon connected to No 60010 *Dominion of Canada*. During June

No 60027 *Merlin* – which was also on the first up train – had a prolonged period working the service.

BR had authorised 1,226 miles of track renewal in 1948, with a further 550 miles of other line work planned in order to reduce the outstanding amount and improve the permissible speeds. This would not be achieved until 1957 when general accelerations of 10 minutes were made to over 150 services. The track renewal during 1949 increased over the previous year to 1,973 miles, which was 39 miles more than had been replaced in 1938. During 1950 only 44 miles were travelled at an average speed of over 60mph and 4,600 at 55mph and higher. *The Engineer* of 11 May 1951 highlighted one area of 90 miles of track that was previously limited to 90mph but at the time had 13 miles restricted to between 50 and 60mph for work to take place. The publication also suggested that the areas with the best track had little other employment opportunities, so men could be found for the work. Nevertheless, the first mile-a-minute schedule of the post-war period was introduced in the winter of 1949 with the 'North Briton', running from Leeds to Glasgow by way of Edinburgh and York. The stretch between Darlington and York – 44 miles – featured the 44-minute timing and this was only a minute slower than the pre-war allowance. In spite of all this activity punctuality in a four-week period in

the summer of 1949 was as much as 94% of trains completing services on time or up to 5 minutes early.

One of the fastest trains during 1949/50 was still the 'Tees-Tyne Pullman', which No 60022 *Mallard* and No 60033 *Seagull* worked frequently over the period with King's Cross stablemates 'A1' Pacifics No 60156 *Great Central* and No 60157 *Great Eastern*, both fitted with roller bearings to all axles. The 'A1s' were also rostered on the 'Night Scotsman' from Newcastle. No 60030 *Golden Fleece* was recorded as running with the 'Flying Scotsman' for a period in the first half of 1950. Other prolonged episodes of intensive work were also noted for Nos 60009 and 60031, which both managed nearly five and six weeks each.

There was a raising of certain speed limits to 90mph over sections of the ECML in 1951 allowing accelerations in some of the express services. The 'Capitals Limited' was rescheduled to complete the journey in 7 hours 20 minutes, while the 'Flying Scotsman' was running at nearly 7 hours 40 minutes and still making stops along the way. As the Festival of Britain was taking

BELOW Heading the 'Tees-Tyne Pullman' north out of the 528-yard-long Gas Works Tunnel is No 60026 *Miles Beevor*.
Eric Treacy

RIGHT No 60027 *Merlin* takes well-earned refreshment at Wiske Moor troughs while working the down 'Capitals Limited' on 1 August 1951. The next set at Lucker was nearly 100 miles away. *IAL*

LEFT No 60011 *Empire of India* traverses the Forth Bridge with an Edinburgh to Aberdeen slow train on 19 June 1952. *IAL*

BELOW No 60034 *Lord Faringdon* bursts out of Hadley Wood South Tunnel with the down 'Capitals Limited' during September 1952. *J. Davenport*

ABOVE The 'A4s' could work freight services when required, and
No 60001 *Sir Ronald Matthews* has been employed on such a duty,
heading a train out of York c1952. *Kenneth Field*

place, the opportunity to introduce some new trains was seized
and the ER saw the 'Heart of Midlothian' begin, serving York
after departures at 2.00pm from both ends of the system. The
allocation of the class was also simplified to just three sheds.
King's Cross had 19 – Nos 60003, 60006, 60007, 60008, 60010,
60013, 60014, 60015, 60017, 60021, 60022, 60025, 60026,
60028, 60029, 60030, 60032, 60033 and 60034; Gateshead had
eight – Nos 60001, 60002, 60005, 60016, 60018, 60019, 60020
and 60023; and Haymarket seven – Nos 60004, 60009, 60011,
60012, 60024, 60027 and 60031.

A log of the 'Capitals Limited' was made by O. S. Nock in
1951 and appeared in *The Engineer* of 2 July 1954. The
locomotive was No 60029 *Woodcock* and the load was 12
carriages or 465 tons. As a result of tardiness in arriving from
Top Shed the train was 13 minutes late making a departure,
then problems were encountered in raising stream with the
pressure being some 70lb per sq in less than the stated maximum.
Just over 100 minutes were required to reach Essendine (88¾
miles), then further delays were encountered after the train
travelling in front of the express was required to stop and check
a fault. Passing Grantham, the 'Capitals Limited' was 30
minutes late and struggling to keep the boiler pressure at 200lb
per sq in. The crew endeavoured to redeem 5 minutes running
time at Doncaster and an additional 7 minutes 30 seconds were
back at Newcastle. After a good finish on the remaining section,

Woodcock came to a stand in Edinburgh at 4.54pm – only a few
minutes late. There was plenty of recovery time in the schedule
and as much as 14 minutes were given for the 'Capitals Limited'.

For the same journal E. H. Livesay also recorded a trip on
the train from the footplate of No 60024 *Kingfisher* with initially
Driver Howard, Fireman Ward and Inspector Hart, before
Driver Gimel and Fireman McConnell took over. The train
weight was 450 tons gross, and 40% cut-off with half regulator
was used to get up to 45mph at Hornsey, but this then fell away
progressively up to Potters Bar where the rate of travel was
around 30mph; 21 minutes were taken for the 13 miles. The
cut-off then became 15% with half regulator and there was
about 230lb per sq in pressure in the boiler. The 27 miles from
Hitchin to Huntingdon were completed in 22 minutes 30
seconds, the latter being passed at 60mph before this fell away to
40mph on the 1 in 200 to Abbots Ripton. A peak of 75mph was
allowed on the following section to Peterborough, and the total
time was 82 minutes 30 seconds. A few delays were experienced
on to Grantham and a further 35 minutes elapsed, making the
train a couple of minutes late at that point. Uninterrupted

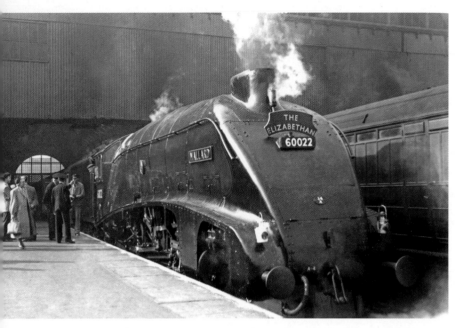

LEFT No 60022 *Mallard* waits at King's Cross with the 'Elizabethan' towards the end of the first season. *IAL*

58.2mph. As part of the celebrations several other named expresses were also accelerated, including the 'Tees-Tyne Pullman', the 'Queen of Scots' Pullman and the 'Heart of Midlothian'. The first 'Elizabethan' left King's Cross at 9.30am on 29 June behind No 60028 *Walter K. Whigham*, while No 60009 *Union of South Africa* was at the head of the southbound train, which left slightly later at 9.45am. The down service had several high-speed sections such as the 73.6mph average necessary between Hitchin and Huntingdon, 70.1mph between Grantham and Newark, 70.5mph between Northallerton and Darlington, and 68.5mph from Dunbar to Drem. Two sections deliberately contained recovery time: Retford to Doncaster, 4 minutes, and King Edward Bridge Junction to Newcastle, 2 minutes. The up train required a high average speed between Dunbar and Drem, Grantshouse to Marshal Meadows (67.1mph), 70.5mph from Darlington to Northallerton, Stoke to Werrington Junction (77.3mph), and Huntingdon to Hitchin (68.9mph). There was an allowance of 3 minutes between Selby and Shaftholme Junction and 8 minutes between Hatfield and King's Cross for the Potters Bar widening scheme, which was increasing the number of lines from two to four.

Nos 60009 and 60028 were recorded at work on the 'Elizabethan' during the first week. *Union of South Africa* headed north and had five permanent way restrictions and three signal checks, one actually stopping the train for over 1 minute. In total these delays amounted to nearly 20 minutes, but Drivers Stevenson and Smith managed to reclaim these losses over the course of the journey and the arrival was right time at Waverley. R. Nelson timed *Walter K. Whigham* on 30 June returning to London and a similar number of restrictions and signals were encountered, but arrival was still made 5 minutes 30 seconds early. Towards the end of the summer No 60011 *Empire of India* was the star performer and was used on the train for three weeks before the start of the winter timetable. Overall, several engines were used for spells of varying periods including Nos 60004, 60009, 60017 and 60031.

O. S. Nock was on the footplate of No 60017 *Silver Fox* to record an up journey on the the 'Elizabethan' in July 1953. The weather conditions were unseasonably windy and this was blowing head-on to the locomotive for much of the trip, increasing the work done by almost a quarter. On the first section from

progress was made to Doncaster, allowing the losses to be regained together with an additional 1 minute 30 seconds. Three minutes were dropped to York after signals at Shaftholme Junction and Balne coupled with restrictions at Selby, Riccall and Escrick. For an unexplained reason No 60024 was running 10 minutes behind at Newcastle. Northward at Alnmouth 20% cut-off and two-thirds cut-off was used for the 4 miles at 1 in 170 to Little Mill. *Kingfisher* pressed on and after reaching Grantshouse maintained an average of 70mph to Longniddry Junction. Just under 10 miles from Waverley the 'Capitals Limited' was on time, then a clear run into the station resulted in an arrival 5 minutes early.

After several improvements had been made to the route a test was performed in mid-1952 to ascertain whether further cuts could be made to running times. 'A4' No 60003 *Andrew K. McCosh* was used between King's Cross and Doncaster with trains of three weights: 350 tons, 400 tons and 500 tons. The results led to new timings being set for these loads, respectively, of 154 minutes 30 seconds, 163 minutes 30 seconds, and 168 minutes. This latter was only just quicker than the timing for the 'Capitals Limited', which generally had a train of 450 tons. By this time the train was running at 7 hours 6 minutes down and 7 hours 7 minutes up. Nos 60017 *Silver Fox*, 60027 *Merlin* and 60033 *Seagull* were familiar sights at the head of the express during 1952 and were supported by Nos 60011 *Empire of India*, 60024 *Kingfisher* and 60034 *Lord Faringdon*.

With the accession to the throne of Queen Elizabeth II in 1953 BR followed the lead of the LNER some 16 years earlier by naming a train to commemorate the event. The 'Elizabethan' replaced the 'Capitals Limited' as the non-stop service between King's Cross and Waverley and the schedule was improved to 6 hours 45 minutes with the overall average speed necessary being

Waverley to Newcastle the locomotive took 133 minutes 25 seconds and was 3 minutes late with an average speed of 56mph; the pressure had been kept high and full regulator with 15% cut-off was used. Travelling on to York *Silver Fox* was interrupted south of Northallerton because of a permanent way restriction but was still able to regain 1 minute 39 seconds. The King's Cross driver pushed the engine to 20% cut-off with pressure over 230lb per sq in, but this caused the fireman to work harder and the engine could not sustain the setting. By Doncaster gains had been made and the train was early at this point, but signals and further track limits saw these lost by Retford. Time continued to be dropped all the way to Hatfield – despite an average speed of 79.6mph between Stoke

ABOVE RIGHT No 60033 *Seagull* hauls the 'Elizabethan' out of Waverley station in the mid-1950s. *Eric Treacy*

BELOW No 60030 *Golden Fleece* has just passed through Calton Hill Tunnel, Edinburgh, with the 'Elizabethan' on 1 July 1954. As usual the engine for the train is immaculate. *E. D. Bruton*

summit, which was passed at 56mph, and Werrington Junction, with a peak of 88mph – the coal was running low and the weather conditions became increasingly wet. The final leg into King's Cross was completed just under 8 minutes early, wiping out the losses and giving 2 minutes 35 seconds to the train.

For the summer timetable of 1954 – beginning on 14 June – there were more accelerations all over the system. On the WR the 'Bristolian' was to run between Paddington and Bristol (118.4 miles) at an average speed of 67.6mph The 7.50am from King's Cross to Leeds and Bradford, which had previously been the fastest train in Britain, was also sped up from 65.9mph to 67.2mph; between Hitchin and Retford the average was 66.3mph. The principal change was to the 'Elizabethan', which would now be required to complete the 392 miles in 6 hours 30 minutes non-stop at an average of just over 60mph.

The changes might have been prompted by several expresses gaining time on the schedules, especially on the ER. Around the new year No 60007 *Sir Nigel Gresley* was in charge of the mid-morning express from Leeds (formed of 12 carriages) arriving at King's Cross several minutes before time; likewise No 60010 *Dominion of Canada* on the 'Tees-Tyne Pullman' (330 tons) arriving at 1.49pm, or 11 minutes early after completing the 228 miles from Darlington in 212 minutes with an average speed of 63mph. No 60029 *Woodcock* had accomplished a similar feat with the train a few days earlier. Not to be outdone, the Peppercorn 'A1' Pacifics were recorded on two consecutive occasions arriving at King's Cross with the 450-ton 'Yorkshire Pullman' 10 minutes early. *Lord Faringdon* was also kept busy over an eight-day period when locomotive availability was low. The engine ran from King's Cross to Leeds and return four times, worked the King's Cross to Newcastle, returning south on the

'Tees-Tyne Pullman', then two services to Grantham were completed. The engine finished off with a turn on the 'Yorkshire Pullman', bringing up a mileage of 2,450.

The first 'Elizabethan' of 1954 ran on 28 June behind No 60030 *Golden Fleece* (down) and No 60009 *Union of South Africa* (up). Both engines recorded early arrivals, the former 3 minutes and the latter 5 minutes. The *British Railways: Eastern Region Magazine* reported that the remainder of the week generally saw an early arrival of 5 minutes at King's Cross and 2 minutes at Waverley. On 30 June the train was 7 minutes early into King's Cross. The magazine adds that the train had been televised as part of the popular programme *Guess My Story*. No 60017 *Silver Fox* also starred in the British Transport Films' *Elizabethan Express*, made during the previous summer and released in 1954.

Nos 60009 and 60030 were joined in employment on the service by No 60032 *Gannet. Union of South Africa* would prove to be the most consistent performer during the summer, amassing 63 trips at the head of the 'Elizabethan', or 24,743¼ miles run on the train, without taking into consideration other workings. The locomotive had undergone a General repair two months prior to the beginning of the summer timetable, ensuring top-class mechanical condition; this practice was traditional for engines selected to work the non-stop. A curio fitted to the locomotive at this time was a plaque of a springbok on the left-hand-side of the boiler, presented by a South African newspaper owner. Later in the year shedmate No 60024 *Kingfisher* had a similar plaque fitted to both sides of the boiler featuring the emblem of HMS *Kingfisher*. This was presented to the engine and regular Drivers A. McLeod and W. McLeod by Lt A. F. Mortimer. C. J. Allen timed No 60009 during the summer but unhappily for him a freight derailment caused a diversion via

Carlisle and the Waverley route. Up to Newcastle the train had been running as much as 10 minutes behind and after the diversion arrival was made at Waverley 2 hours 30 minutes late. When Allen travelled back to London on board the 'Elizabethan' a few days later No 60008 *Dwight D. Eisenhower* was at the front and fared little better with regard to keeping to schedule, and 20 minutes were lost and a late arrival occurred.

O. S. Nock had better luck on his journey south behind No 60030 *Golden Fleece* as several relatively high speeds were produced on the Waverley to Newcastle section. The first was

LEFT Receiving attention in 2-bay of the Crimpsall Repair Shop at Doncaster is No 60029 *Woodcock. Colour-Rail*

77mph at Drem Junction, then 81mph down the 1 in 190 at Marshal Meadows, followed by 82mph on the level at Beal. The final one was 75mph at Alnmouth, where the gains on the timetable amounted to 1 minute 30 seconds. The final time to Newcastle was 124 minutes 8 seconds or just under 1 minute early, and an average speed of 60.2mph had been produced. After a signal check south of Newcastle the engine was 3 minutes down at Durham, but with the speed not dropping below 75mph between Darlington and Alne the 'Elizabethan' was running 1 minute 30 seconds in front at York. The average speed over the section was 79mph. By Doncaster uninterrupted running had allowed *Golden Fleece* to add a few more minutes to the time in hand and this persisted to Grantham, although a track restriction at Crow Park removed a couple of minutes. From Stoke summit to Tallington the time taken was 11 minutes 2 seconds and a peak of 96mph was attained through Essendine and the average speed was 81.6mph for the 15 miles. Two permanent way checks, both north and south of Peterborough, brought the train closer to right time, but No 60030 kept just in front to Hatfield and, with a good final run into King's Cross, the arrival was under 5 minutes early and the net time was close to 370 minutes for the 392¾ miles. Several other performances in this vein were noted over the course of the summer. A small number of failures also occurred and brought an interesting variety of replacements to the head of the train.

After the maintenance of the 'A4' class had reached a low ebb during the war and towards the end of the 1940s, a recovery was made during the 1950s allowing the locomotives to become generally more reliable. The average annual mileage of the class in 1950 and 1951 was over 56,000 and 52,000 miles respectively,

and in 1956 over 65,000 miles was achieved with around 70% availability. Generally, the Haymarket 'A4s', although outnumbered by their English classmates, ran higher average mileages over a 12-month period. In the early 1950s the 'A4s' north of the border ran approximately 60,000-65,000 miles, then in the latter part of the decade the average went to over 70,000 miles, with similar advances in availability. These increases were partly due to an improvement in the workforce and an ease in obtaining materials following the years of austerity. The appointment of Mr K. J. Cook as Mechanical & Electrical Engineer North Eastern and Eastern Areas in 1951 also played a part. Cook had been educated at Swindon Works and had risen to be the Works Manager there in 1937, then becoming the Mechanical & Electrical Engineer Western Region.

Once at Doncaster, Cook set about improving workshop practice in order to increase the reliability of all the locomotives repaired there. One method introduced was optical alignment of the cylinders, frames and axleboxes in order to reduce stresses when running, either arising from the track or the movement of the valve gear. Cook argued that the greater the accuracy in the set-up of the axles on which the different parts moved, the lower the maximum stresses caused. A high standard of set-up would also lead to reduced tolerances, which in the Gresley Pacifics had always been quite generous. The result of improving the latter was that the rate of wear and play in the joints of the motion would be much reduced, leading to higher mileages

ABOVE On shed at Edinburgh Haymarket on 31 July 1955 is No 60011 *Empire of India*. D. Marriott

between repairs. Traditionally the centre lines of the cylinders and the lining up of the axle centres from the former was achieved via fine lengths of wire that had been positioned by finding the centres through the use of callipers. Optical devices were pioneered for the process in the 1920s and were subsequently adopted by the GWR and used at Swindon for many years. In his paper on the method, delivered to the Institution of Mechanical Engineers in 1955, Cook commented on the procedure and the background to the introduction at Doncaster.

He said: 'At the Mechanical Tool Exhibition in 1952 a British optical exhibit was noticed which appeared to be capable of development although at that time it had no reference to locomotives. The makers became very anxious to cooperate and quite quickly a method much simpler than the German, and capable of proceeding very much further in the quest for accuracy, was produced. It became known as the Auto-Reflection method, using instead of a collimator a reflecting mirror fixed parallel to and in line with a straight edge. The auxiliary apparatus and measuring rods are also much simpler.'

P. N. Townend, who was shedmaster at King's Cross during the 1950s and 1960s, recalls – in his excellent book *Top Shed* – that the introduction of the optical alignment method was not an immediate success with the locomotives as during one period up to 11 'A4s' were out of service because the tolerances were too fine, causing the driving axlebox on the right-hand side to run hot. This incident was made worse by the fact that standard axleboxes could not be taken out of stores for machining to the correct size at the shed as had been the case previously, but had to be sent direct from Doncaster. This could take several days, triggering a serious shortage of motive power. Doncaster

increased the tolerances as a result and would send spare sets of axleboxes with overhauled 'A4s' back to King's Cross in case they were needed. Townend explains that King's Cross investigated the general tendency for the overheating of the right-hand driving axlebox and found that this generally happened after the engine had run 40,000 miles. As a result, a decision was made to renew the boxes when the 36,000-mile examination was carried out and the number of instances dwindled to nearly zero.

In addition to the optical alignment method of set-up, Cook brought the Churchward/de Glehn type of big end bearing from Swindon. Gresley's original 'marine' type bearing was made of two parts of bronze, which had two sections each of white metal inserted $^3/_8$ inch deep into the bearing. The Swindon type was a continuous white metal surface set on to a brass surface. There were two gaps at the bottom and the top to allow felt pads to lubricate the metal; these had to be very carefully fitted or the component would fail. The bearing was cautiously machined to ensure the correct fit around the axle. The success of the new type of bearing was coupled to vigilant maintenance and religious inspection every 12,000 and 24,000 miles. P. N. Townend also notes that reliability was considerably improved by having the 'A4s' sent to Doncaster Works for their 36,000-mile inspection, when the motion, piston valves and cylinders would be comprehensively examined. This was done because a number of the components would have to be shipped to Doncaster for repair and the axleboxes had to come the other way, so for the ease of everyone concerned the task was delegated to the works.

Before the war Gresley had kept the 'A4s' in top condition by stipulating that a General repair would be carried out every 60,000-80,000 miles. After the above changes were made to the 'A4s' the locomotives were able to run to 100,000 miles and even more in some instances, remaining at work on the long-distance expresses with a high factor of reliability. In 1955 the 'Elizabethan' was run without a single failure, and No 60033 *Seagull* ran 50 of the trains, accumulating nearly 20,000 miles on this duty alone. Another Kylchap-fitted engine was also heavily involved, with No 60034 *Lord Faringdon* completing 24 journeys; on one the time for the 124½ miles between Edinburgh and Newcastle was 113 minutes. No 60033 was also recorded making high speeds over several sections of the line and a number of instances of net times just totalling over 6 hours for the 392 miles were recorded over the summer. In 1956 *Seagull* went eight better than 1955 and was equalled by Haymarket's No 60011 *Empire of India*, both being supported predominantly by Nos 60010 and 60012. No 60033 was documented reaching 100mph when passing Essendine on one up train after 69½mph at Stoke summit. Arrival was made at King's Cross over 7 minutes early after a superlative dash between Grantham and King's Cross, which was slightly more than 90 minutes net for the 105½ miles.

ABOVE Travelling out of King's Cross past Copenhagen signal box with an express to Leeds is No 60022 *Mallard*. On the right, waiting to be called to the station, is No 60010 *Dominion of Canada*. *Eric Treacy*

BELOW Kylchap-fitted No 60017 *Silver Fox* is coupled up to an express at Grantham on 8 May 1960. *Bill Reed*

The Kylchap blastpipe and double chimney played a significant role in such performances being possible – Gresley had intended to have the apparatus fitted to the class, and others, after the rights had lapsed during the 1940s, but his death stopped this from occurring. None of the succeeding engineers seem to have considered altering any of the Pacifics or the 'V2s', despite having the apparatus present on their own engines. In 1953 steps were taken to improve the draughting of the 'A4s' by altering the chimney and blastpipe arrangement to those found satisfactory in conjunction with 'V2' class No 60845 tested at Swindon. At the end of 1953 No 60006 *Sir Ralph Wedgwood* and No 60015 *Quicksilver* had blastpipes of 5³⁄₈-inch diameter fitted with a chimney of 1ft 4¾in diameter at the top and 1ft 3in diameter at the choke. After tests were conducted the coal consumption was found to have increased and the steaming was no better than with the old arrangement. The blastpipe diameter was duly reduced to a 5¹⁄₈-inch diameter, but a deterioration in performance was experienced when working hard. No 60008 *Dwight D. Eisenhower* and Nos 60001, 60002, 60016, 60018 and 60023 of Gateshead followed in receiving the setting, but any improvements detectable were marginal at best. The reason for the Kylchap apparatus not being adopted immediately was apparently that the alterations would be difficult and costly to carry out, with the cowls also making the cleaning of the tubes more labour intensive. The reality was that there was little alteration to the locomotive necessary and

the cost was approximately £200. With authorisation for conversion not forthcoming, tests were arranged at King's Cross that showed the fuel economy of a Kylchap-fitted engine to be 7lb per mile over a single-chimney 'A4', and this prompted the alteration of the remainder of the class. The first to be changed was No 60017 *Silver Fox* in May 1957 and the last was No 60032 *Gannet* in November 1958. The 'A4s' were not the only engines modified, as King's Cross shed pushed for the 'A3s' to be altered and this took place between June 1958 (No 60055 *Woolwinder*) and January 1960 (No 60079 B*ayardo*). The Kylchap exhaust arrangement brought about a definite renaissance to both classes' performance, and steaming troubles largely became problems of the past, even with poor-quality coal, which was often being supplied at sheds even for express passenger work.

Unfortunately for the Gresley Pacifics and steam locomotives in general such enhancements were coming late in the day. The British Transport Commission's *Modernisation and Re-Equipment of British Railways* of 1955 outlined that expenditure totalling £1,200,000,000 had been authorised for the improvement of the network and the rolling stock up to 1970. Of the aforementioned figure, £105,000,000 was to be spent improving the track and the infrastructure to make higher speeds possible, the aim being 100mph over long stretches. A further £100,000,000 was set aside for the improvement of signalling, with the main feature of the plan being the introduction of power signal boxes and centralised traffic management. The biggest upgrade was the introduction of diesel and electric locomotives and the progressive scrapping of the steam fleet, with the construction of steam locomotives being stopped soon after the announcement. The reasons for the decision given in the report were the dearth of suitable coal for locomotive purposes and the dirt and grime associated with the fuel's use; the imminent introduction of the Clean Air Act to reduce pollution also served to deter the future use of steam engines. Another reason cited was the difficulty in recruiting staff for the work associated with servicing, and that new units were necessary to attain the envisaged average speeds of BR's new express services. Around 2,500 diesel locomotives were expected to be in service by 1970 with some £125,000,000 being spent.

The 'A4s' evidently did not hear this death knell sound as the overall standard of performance and reliability continued to increase throughout the second half of the 1950s. No 60014 *Silver Link* – then over 20 years old – was recorded on the 'Flying Scotsman' travelling between Grantham and King's Cross with 500 tons in just over 100 minutes at an average speed of 62.2mph. This is made more impressive as several signals were against the engine. No 60021 *Wild Swan* produced the same time in the opposite direction in the same circumstance but with 510 tons. No 60030 *Golden Fleece* was also noted on the 'Flying Scotsman' for the best part of three weeks towards the end of 1958, travelling as far as Newcastle, then returning with the heavy evening express.

With the summer services of 1955 came a change to locomotive running practice. On the 'Flying Scotsman' – and other long-distance trains – engines would generally be worked to Newcastle without being remanned. A new train inaugurated at this time was the 'Anglo-Scottish Car Carrier', which also offered sleeping carriage accommodation for tourists taking a holiday in Scotland. The train ran at 7.45pm from King's Cross on Wednesdays and Sundays returning from Perth at 8.00pm on Saturdays and Tuesdays. In 1956 the 'Talisman' was introduced and was a lightweight formation of eight carriages (generally 280-300 tons) running between King's Cross and Edinburgh Waverley in 6 hours 40 minutes. Leaving the capitals at 4.00pm, the

BELOW Preparing to move off Haymarket shed to Waverley station for the 'Talisman' on 11 April 1957 is No 60031 *Golden Plover*. Bill Reed

northbound train was allowed 4 hours 28 minutes to the stop at Newcastle and the average speed necessary was 60mph. The stock used was an assortment of BR Mark 1 coaches, Thompson dining cars and Gresley firsts, which were from the spare 'Coronation' set. The train was a success with the travelling public and at the start of the second quarter of 1957 a 'Morning Talisman' was introduced, leaving at 8.00am. This was followed by an extension to Perth in October, being named the 'Fair Maid'. Unfortunately this was not as successful and was discontinued just over a year later. The first 'Talisman' was run on 17 September with No 60025 *Falcon* travelling northward from King's Cross and No 60019 *Bittern* running south. No 60025 had Driver P. Heavens on to Newcastle where No 60031 *Golden Plover* and Driver T. Smith were waiting to take over and were kept back a few minutes after No 60025 lost a lot of time to delays. *Golden Plover* did make up some time on the final section and the first 'Talisman' was only 2 minutes 15 seconds late. The locomotive was at the head of the up train on 18 September and No 60018 *Sparrow Hawk* took the service from Newcastle to King's Cross, taking 261 minutes.

British Railways: Eastern Region Magazine of January 1957 reported that the 'Talisman' of 5 November 1956 had made an excellent run north despite experiencing heavy delays starting due to problems with the coaching stock. Departure was made 23 minutes late by No 60026 *Miles Beevor* with Driver B. Hoole and Fireman L. Hammans on the footplate. Amazingly, arrival was made at Newcastle for the first stop 6 minutes early. Nearly

10 minutes had been recovered to Peterborough, a further 10 to Doncaster, 4 minutes between York and Darlington, and 7 minutes to Newcastle. Driver Hoole was keeping up this good work when only a few days later he worked the 'Talisman' with No 60025 *Falcon*. Over 26 minutes late in starting, the losses were cut by half at Newcastle with excellent high-speed running from just past Hitchin to Tempsford, with nearly 100mph sustained for the 15 miles, and Stoke summit was passed at approximately 65mph. The time was 281 minutes 30 seconds gross, but the net time was 220 minutes 30 seconds. In mid-1957 No 60017 *Silver Fox* had 280 tons on the 'Morning Talisman' and lost time out of London due to delays but soon attempted to convert the situation with an 88mph average speed for the 13 miles from Stevenage to Biggleswade, and over 90mph on the level at Holme. The 15¼ miles from Tallington to Stoke were reeled off in 11 minutes 4 seconds and the average speed was 82.7mph; the speed at Tallington was 77mph and increased to 78mph at the summit.

The first 'Fair Maid' left King's Cross with No 60015 *Quicksilver*. The 325-ton train was timed at a mile a minute to Darlington, but Driver Hoole had this rate higher on

BELOW No 60015 *Quicksilver* is admired by a number of young enthusiasts at King's Cross before taking out the 'Talisman' in August 1959. At the adjacent platform is 'A3' No 60063 *Isinglass*.

5 November 1957 as he averaged 65.2mph for the 232¼ miles with No 60003 *Andrew K. McCosh*. The run started with 11 minutes lost getting out of the station, but speed was soon gained and a dent was made in the shortfall by Hatfield. After a speed restriction there, the acceleration was phenomenal and 107.5mph was attained near Sandy. Incredibly, the train had recovered the losses and a further 10 minutes when passing Doncaster. Some of this was lost to Darlington, but the 'Fair Maid' was still in front after Hoole's whirlwind performance, and the net time was 188 minutes 15 seconds.

The 'Elizabethan' was slightly hampered by engineering work taking place during 1957 and the schedule had to be increased to compensate for this, forcing a drop in the average speed to below 60mph. Nevertheless a high level of performance was kept up by the 'A4s' and No 60012 *Commonwealth of Australia* worked the train for several weeks, totalling 78 journeys, a number of which were in a consecutive spell. No 60022 *Mallard* provided one of the few 'black marks' as the engine failed in early July and had to be replaced at Peterborough. A few years earlier in 1954 *Mallard* was showing what a well-maintained 'A4' could achieve by completing approximately 120,000 miles since the last General repair at Doncaster, which was in July 1952. The engine did have a Non-Classified repair in mid-1953 but would not return to the works until 4 March 1954. No 60022 was recorded by O. S. Nock in the period just before entry, when at the head of the 'Yorkshire Pullman' between King's Cross and Doncaster, with 450 tons gross behind the tender, *Mallard* was up to 56mph at Wood Green but progressively lost speed up the bank and was not helped by a speed restriction of 5mph going through the station, which was being rebuilt for the widening. The acceleration was rapid to recover speed, which was over 65mph passing Hatfield and was

up further still to 75mph at Hitchin where the 32 miles from King's Cross had been completed in 43 minutes 41 seconds. On to Huntingdon the 27 miles took 22 minutes to travel at an average of 73.6mph. A bad signal check almost stopped the train before Peterborough, but *Mallard* was running at 65mph at Tallington and proceeded to Stoke summit in a time of 15 minutes 49 seconds. To Grantham the engine had taken 117 minutes 28 seconds. The remaining 51 miles to Doncaster occupied 52 minutes 47 seconds at a speed of 55mph.

No 60029 *Woodcock* demonstrated the capabilities of a freshly overhauled 'A4' later in the year on the 'Tees-Tyne Pullman' southbound with O. S. Nock again recording the performance. *Woodcock* had been overhauled after about 18 months in traffic and was just about run-in when timed. With 335 tons the locomotive stormed through Grantham at 75mph, then dropped to approximately 65mph on the 5 miles of 1 in 200 to Stoke. Down the opposite side the engine was 'let loose' and 3 miles on at Corby *Woodcock* was reaching 90mph through the station; 5 miles later, after passing through Little Bytham, it was travelling at over 100mph, peaking at 103½mph. From Stoke to Essendine (11¼ miles) the time was 7 minutes 38 seconds and the average speed was 88.4mph.

Even though the Peppercorn Pacifics were highly capable engines and very reliable, the 'A4s' were never ousted as the prime locomotives running on the ECML during the late 1940s

terminus in 147 minutes 30 seconds from Doncaster, and the average speed was 63.5mph. No 60014 worked a second train, again with Driver Hailstone, the next Sunday, which capped the week-long celebrations. *Silver Link* took the train north on this occasion after the Atlantics had worked up in the morning. In damp conditions the locomotive went up to Potters Bar with a minimum of 59mph before slowing for the limit at the station. The section between Hitchin and Huntingdon was covered at an average speed of 87mph, with a high of 98mph, then at Stoke No 60014 passed the summit at 69½mph after a top speed of 79mph on the bank. The engine went on to Leeds after stopping at Doncaster, and on the 1 in 106 at Ardsley – after a speed restriction at Wakefield of 10mph – went up the bank at 44½mph with 375 tons.

Two other centenary celebrations had occurred the previous year: the opening of King's Cross station and the 'Towns Line' between Peterborough and Retford. Festivities were organised and on 28 September these included a special train from King's Cross to York called the 'Centenaries Express'. 'A4' No 60007 *Sir Nigel Gresley* was the locomotive given the honour of hauling the 10-carriage train, which had a schedule of 3 hours 15 minutes. In the event a number of restrictions and a diversion at Doncaster caused disruption to this, but No 60007 still managed to maintain an average speed of 63.1mph to Doncaster and arrived 1 minute early at York.

In mid-July 1951 No 60008 *Dwight D. Eisenhower* was an attraction at the exhibition that was held at Boston station for the American Pilgrimage. The naming of Thompson 'B1' class 4-6-0 No 61379 *Mayflower* at King's Cross by Commander Harold L. Goodwin of the US Navy preceded the event as the engine was scheduled to take the pilgrims to Boston. *British Railways: Eastern Region Magazine* of September 1951 comments that the 'A4' was the centrepiece of the ensuing festivities as 'long queues formed when facilities were provided for the public to inspect it in the down platform'. The article added: 'Considerable interest was derived from the privilege of being allowed to walk through [the] locomotive's corridor tender on

and throughout the 1950s. This is demonstrated by their use on the majority of the named trains and the principal expresses as well as numerous special trains and railtours that took place during the period. Shortly after nationalisation on 17 and 18 July Doncaster 'Plant' Works Exhibition was held and featured No 60029 *Woodcock* among the exhibits. There was also No 60114 (later named *W. P. Allen*), the first Peppercorn 'A1' Pacific, and Ivatt Atlantic No 251, which had by then been preserved. In partnership with the latter and No 990 *Henry Oakley*, 'A4' class No 60014 *Silver Link* worked a special train from King's Cross to Doncaster for the centenary of the opening of Doncaster Works on 20 September 1953. The two veterans were given the task of heading north with a stop at Peterborough for the Atlantics to be refreshed. *British Railways: Eastern Region Magazine* said that hundreds of people lined the route to see them back on the main line and the engines were practically mobbed by people when taking water. The Atlantics had managed to arrive 4 minutes early and carried the majority of this on to Doncaster. No 60014 came on to the 425-ton train for the return to King's Cross with Driver E. Hailstone. There were a number of excellent moments on the trip, particularly down from Stoke as a top speed of 96mph was attained. Arrival was made at the

TOP The 'Stephenson Jubilee' special at Doncaster; *Sir Nigel Gresley* reached 112mph on the return to King's Cross.

ABOVE Driver B. Hoole and Fireman A. Leech in the cab of No 60032 *Gannet* at King's Cross, c1955.

to the footplate.' No 60008 was also used to transport BR officials from King's Cross on 17 September 1954 for the official opening of the Woodhead route between Sheffield and Manchester, which was a pioneer in the use of electricity supplied from overhead cables. The scheme had been instigated by the LNER and the first locomotive had been designed by Gresley. No 60008 also returned the distinguished passengers to the capital and showed off with several high speeds.

Earlier in 1954 the International Railway Congress was held in Edinburgh and two 'A4s' were chosen to haul the special trains north – these featured the 'Coronation' observation cars for one of the few occasions that they ran on the main line after the war. The time booked was 6 hours 45 minutes and No 60022 *Mallard* left first at 7.55am, followed by No 60034 *Lord Faringdon* at 8.05. The former arrived early after running at an average speed of 58.9mph, but the latter was delayed due to a water stop being necessary.

At the end of 1953 *Mallard* was given the task of conveying HRH The Duke of Edinburgh and other important persons from King's Cross to Sheffield Victoria for a business exposition being opened in the city. The engine made a good impression as the service was completed 3 minutes ahead of the booked 2 hours 58 minutes, and an additional minute was saved on the return to the capital with a slightly longer allowance of 3 hours 12 minutes. About a year later *British Railways: Eastern Region Magazine* told how the Duke of Edinburgh had been attracted to a talk held at the City of London College where a paper was being read on 'The Development of Steam Locomotives', which featured reference to the 'A4' class Pacifics and in particular the world speed record-holder *Mallard*. As a coincidence, the Duke and HM Queen Elizabeth II were travelling later that night from King's Cross to the West Riding of Yorkshire behind No 60026 *Miles Beevor* as far as Retford, where 'B1' class engines took over. In June 1956 the Royal Train again travelled on the ECML as the Queen was carried to York with No 60007 *Sir Nigel Gresley* at the head and Driver Hoole on the footplate.

Another important royal occasion entrusted to the 'A4s' was carrying the Royal Family and other VIPs from King's Cross to York for the wedding of HRH Prince Edward, Duke of Kent, on 8 June 1961. In total three special trains were run, with No 60028 *Walter K. Whigham* leading the procession followed by Nos 60003 *Andrew K. McCosh* and 60015 *Quicksilver*. Should No 60028 have succumbed to any mechanical or other troubles, No 60014 *Silver Link* was prepared to step in, but fortunately all three were in top condition and the trains were run to York and back in excellent fashion.

Like No 4492 *Dominion of New Zealand* 21 years earlier, No 60010 *Dominion of Canada* was used to take members of a shipping community north to witness the launch of a new ship – in this instance the Canadian Pacific Steamships Limited's *Empress of Canada*. The party went north on 10 May 1960 and the engine was specially prepared at King's Cross shed, being selected despite running nearly 100,000 miles since the last General repair. P. N. Townend recalls in *Top Shed* that *Dominion of Canada* spent five days being thoroughly fettled, including

receiving a new coat of paint; the engine would remain in traffic for a further three months after the event before being called into Doncaster Works for overhaul.

An instance of 'A4s' hauling football fans' specials was recorded in January 1955. No 60014 *Silver Link* and No 60017 *Silver Fox* were in charge of two trains that had originated at Hastings and were destined for Sheffield for an FA Cup third-round tie at Hillsborough. Unfortunately for Hastings United there would be no 'giant killing' but a swift return to the south coast as the team was overcome 2-1 by the Owls. No 60007 *Sir Nigel Gresley* was also employed on an FA Cup special, departing from King's Cross with a train full of Tottenham Hotspur supporters bound for Gateshead.

Perhaps the most famous special to be run by an 'A4' was the Stephenson Locomotive Society's 'Golden Jubilee' railtour organised for 23 May 1959 and travelling between King's Cross and Doncaster via Lincoln, returning direct. The driver chosen for the occasion was Bill Hoole – assisted by Fireman A. Hancox – and the engine was to be his regular No 60007 *Sir Nigel Gresley*. The trip was several months in the planning and the ER hierarchy took some persuading to allow the maximum speed of 90mph to be lifted on some sections, especially for the run down Stoke bank. On the day the train was formed of a modest eight carriages and the weight was 295 tons gross. Standing at Platform 5, the departure was set for 9.48am and also in the cab of No 60007 was Alan Pegler, Chief Inspector B. Dixon and C. Palmer, Motive Power Officer.

BELOW No 60027 *Merlin* at Perth shed. *Bill Reed*

After setting off, Driver Hoole selected 40% cut-off with full regulator to haul the train out of London, and in 2½ miles to Finsbury Park the speed was 53mph, having taken just over 5 minutes 30 seconds. At Harringay the cut-off was brought back to 20% as the speed rose to 64mph towards Wood Green; a short distance further on the safety valves lifted as the train progressed steadily to Potters Bar at around 60mph. Hatfield was passed in 20 minutes 3 seconds. The next 14¼ miles to Hitchin took 12 minutes 7 seconds including a slowing for water to be picked up at Langley. The speed pushed close to 100mph at Three Counties and Arlesey, but an inaccurate speed recorder kept Hoole from pushing the mark. The cut-off was 15% with a half-open regulator, and the time to Huntingdon was 19 minutes 41 seconds for the 27 miles at an average speed of 82.3mph. Several restrictions were then observed between Huntingdon and Peterborough with the total time when passing the latter being 69 minutes 24 seconds. Hoole then tried to push *Sir Nigel Gresley* back up to speed from the restriction through the station in preparation for the climb to Stoke summit but was hampered by a permanent way restriction at Werrington Junction. After passing this, Hoole used 30% cut-off to get the engine running at 79mph going through Tallington and there was a high of 83mph between Essendine and Little Bytham. On to Corby the speed dropped slightly to at least 79mph before Hoole countered with an increase in cut-off to 36% and 83mph was again reached on the level through the station. On the 3 miles of 1 in 178 to Stoke the speed fell again to 80mph but another increase in cut-off saw No 60007 top the summit at 82mph. The time to Grantham was approximately 97 minutes. The remainder of the trip to Doncaster via Lincoln passed without incident and the train entered the station just early on the 3 hours 5 minutes booked. Before taking a well-earned rest Hoole was presented with a clock by Alan Pegler to mark the occasion.

The departure at 5.46pm was missed by 2 minutes, giving the large crowds at Doncaster a few more minutes to admire *Sir Nigel Gresley*. Hoole immediately sought to regain the time and in 4 miles he had the train moving at 70mph, then, after a restriction to 40mph, 80mph was attained prior to another restriction through Retford station. On the gradient to Markham summit just south of the latter, No 60007 accelerated up the bank, reaching 72mph, and there was then over 80mph achieved going down the opposite side. The engine was handled steadily on to Grantham, which was passed at 80mph – some 10mph over the limit – but the train was 3 minutes late at this point. The speed only dropped by 10mph up the following incline, then once on the falling gradient the engine was soon above 100mph and a further 10mph was added when the train rushed through Little Bytham station. Before Essendine was reached the speed had peaked at 112mph – setting a post-war speed record for steam in Britain. Hoole would have taken the engine higher if Inspector Dixon had not pulled on the reins. From Corby to Tallington the average speed was 104mph, but Hoole was not finished there as he took another run at 100mph on the level from St Neots to Sandy and this was easily achieved. The average speed from Huntingdon to Hitchin was 84.4mph and the time 19 minutes 12 seconds. Arrival at King's Cross was made 4 minutes 18 seconds early after a total time of 137 minutes 42 seconds was recorded from Doncaster for an average speed of 68mph.

This was a fitting tribute to Hoole and to the other drivers (not forgetting the firemen) who spent years learning the road and the methods necessary to travel successfully from point to point on the main line, whatever the circumstances. Hoole retired a short time later in early July after working a return trip on the 'Elizabethan' with No 60027 *Merlin*. There was to be a final 100mph down Stoke but fate intervened in the form of an adverse signal and the journey ended in just a punctual arrival.

By the end of the 1950s BR's Modernisation Plan was beginning to take effect and a large number of branch lines were being serviced by diesel multiple

LEFT The prototype diesel locomotive DP1, or *Deltic*, at Grantham in September 1960. After withdrawal in 1961 the unit was preserved, but unfortunately not in working condition. *Bill Reed*

ABOVE Crossing the River Idle at Retford with a down express is No 60019 *Bittern*. *Bill Reed*

units, which brought a certain amount of efficiency and monetary saving to their operation; passenger numbers also improved as a result. On the ECML five Type 4 diesel locomotives that produced over 2,000 horsepower were taken on trial in mid-1958; a further five ordered by the ER as part of the Pilot Scheme were put to work between Liverpool Street and Norwich. On both lines the locomotives were found to be less than capable than the steam engines at work because up to a quarter of the stated power was not transmitted to the track. Nevertheless, BR saw fit to order another 190 and these would appear before 1962. The ER declined to take all but a few examples and the rest were spread over the NE Region, Scottish Region and LM Region. The upper hierarchy had their eyes set on more powerful locomotives to run trains at average speeds round 75mph and such a design happened to be on test on the LMR at the time. This was the DP1 locomotive, or *Deltic*, constructed by English Electric in 1955 as a prototype to demonstrate the capabilities of the Napier engines that had previously been used for marine purposes. Two diesel units were employed and these generated 1,650 horsepower each, or 3,300 total, with the tractive effort being 50,000lb. The authorities on the LMR were not confident in

the design, even though some good performances were made. The ER evidently took note of these and did not hesitate in ordering 22 'Deltics' on 1 May 1958. The prototype was eventually sent to the ER in January 1959 to run on the ECML, with Driver Hoole bringing the engine down from York to Hornsey. He was specially trained in the working of the locomotive and was on hand to teach other drivers the intricacies of the contraption's operation. Hoole was also involved in several trials with *Deltic*, including one where the 27 miles between Huntingdon and Hitchin were covered in just 16 minutes, while another occasion saw the locomotive's maximum speed of 105mph reached when heading south from Stoke. As BR abandoned a gradual approach to the introduction of diesel locomotives and flooded the market with orders, the construction of the first production 'Deltic' was not completed until January 1961. After acceptance tests were carried out, the first locomotives finally entered service at the end of February. The remainder trickled into traffic up to

May 1962 and were distributed to the new diesel depots at Finsbury Park (eight), Gateshead (six) and Edinburgh Haymarket (eight).

Before the beginning of the 1960s a landmark for British roads was reached as the first motorways began to open, including the initial section of the major trunk route – the M1 – which stretched from Watford to Rugby, later being extended to Sheffield and Leeds. This, and other roads, served to ease congestion on increasingly crowded A roads, catering to the ever-growing private transport industry. In the same period BR's freight receipts were a third of the investments that hauliers were making and rail was moving 3,400 million tons of freight less than roads. There were 4.5 million cars and 50,000 million miles were being travelled by them. This compared to 25 million passenger miles run by BR. With quicker times to deliver goods being achievable after the introduction of the new motorways

and cheaper prices being offered, BR was fighting a losing battle to keep the freight business afloat.

T. R. Gourvish in *British Railways 1948-1973: A Business History* details some of the figures relating to passenger traffic and those negatively affecting the company's operations. The total number of passenger miles as part of the market share fell from over 21% in the early 1950s to 14% at the start of the 1960s, but the passenger mileage actually increased to 25.3 million miles at the end of the decade. Overall BR's situation was similar to the LNER's some 30 years earlier, as the 1950s started off as promising for the future but matters quickly deteriorated and the losses steadily grew. In 1958 the shortfall for BR was a total of £90.1 million, in 1959 the tide was partly stemmed, but in 1960 the loss was £112.7 million and in 1962 £159 million. The situation was not helped by continually rising costs incurred by running trains: coal prices were up by 40% from the late 1940s and the quality was deteriorating; labour charges were 70% greater in 1962 than 1953; and steel prices rose considerably during the mid-1950s before settling and holding at about 50% of the cost at the start of the 1950s. Against this BR was restricted in the charges that could be levied

BELOW No 60028 *Walter K. Whigham* receives fuel from King's Cross shed's 500-ton mechanical coaler before working the 'Elizabethan'. *Eric Treacy*

ABOVE A dramatic shot of No 60006 *Sir Ralph Wedgwood* leaving King's Cross with an express;
a Brush Type 2 diesel can be glimpsed on the right. *IAL*

LEFT At 26 years old No 60014 *Silver Link* was still doing sterling work on the expresses. The engine makes an enforced stop at Helpston Crossing with the 'Elizabethan' to Edinburgh on 24 July 1961. *D. C. Ovenden*

for the carriage of passengers and freight as the Government was particularly keen to not have prices rise too much for fear of upsetting the voting public. Passenger fares for ordinary services were kept under 2d per mile for the second half of the 1950s and became 3d in 1962; in real terms this was actually of lesser value than the 1.4d charged at nationalisation.

In the summer of 1958 the timetable featured 35 services running at an average speed of over 60mph, 11 more than in 1957, and the number of miles came to 2,436, which constituted a quarter of the overall national figure. The Type 4s did not begin regular work until the mid-point of the season, working sections of named-train routes such as the 'Heart of Midlothian' and 'White Rose' to Peterborough and Doncaster respectively. In the winter timetable dedicated diesel services were introduced both on the ECML – to Newcastle – and to Sheffield with the 'Master Cutler' Pullman, which travelled north in 2 hours 35 minutes with one stop at Retford. The 'A4s' were not too seriously affected by this development as the new locomotives' reliability left a lot to be desired and their numbers were not sufficient to cause any unemployment. If anything, the class were generally working as hard as ever. R. A. H. Weight reported in *The Meccano Magazine* of June 1958 that No 60019 *Bittern* had been fully employed during the previous winter, being rostered on the up 'Talisman', then working back the next day with the 10.10am to Glasgow as far as Newcastle. From there the engine was used on the night sleeper to Edinburgh, and this spell ended with the up 'Flying Scotsman' as far as Newcastle, where No 60158 *Aberdonian* relieved. This train was formed of 11

carriages weighing in excess of 400 tons, and *Bittern* had no problem in making Dunbar in less than half an hour, in addition to attaining 83mph between there and Berwick. With some steady speeds onward, the time to Newcastle was 4 minutes 30 seconds early. The four workings totalled 786 miles and required a high standard of running. R. A. H. Weight also noted some of the arrivals at King's Cross during the summer of 1958, and the 'Fair Maid' was behind No 60026 *Miles Beevor*, the 6.06pm from Leeds was with No 60021 *Wild Swan*, and the 6.40pm ex-Glasgow was with No 60033 *Seagull*, all running ahead of time. No 60013 *Dominion of New Zealand* let the class down with time booked against the engine on the 'Elizabethan'. No 60034 *Lord Faringdon* was also recorded as taking the down 'Talisman'. Only one diesel was seen at work – No D207 – and this locomotive was on the 'Northumbrian'. With regard to the 'Elizabethan', the 1958 season featured several 'A4s' with none appearing to dominate proceedings as in previous years. There is also the suggestion that three failures occurred during the period.

No 60022 *Mallard* was making sure that performance was not ebbing away later in the year when R. A. H. Weight was again on hand to detail the running with the 'Morning Talisman', which weighed approximately 330 tons. Starting from Darlington, *Mallard* was soon up to speed and sustained around 90mph for a period before the first of a number of restrictions set in and these continued on to Newark with a total of seven experienced to that point, making the train 14 minutes behind time. An adverse signal before Stoke tunnel ruined the climb, but the engine peaked at 90mph down the bank and averaged 83mph to Tallington. This rate only dropped to 78mph for 41 miles beginning at Huntingdon and ceasing at Hatfield. No 60022 had nearly regained the losses at this point but delays into London made the train just over the scheduled arrival time. The 76 miles from Peterborough were completed in 67 minutes at an average speed of 68.3mph. The year ended with No 60030 *Golden Fleece* working the 'Flying Scotsman' for almost two weeks, and another week working other services gave the engine an impressive mileage figure for the period.

RIGHT At Peterborough with an up Leeds train on 17 February 1962 is No 60025 *Falcon*. *P. H. Wells*

BELOW Gateshead's No 60018 *Sparrow Hawk* takes the Bristol to Newcastle express out of York. *Eric Treacy*

Diesels did not make any notable inroads into the timetables during 1959, although the less-powerful Type 2s were finding employment on local passenger services. Another sample of workings, taken during the year, saw No 60010 *Dominion of Canada* working the 'Northumbrian', No 60014 *Silver Link* at the head of the 'Flying Scotsman', No 60015 *Quicksilver* bringing a Hull express from Doncaster, and No 60031 *Golden Plover* on an express from Edinburgh. Haymarket shedmate No 60027 *Merlin* was the mainstay of the 'Elizabethan' during the summer, accumulating 62 trips with the train, 40 of which were consecutive. The engine was closely followed by King's Cross's No 60028 *Walter K. Whigham*, which was rostered 53 times. Only two failures were recorded on the train.

Early in 1960 *Mallard* was keeping busy by working a prolonged spell on the 'Flying Scotsman'. This was taken further by Haymarket's No 60027 *Merlin* on the 'Elizabethan' as a total of 76 journeys were made between the capitals and 46 of these were undertaken consecutively early in the summer, followed by a further 22 back-to-back before the winter timetable came into effect. The locomotive had started the summer season from Waverley on 13 June with No 60032 *Gannet* travelling in the other direction. This latter engine produced the only failure on the train, which occurred late in September. Other engines recorded with the 'Elizabethan' included Nos 60024 *Kingfisher*, 60025 *Falcon* and 60029 *Woodcock*. No 60007 *Sir Nigel Gresley* also had a busy summer working other trains and was noted as accumulating nearly 10,000 miles over a short period.

The winter timetable commenced on 12 September with diesels dominating the mileage run for passenger services, the ratio now being 60:40. Generally there were no accelerations and some time was actually added due to the engineering works taking place all along the main line. Early in 1961 many of the principal trains were noted as being in the main diesel-hauled from the northern end of the line, which was due to the relatively large numbers of Type 4s being delivered to the NE and Scottish Regions. In early 1961 No 60015 *Quicksilver* was working the 'Tees-Thames Express' – introduced for the new diesels and running between King's Cross and Saltburn – weighing 455 tons, and at Grantham responsibility was handed over to Type 4 No D284. The performance by the veteran was very good as a 2-minute delay at King's Cross was made up despite track work and signals before Peterborough. On to Grantham further interruptions did not stop a gain of 2 minutes being made, and a high of 90mph was recorded from *Quicksilver*. On another occasion No 60018 *Sparrow Hawk* made the same journey in 102 minutes net with the average speed being 62mph.

When the summer services were announced in 1961 diesels had a slightly higher share of the traffic, but the 'Elizabethan' was still 'A4'-hauled, although this would prove to be the last season of the train being worked by steam. The influx of 'Deltics' over the remainder of the year would make many of the Pacifics redundant. Fittingly, No 60014 *Silver Link* was a regular at the head of the service and amassed 41 trips between the capitals. Playing a supporting role were other regulars from previous years: Nos 60009 *Union of South Africa*, 60024 *Kingfisher*, 60028 *Walter K. Whigham* and 60031 *Golden Plover*. The last steam-hauled 'Elizabethan' left King's Cross behind No 60022 with Driver H. Birkett, while at Waverley No 60009 was at the head with Driver R. Currie. The latter locomotive was recorded between Grantham and King's Cross late in the season completing the 105½ miles in 100 minutes after stopping for water following tender scoop problems. The average speed was 63.3mph and the engine nearly reached 100mph down Stoke bank.

Eleven Deltics were in service by September 1961 and considerable accelerations were made. The fastest of these was the 'West Riding', which was cut by 44 minutes and was booked to run the 106 miles between Hitchin and Retford in 89 minutes at an average speed of 72mph. The biggest acceleration was to the early morning Newcastle to King's Cross service, which saw 59 minutes excised, and this was followed closely by the early evening Bradford to King's Cross, which was cut by 55 minutes and had a total running time of 3 hours 13 minutes. Before the winter service began 'Deltic' No D9003 *Meld* was recorded on the down service (timed at 189 minutes) and the up (185 minutes) in the *British Railways: Eastern Region Magazine*. Generally the locomotive had no problems keeping just in front of the point-to-point times, despite five permanent way restrictions on the northbound journey and a slowing for signals at Hitchin. There had been an acceleration with the 376-ton train up the bank to Potters Bar, reaching 70mph at Hadley Wood and peaking at 72mph through the station. From Arlesey to St Neots No D9003 sustained 92mph for 14 miles before slowing to 70mph through Offord. A swift rise in speed followed Peterborough and at Helpston 90mph was kept from there to Essendine, just falling by a minimum of 5mph on the next 11¼ miles to the top, the average for this being 88mph. At Leeds arrival was made 3 minutes early. On the return, with the same load, the locomotive gained 3 minutes between Doncaster and Retford and would keep these for the remainder of the run. No speeds over the limit were attempted down Stoke, but 89mph was averaged. The 185½ miles were completed in 182 minutes 20 seconds and the average speed was 61mph.

The 'A4s' continued to be used where possible from this point, but were no longer the primary motive power for the main line. The named expresses usually featured the 'Deltics' or Type 4s, and the Pacifics were generally only brought in for a failure or to cover the services without an available diesel. An event perhaps signifying how the position had changed occurred in 1962 when the 100th anniversary of the 'Flying Scotsman' was celebrated on 18 June. The first train – with a new timing of 6 hours – was taken north behind an unidentified 'Deltic'.

As steam was being wound down the 'A4s' were still in demand by enthusiasts who wanted members of the class to

BELOW No 60034 *Lord Faringdon* is turned at York prior to working back to London on 10 August 1962. *R. J. Farrell*

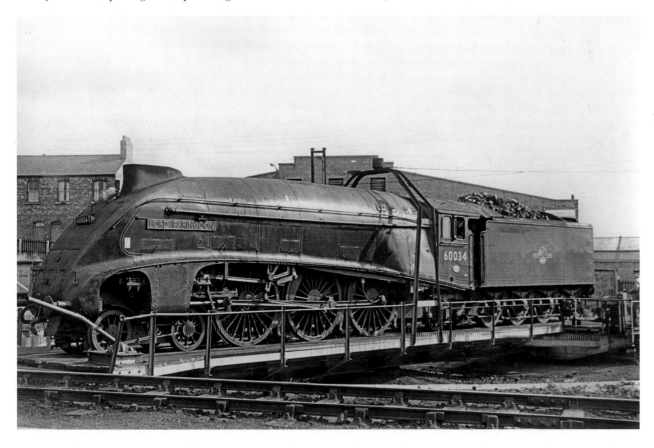

transport them to various places of interest – railway or otherwise – all over the country. No 60022 *Mallard* was employed for a tour taking place on 4 June 1961 organised by the Home Counties Railway Club, travelling between King's Cross and Doncaster. At the end of the summer No 60022 was again in demand, this time hauling the 'Northern Rubber' special from Retford to Blackpool, via Wakefield, Sowerby Bridge, Blackburn and Preston. The return saw Midland Railway Compound 4-4-0 No 1000, which had been preserved two years previously, pilot *Mallard* for an appreciable distance from Blackpool. After working the 'Ian Allan Locospotters Special' from King's Cross to Doncaster for a tour of the works in May 1962, No 60022 was chosen to take the first of two journeys to Edinburgh. The first was for the Gainsborough Model Railway Society, leaving Lincoln on 26 May and heading north to the Scottish capital where a brief journey was made to the Forth Bridge with No 60004 *William Whitelaw*. Both engines were then used just a week later by the Railway Correspondence & Travel Society and the Stephenson Locomotive Society for the jointly organised 'Aberdeen Flyer' on 2 June. This was said to be the last non-stop journey between the capitals performed by a steam locomotive. No 60022 was given this honour, with an allowance of 6 hours 30 minutes and a train consisting of eight carriages. No 60004

was waiting to take this on to Aberdeen, but the stay was to be brief in the 'Granite City' as two LMR 'Princess Royal' class Pacifics were to whisk the train back south later that evening via the WCML. In the event *Mallard* was held up by a freight wagon running hot, causing a stop south of Berwick, and the engine was late into Waverley. *William Whitelaw* took up the challenge of completing the difficult 130 miles in the 3 hours 10 minutes allowed – including a water stop – and succeeding in doing so with 5 minutes to spare.

As 20 'Deltics' had entered traffic by the end of 1962 the ER authorities saw fit to condemn a number of 'A4' locomotives for scrap. A total of five from King's Cross were selected, these being Nos 60003 *Andrew K. McCosh*, 60014 *Silver Link*, 60028 *Walter K. Whigham*, 60030 *Golden Fleece* and 60033 *Seagull*. In April 1963 – two months after the final 'Deltics' had been delivered – two more Pacifics were released from traffic: Nos 60015 *Quicksilver* and 60022 *Mallard*. The summer timetable began in June 1963 with several of the top expresses being given average

BELOW No 60009 *Union of South Africa* passes Sulzer Type 4 'Peak' No D11 as a start is made with the 'Elizabethan' out of Edinburgh Waverley on 30 August 1961. *Eric Treacy*

speeds of 70-75mph. At the same time King's Cross shed was closed and all the engines transferred away, including the 'A4s', which went to Peterborough New England depot. Not long afterwards the first NE Region 'A4' went for scrap – No 60018 *Sparrow Hawk* – and was followed by No 60008 *Dwight D. Eisenhower*. Steam was also officially discouraged from working south of Peterborough.

On 30 June 1963 No 60023 *Golden Eagle* was used on the RCTS's 'Three Summits' railtour from Leeds to Carlisle. Unfortunately troubles with the injectors caused as much as an hour's running time to be lost, but when function returned a good climb was made to Ais Gill summit and the speed rose to 90mph down the bank.

The timing for the 76.8 miles was 90 minutes and *Golden Eagle* completed this in 82 minutes 30 seconds. No 60004 was involved in a small portion of the tour between Auchinleck and Carlisle, handing back the reins to No 60023 for the return to Leeds. The engine gained over 4 minutes by Plumpton but a bad signal check deleted these. No 60023 worked hard to maintain 55mph on the 7 miles to Shap summit, taking 13 minutes 53 seconds, accumulating 8 minutes and 41 seconds of gains, with over 80mph touched descending from the top.

The 25th Anniversary of *Mallard*'s record run occurred on 6 July 1963 and to mark the event the Locomotive Club of Great Britain organised a special train running from King's Cross via Cambridge and Lincoln to Doncaster, then on to York before returning on the ECML. The locomotive used was No 60007 *Sir Nigel Gresley* and another speed of 100mph was recorded down Stoke bank when the party was returning to London. The average speed for the 188 miles was 60.1mph.

After the summer of 1963 more 'A4s' were taken out of traffic. The casualties in October were No 60017 *Silver Fox*, which worked the last timetabled train out of King's Cross by an 'A4', and Nos 60021 *Wild Swan*, 60025 *Falcon*, 60029 *Woodcock* and 60032 *Gannet*. The majority of the 'A4s' left in the stock of the Eastern and North Eastern Regions were then sent to the Scottish Region. Edinburgh Haymarket had dispensed with the majority of the 'A4s' stationed there by this time, as two – Nos 60027 *Merlin* and 60031 *Golden Plover* – had been transferred to St Rollox, Glasgow, to find new employment opportunities. Nos 60004 *William Whitelaw*, 60009 *Union of South Africa* and 60011 *Empire of India* became the first 'A4s' to be allocated to Aberdeen after leaving Edinburgh. The

ABOVE A number of 'A4s' were deserving of preservation but none perhaps more so than No 60014 *Silver Link*, which set the tone for those that followed. Unfortunately the engine was sent for scrap and the process has just begun at Doncaster Works in September 1963.

first-mentioned was actually transferred back in late 1962 and continued to be on the roster with No 60012 *Commonwealth of Australia* and No 60024 *Kingfisher* until mid-1963. With the influx of the English 'A4s' into the Scottish Region, many found themselves being put into store at several locations, including Edinburgh's Dalry Road and St Margaret's sheds, Bathgate and Galashiels.

The Scottish Region had begun the process of dieselisation in the late 1950s and, in addition to taking some Type 4s, had a number of Type 2s provided by the North British Locomotive Company and BR workshops with engines from Sulzer. The NBLC units proved to be extremely unreliable – the diesel engine would end up having to be replaced – and neither were the latter mentioned to a degree. This left a void between the motive power available and the requirements set down in the timetable. The Glasgow Buchanan Street to Aberdeen service, which was traditionally a Caledonian Railway/LMSR undertaking, was run in 3 hours just before the war being named the 'Granite City' along with the 'Saint Mungo' and 'Bon Accord'. Making the main titled services on the line a quartet after nationalisation was the 'Grampian'. From the mid-1950s the best steam time was 3 hours 30 minutes, and with the introduction of diesels the authorities intended to return this timing to 3 hours. As the new engines proved to be a let-down, replacements were sought and, with the 'A4s' being ousted from Haymarket and also from England, several of the class were given an opportunity to continue in traffic. No 60031 *Golden Plover* was taken on at St Rollox for an initial trial in early February 1962, but got off to a bad start by failing with a mechanical fault. No 60027 *Merlin* was then sent over from Haymarket and worked the test later in the month with no problems, taking around 2 hours 30 minutes there and back, excluding stops, with an eight-carriage train. The four services were introduced with accelerations for the summer of 1962. Leaving Glasgow at 8.25am was the 'Grampian' and the corresponding train from Aberdeen was the 7.10am 'Bon Accord', which returned at 2.05pm in 3 hours 35 minutes with stops. In the early evening the 'Saint Mungo' left Glasgow at 5.30pm and the 'Granite City' headed south at 5.15. No 60027 *Merlin* was recorded on the latter during this first summer with an eight-car train weighing 265 tons gross. The locomotive reached 56mph on the difficult climb out of Aberdeen and did this within the allowance of 19 minutes. After stopping at

Stonehaven *Merlin* completed the 41 miles to Forfar at an average speed of 57.2mph, despite the inclusion of a steep climb past Bridge of Dun to Glasterlaw. Onward to Perth a signal check interrupted a spell at over 75mph – which was the ScR speed limit – before the train made a late stop at the station. This situation persisted after departure, then a change in weather to damp conditions, coupled with more signal checks and speed restrictions, meant that entry into Buchanan Street was late despite the best efforts of the crew and engine.

The 'A4s' continued to work these services throughout the winter of 1962 and into the summer of 1963, but several failures were noted, including both supporting 'A3s' (Nos 60090 *Grand Parade* and 60094 *Colorado*), which allowed Peppercorn 'A2s' and 'V2s' to substitute, performing creditably. At the end of 1963 diesels were trialled on the trains but could not force their way in, allowing several 'A4s' to be taken out of store to join in with the summer schedules of 1964, including Nos 60006, 60007, 60016, 60023, 60026 and 60034. No 60005 *Sir Charles Newton* and No 60010 *Dominion of Canada* were in work at Aberdeen from late 1963, but the former did not last too long and was withdrawn in March, soon to be followed by Nos 60011, 60012 and 60023. Gateshead depot had kept three 'A4s' but these dwindled away by the end of 1964. No 60020 *Guillemot* and No 60002 *Sir Murrough Wilson* were sent for scrap in March and May respectively, while

BELOW Next in line for the cutter's torch at Doncaster is No 60017 *Silver Fox*, pictured in January 1964.

No 60001 *Sir Ronald Matthews* lasted until mid-October, ending an association of over 26 years with the shed.

The year finished with two railtours. The first featured No 60007 *Sir Nigel Gresley* and No 60009 *Union of South Africa* on the RCTS 'Scottish Lowlander' on 26 September 1964. No 46256 *Sir William A. Stanier F.R.S.* – making a final appearance before withdrawal – was used for the first leg between Crewe and Carlisle, where No 60007 was waiting to take over the 450-ton train for the next section over the Waverley route. No 60009 would then take the excursion via Kilmarnock and Dumfries back to Carlisle. Driver Maclaren and Fireman Whiteman were on the footplate of *Sir Nigel Gresley* and the two Carlisle Kingmoor men had the engine running up to Whitmore summit, which consisted of 8 miles at 1 in 75 and 1 in 80/90, with an average speed of 40mph. Going down the opposite side of the bank to Hawick nearly 4 minutes were gained on the allowance, added to 2 minutes already in hand. For the rise to Falahill the engine was travelling at approximately 60mph at the foot of the incline before accelerating on the first section to Stow, which was made up of sections at 1 in 120, 1 in 99 and 1 in 75, to 63mph. Some speed fell away to Falahill summit and was 46mph at the peak. The 15.6 miles had taken 20 minutes 5 seconds at an average speed of 46.6mph, and the gains were now nearly 8 minutes. Some signals were against the engine on to the changeover, but No 60007 had taken 128 minutes 10 seconds for the hard 98.2 miles, which was a very good time for the route and the weight of the train. No 60009 was also used for the RCTS/SLS 'Jubilee Requiem' service on 24 October 1964, travelling from King's Cross to Newcastle and back, and would prove to be the last time an 'A4' would visit the former while in BR service. The northbound run experienced heavy delays but coming south from Newcastle *Union of South Africa* had a clear road and recorded over 95mph down from Stoke summit, and arrival at the terminus was approximately 27 minutes early, albeit on a timing that was over 5 hours long.

The last steam locomotive to be repaired at Doncaster Works was *Union of South Africa* in November 1963. The 'Plant' had kept the engine fresh for over 26 years and over 1.6 million miles. According to *Locomotives of the LNER Part 2A*, No 60009 held the record for the highest mileage achieved by an 'A4' between General repairs, with 126,814 in 21 months between 1950 and 1952. In the early 1960s any attention required could result in the scrapping of an engine, but some repairs were carried out on shed in Scotland or at Darlington, Cowlairs and Inverurie Works. No 60012 *Commonwealth of Australia* had made a visit to Cowlairs in 1961 and would later be followed by No 60031 *Golden Plover* and No 60019 *Bittern*. Darlington received Nos 60019, 60023, 60009, 60004 (twice) and 60034 and returned them to traffic for further service, but Nos 60010 and 60011 were condemned there in May 1965 and May 1964 respectively. Being in close proximity to Aberdeen, Inverurie Works also allowed 'A4s' Nos 60004, 60006, 60007 (three times), 60011 (three times) and 60019 to prolong their careers.

Some 'A4s' were still fully employed into early 1965 on express passenger services between Aberdeen and Glasgow and to Perth and Edinburgh. Freight trains were also handled, including the mail from Aberdeen. With the passenger trains generally being under 300 tons, the 'A4s' had no trouble in keeping to the schedules or making up lost time if delays were encountered. Early arrivals of up to 10 minutes were not uncommon and such performances kept the 'A4s' in charge for the majority of the year. The rebuilt Type 2s from the

NBLC did come into service towards the end of the year and worked for spells, but the reliability was not too much improved. The ranks of the 'A4s' were further thinned during the year for both mechanical reasons and to reduce the steam stock. No 60016 *Silver King* was the first casualty in late March followed by No 60006 *Sir Ralph Wedgwood* and No 60027 *Merlin* in September, No 60031 *Golden Plover* in October, and No 60026 *Miles Beevor* in December, leaving just six 'A4s' still in traffic. No 60031 had a final send-off of sorts when the engine worked the 'Scottish Rambler' in April, running from Glasgow Queen Street to Glasgow Central via Edinburgh, the Waverley route and Carlisle. In September No 60026 was used for the 'LNER Pacific' railtour with No 60052 *Prince Palatine* running from Aberdeen to Glasgow then Edinburgh Waverley.

There was a reduction in the use of the 'A4s' on the expresses in early 1966, causing the withdrawal of No 60007 *Sir Nigel Gresley* on 1 February. The five remaining held on for the summer services but mechanical issues restricted the number of appearances made. No 60009 left traffic in June, followed in succeeding months by Nos 60004 and 60034. Nos 60019 and 60024 persisted and were honoured by the ScR

ABOVE The 'A4s' became a regular sight at Glasgow Buchanan Street station in the mid-1960s. No 60026 *Miles Beevor* is at the platform ready to depart with an express on 15 May 1964. *Bill Reed*

OPPOSITE TOP No 60031 *Golden Plover* was one of only two 'A4s' to receive the yellow warning strip signifying that Crewe was the limit of their operation due to electrification. The engine was a long way from there on 20 August 1965, being seen here at Perth about to take water. *Bill Reed*

OPPOSITE BOTTOM No 60019 *Bittern* receives a quick check-up before leaving Perth to continue with the 08.25 Glasgow to Aberdeen express on 25 June 1966. *M. Dunnett/K. Groundwater*

authorities as the scrapyard loomed, with the 'A4 Farewell' special from Glasgow to Aberdeen and back on 3 September behind *Bittern*. On the 5th both engines were then condemned. *Kingfisher* was allowed a final fling at the head of the 17.15 to Glasgow on 13th September, returning to Aberdeen the next morning with the 08.25 express.

NEW PASTURES, 1963-2015

The cycle of life for a locomotive has been determined since the beginning of their existence in the mid-1800s. Specifically, this sees them being employed for as long as the design is useful for the intended purpose (or in some instances after a redeployment on a secondary duty), then when this ceases the engine is sent to be scrapped. However, on occasion this sequence has been broken by locomotives or designs that have been selected to be preserved – either in working order or in pristine cosmetic condition – by companies, public bodies or private individuals for their historical, social or nostalgic value. The earliest steam locomotive preservation was the Stockton & Darlington Railway's *Locomotion No. 1*, which was the first engine to be used on a public railway. After being stored briefly the engine was put on display for many years at Darlington Bank Top station – along with *Derwent*, also used by the S&DR – to honour the area's contribution to the birth of the railways.

This process continued into the early 1900s and by the Grouping the 'Big Four' companies had a collection of locomotives, rolling stock and railwayana. There were no museums for displaying the items until 1928 when the LNER dedicated part of the old York Works buildings for the purpose. The LNER's exhibits were joined by items loaned by the other companies, such as the GWR's 'City' class 4-4-0 No 3440 *City of Truro*, which was specially restored to enter the museum. The Stephenson Locomotive Society also donated London, Brighton & South Coast Railway 'B1' class 0-4-2 locomotive No 241 *Gladstone*. Closure occurred after the outbreak of war but the museum was reopened by Sir Ronald Matthews in mid-July 1947.

After the Modernisation Plan was announced, BR formed the Consultative Panel for the Preservation of British Transport Relics to select items to enter the LNER museum's collection, or that of any other institution. In 1961 a list of over 30 locomotive classes was drawn up for a member to be saved, and amongst these were 'V2' No 60800 *Green Arrow*, Standard Class 7 Pacific No 70000 *Britannia*, Standard Class 8 4-6-2 No 71000 *Duke of Gloucester*, BR '9F' class No 92220 *Evening Star* (the last main-line steam locomotive to be built), Stanier 'Coronation' class Pacific No 46235 *City of Birmingham* and GWR 'King' class 4-6-0 No 6000 *King George V*. 'A4' class Pacific No 60022 *Mallard* was perhaps the most obvious locomotive still at work to be included, and after withdrawal was taken to Doncaster Works for a cosmetic restoration. In the event a lot more attention was bestowed upon the engine and, when completed in early 1964, *Mallard* was in very good condition. The locomotive's identity reverted to the LNER's when refurbished and Garter Blue livery was applied, as well as the original number. In the main the features were historically correct for when the engine was built in 1938, but there was a 'cover up' concerning the tender. The original non-

ABOVE No 60022 *Mallard* was the first 'A4' to be preserved and was restored to LNER condition at Doncaster Works in 1963/64. Here, the engine is being reunited with the streamlining casing in the Crimpsall's 4-bay.

corridor type (No 5642) had been uncoupled from the locomotive a number of years earlier and was still in traffic behind No 60026 *Miles Beevor*. Non-corridor tender No 5670 was separated from the recently withdrawn No 60003 *Andrew K. McCosh* and substituted, being renumbered 5642. The locomotive was to take centre stage at the Museum of British Transport, Clapham, which was opened in an old tram shed in 1963. No 4468 was transported to London at the end of February 1964 and was kept at Nine Elms shed until moved to Clapham by road. This was not trouble-free as the low-loader became stuck, but *Mallard* eventually entered the museum for the beginning of March 1964.

With the official selection of locomotives for preservation not being comprehensive, enthusiasts from all over the country decided that in order to save the nation's heritage they needed to act themselves or many more engines would end up in the scrapyard. A spur to this was the private purchase from BR in 1963 of 'A3' Pacific No 60103 *Flying Scotsman* by Alan Pegler

and the subsequent widespread public attention this generated through the many railtours run over the next few years. This was not the first private locomotive purchase, as the first from BR had taken place in 1959 with 'J52' class 0-6-0ST No 68896 (Ivatt GNR Class J13). However, Pegler was at an advantage through his position on the BR Board allowing him to negotiate a contract that saw *Flying Scotsman* able to travel across the network for 10 years. Also during 1963 the 'Beeching Axe' fell on many branch lines (and some main routes) around the country and a swift closure was to be experienced by many in order to save money. There was a similar determination to save some of these routes and the first to be rescued was a section between Sheffield Park and Horsted Keynes near the south coast, being named the Bluebell Railway.

No 60008 *Dwight D. Eisenhower* was withdrawn a short time after *Mallard* and the engine was also chosen to be preserved, but not in this country. BR offered the locomotive to the American National Railroad Museum in Green Bay, Wisconsin, and was accepted. Again the engine was taken to Doncaster Works, but only a minimal refurbishment was performed on the BR livery. When this was completed in early 1964 No 60008 was sent south via the ex-GCR line to Eastleigh shed and from there was towed to Southampton

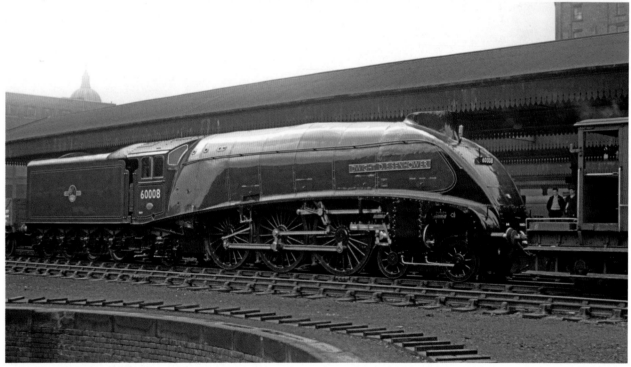

TOP No 60008 *Dwight D. Eisenhower* as externally restored at Doncaster Works in 1964.

ABOVE During April 1964 No 60008 was transported for shipment to America via the ex-GCR line. The locomotive is seen here pausing at Nottingham Victoria before continuing south. *Bill Reed*

Docks by 'Merchant Navy' class Pacific No 35012 *United States Lines* on 24 April. The latter also brought BR officials from London for the official handover, where Dr Beeching gave No 60008 to the President of the National Railroad Museum, and the locomotive was then loaded on to the ship *American Planter*. The voyage to New York took a couple of weeks and arrival was made in early May. *Dwight D. Eisenhower* then travelled approximately 1,000 miles to the museum, taking a berth there at the end of the month. The locomotive would be joined in March 1968 by LNER carriages Nos 1591 and 1592,

ABOVE No 60008 in the National Railroad Museum, Wisconsin, on 29 September 1989 when partially exposed to the weather. The engine has subsequently found accommodation in a dedicated building. *Bill Reed*

RIGHT No 60010 is loaded on to the ship. *IAL*

which had formed part of General Eisenhower's train while he travelled in England late in the war.

Two years would elapse before No 60010 *Dominion of Canada* was reprieved. The locomotive was stored at Darlington shed after withdrawal and was there for over a year until August 1966, then being sent to Crewe for a fresh coat of paint to be applied. *Dominion of Canada* was transported to Royal Victoria Docks, London, and on 10 April 1967 was loaded on to *Beaveroak* by the floating crane *Mammoth*. Once aboard, John Ratter of BRB gave the engine to Geoffrey Murray, Acting High Commissioner of Canada, who – on behalf of the Canadian Railroad Historical Association – accepted No 60010 as a gift from Britain for the Canadian Centennial. Upon arrival, No 60010 was taken to the Canadian Railway Museum, Montreal.

While these official preservations were taking place, a group of young men came together to plan the purchase of an 'A4' class locomotive from BR. The A4 Preservation Society (later the A4 Locomotive Society) was duly formed in 1964 with the aim of buying No 60007 *Sir Nigel Gresley*, and negotiations for the transaction began in 1965, as did the fundraising efforts. Donations large and small were welcomed and to push matters along the society organised an excursion headed by the object of their affection on 23 October 1965. The 'Paddington Streamliner' ran from Manchester Exchange to London Paddington station via Wrexham and Shrewsbury. The money necessary had come in by early 1966 and the purchase of No 60007 was made soon after withdrawal. To celebrate, a second outing – the 'Victory Railtour' – was organised for 26 March but the motive power in this instance was No 60024 *Kingfisher*, which travelled from Scotland to London Waterloo. From there the engine headed to Southampton, Weymouth and Yeovil before returning. The event not only commemorated the achievement but also helped to add funds to the cost of *Sir Nigel Gresley*'s overhaul. A further railtour involving *Kingfisher* was organised for 21 May and the 'East Coast Limited' departed from Doncaster and travelled north to Edinburgh. During the summer of 1966 No 60007 was brought south to Crewe Works for a full repair as a year had elapsed since the engine's last works visit and as many as four years had passed

since the last General overhaul. This left a lot of work to be carried out, including fitting new superheater flues, elements and small tubes; a new superheater header; replacement smokebox; new piston valves; refurbished axleboxes; second-hand coupled wheels with new tyres (No 60026 *Miles Beevor* was used as a donor engine); replacement cab and boiler cladding; and the tender completely overhauled. The livery applied was LNER Garter Blue with original numbering, but some modern features were kept such as the Kylchap double blastpipe and chimney and AWS equipment.

The work took several months and was eventually finished in early March 1967. No 4498 was subsequently run in and tested from Crewe South shed, even working a local passenger service for BR in the process. Therefore the engine was in good condition for the first railtour of private ownership to take place on 1 April, travelling on the WCML from Crewe to Carlisle – where there was a visit to Kingmoor shed – before heading back via the Settle and Carlisle line to Hellifield, then travelling via Blackburn, Wigan and Warrington to Crewe. The train was 450 tons gross and this was handled well northbound, keeping to the times set, and on the return was hauled just as competently, even though the conditions were not to the locomotive's advantage over the hills and several instances of slipping occurred. As the tour was a success overall another was organised soon after, taking *Sir Nigel Gresley* back to Scotland. The departure and arrival points were Glasgow and Aberdeen respectively by way of Perth, then returning via Dundee and Edinburgh. For the weekend of 3 and 4 June the locomotive was in the south of England for a

ABOVE On 10 August 1967 *Sir Nigel Gresley* is accommodated between railtours in York shed. *Bill Reed*

few runs on SR metals. The Saturday train left London Waterloo and headed south-west to Weybridge, Winchester and Southampton, then continuing on to Bournemouth. After No 4498 had brought the party back to Southampton, Bulleid 'West Country' Pacific No 34023 *Blackmore Vale* (which was still in service) took over for a brief jaunt to Salisbury, and from there *Sir Nigel Gresley* worked the train to Waterloo. On the Sunday the itinerary was the same as far as Bournemouth, where the engine carried on to Weymouth before returning along the route without the detour to Salisbury. On 23 July *Sir Nigel Gresley* was back on the ECML and picked up the train, which had been diesel-hauled from King's Cross, at Peterborough, continuing to Newcastle. This would not prove to be a triumphant appearance as the ER limited the engine to just 60mph and problems were experienced obtaining water, causing delays.

ABOVE Coal is loaded on to the tender of No 60009 *Union of South Africa* **at Lochty in August 1968.** *Bill Reed*

No 4498 was busy over seven days at the end of August 1967 with two railtours scheduled. The first took passengers from Doncaster to Waverley and back on the 20th with a timing of just under 5 hours 30 minutes, followed by a circular tour from Leeds to Carlisle, then Newcastle and York before reaching Leeds. The situation was the same over the weekend of 30 September/1 October as the locomotive worked in partnership with No 7029 *Clun Castle* on the Peterborough to Carlisle 'Splendour of Steam' special. The latter headed north on the first day and the return was later made by *Sir Nigel Gresley*, the opposite arrangement in force the following day. On 28 October No 4498 was on the RCTS's The 'Border Limited' in partnership with several Stanier Class 5 4-6-0s, and was used on the portion running between Crewe and Carlisle, later taking the party on to Skipton. The final steam-hauled portion of the journey also had No 4498 at the head between Accrington and Crewe. The engine performed creditably throughout the day with the 375-ton train, including a maximum speed of 90mph travelling from Crewe and over 50mph at Shap summit, with time also gained on that booked.

No 60009 *Union of South Africa* was condemned only four months after *Sir Nigel Gresley* and was offered for scrap initially before a party of four businessmen headed by John Cameron stepped in and purchased the locomotive. Stored for several months at Aberdeen Ferryhill shed, No 60009 was brought back to life in early 1967 for a railtour organised by BR, which took in many areas of Scotland. On 25 March the engine was partnered with 'Black Five' No 44997 in working the

18-carriage train (weighing 640 tons) from Perth to Aberdeen, taking 87 minutes at an average speed of 61.9mph. The engines rendezvoused with the train at Perth and concluded the tour to Edinburgh Waverley. Shortly after this event *Union of South Africa* was moved by rail and road to Lochty, Fife. There a recently defunct railway – previously a mineral line off the route between Thornton Junction and Leven – was partially restored by Mr Cameron and an engine house was also constructed to accommodate the 'A4'. In June 1967 No 60009 began a period of semi-retirement by working short trips up and down the line for tourists and enthusiasts. This was quite popular when taking place during the summer and soon necessitated the addition of a second carriage for passengers as well as a short extension of the line.

Another group of people, headed by Geoff Drury, came together to buy an 'A4' and from the last two left No 60019 *Bittern* was chosen. The locomotive was quickly dispatched from Aberdeen and took up residence at York North shed. From there No 60019 worked a freight train for BR during the last few months of the year in order to assess the engine's mechanical condition. This was found to be satisfactory but a number of months passed before *Bittern* was back in steam and on 16 July 1967 the engine was employed by the RCTS on a special from Leeds to Glasgow via the Settle and Carlisle line.

Despite interruptions to the trip (in the form of engineering work) the RCTS was evidently content with the locomotive's performance as No 60019 was booked by the society for another tour on 4 November, this time from Leeds to Edinburgh, taking the ECML. Before the end of the month *Bittern* was back in Leeds for the 'Mancunian', organised by the Manchester Rail Travel Society, to head via the Settle and Carlisle line to Lancaster, Wigan, Manchester and Stockport. The return was made through Rochdale and Dewsbury to Leeds.

Both No 4498 and No 60019 would have their new ventures cut short as BR placed a total ban on steam operations on the network in 1968. *Sir Nigel Gresley* was given quarters by the National Coal Board at Lambton Engine Works, Philadelphia, after the closure of Crewe South shed, while *Bittern*, which was similarly evicted from York, took up residence at Leeds Neville Hill depot, later being moved to Dinting Railway Centre.

Thankfully, the attitude within BR changed in the early 1970s and the restriction was relaxed in 1971. There were stipulations to this, including a speed limit of 60mph and the confinement of steam specials to certain sections of the country. The first locomotive to take to the rails was No 6000 *King George V* in October after restoration, and a tour was made of many areas of the West Country. No 4498 was the first 'A4' to start running again in 1972 and was used on the 'Steam Safari' on 17 June between Newcastle and Carlisle. The return

was also performed, but a diesel locomotive was used to take the passengers back to London via Sheffield. *Bittern* made a comeback later in the season, with the engine now in Garter Blue livery with the number 19 applied. The tour – from York to Scarborough and back – was organised in partnership with the RCTS and the City of York and also featured a visit to the North Yorkshire Moors Railway. This section of line between Whitby and Pickering had only just been purchased from BR and would be formally opened in 1973.

A marginally busier year was experienced by both 'A4s' in 1973 and they were even joined on the network by No 60009 *Union of South Africa* after a six-year absence. The 'A4s' started off on 21 April with No 4498 and No 19 joining forces to take tours between York, Scarborough and Hull. Steam returned to Scottish metals on 5 May as *Union of South Africa* ran between Edinburgh and Dundee. Early in the following month the locomotive was used for an open day at Inverness, and *Sir Nigel Gresley* would also put in an appearance at a similar event at Tyseley in June. *Bittern* was on the York-Scarborough line later in the month as part of a tour from Manchester, which also utilised Stanier ' Jubilee' 4-6-0 No 5595 *Bahamas*. No 19 was

BELOW On 31 August 1975 No 4498 and Stirling 'Single' No 1 take part in the Shildon 'Cavalcade of Locomotives'. *Bill Reed*

ABOVE No 4468 *Mallard* is present at 'Railex 125' held in 1978 to celebrate the anniversary of the opening of Doncaster Works. Also joining in are the two Ivatt Atlantics, the Stirling 'Single' and 'V2' No 4771 *Green Arrow*.

out of action soon after and would remain so for a considerable period of time as Geoff Drury could no longer maintain the engine. No 4498 and No 4771 *Green Arrow* were then chosen to be a part of a 'Gresley Commemorative' special organised by the LCGB on 1 July 1973. The former ran from Tyseley to Didcot, while the latter took the return. No 60009's second and last appearance of the year again occurred in Scotland and at this time the locomotive was accommodated for a brief period at Kirkcaldy before finding a permanent residence at Markinch.

Despite *Bittern* being lost, No 4498 and No 60009 continued to be used relatively regularly in 1974, with the latter becoming a favourite of the Scottish Railway Preservation Society. *Sir Nigel Gresley* was also running north of the border with the 'Tyne Dee Coastal' on 22 June from Edinburgh Waverley to Aberdeen and back. In the autumn, after the locomotive had completed the engagements for the year, two superheater tubes were found to be in need of repair if *Sir Nigel Gresley* was to take part in the following year's events. The highlight of these was the 'Cavalcade of Locomotives' at Shildon for the 150th Anniversary of the opening of the Stockton & Darlington Railway. No 4498 was patched up in time and also received a new coat of paint for this special occasion, which featured many famous engines. The interior of the locomotive still caused concern as water was soon seen leaking into the firebox, necessitating a total replacement of the boiler tubes. No railtours were hauled by the engine in 1976 and during the year an agreement was reached for the locomotive to leave the

cramped surroundings of Philadelphia to take a position at Carnforth. There No 4498 would be closer to the routes that were becoming the main focus of the specials being operated. During the period No 60009 continued to be a presence in Scotland, but would also be in need of some maintenance during the mid-point of the decade.

Shortly after the opening of the Museum of British Transport BR began to think that a role in such an undertaking was unjustified and sought to relinquish the collection. In the early 1970s the Science Museum was approached and agreed to take the railway objects, and as a result the National Railway Museum was formed at York in the old North shed, which was provided by BR. In consequence the LNER museum was closed and the Museum of British Transport followed soon after in 1973. The exhibits were transported north behind a Class 45 diesel and No 4468 *Mallard* became the centrepiece of the NRM, which opened in 1975.

No 4498 was ready to resume railtour operations in 1977 and, with No 4472 *Flying Scotsman* and No 4771 *Green Arrow*, worked several from Carnforth to York and Leeds as part of the celebrations for the Queen's Silver Jubilee. Before moving to Carnforth *Sir Nigel Gresley* was invited to a special dinner at the NRM to commemorate the 100th anniversary of the birth of the locomotive's designer and namesake. Regrettably, this had been postponed for several months from the actual date because of the work being carried out, but was a fitting tribute nevertheless. As the 1970s drew to a close No 4498 was regularly employed on railtours to the north-western seaboard as well as to Leeds and York.

In 1980 the 150th anniversary of the Manchester & Liverpool Railway was celebrated with a parade of locomotives, and No 4498 was amongst the participants at Rainhill. By 1982 the condition of the firebox was beginning to deteriorate and at the end of the season the engine was taken out of service for a thorough repair. This included extensive attention to the latter component and the smokebox tubeplate; complete retubing; a new smokebox; and refurbishment of all bearings. These tasks took until mid-1984 to complete, and No 4498's first special was run from Clitheroe to York and back on 9 June. No 60009 *Union of South Africa* also made a return to England for the railtour season, running services from York to Scarborough and on the Carlisle route from Settle. Early in 1985 *Sir Nigel Gresley* hauled the first train out of London under steam for the first time in around 20 years. This event occurred on 21 January as Royal Mail launched a set of 'Famous Train' stamps.

After *Mallard*'s transfer north to York the movement of the engine outside the confines of the museum was made feasible due to the connection between the NRM and the network. In 1977 the locomotive was displayed at York for the

anniversary of the opening of the new station and in the following year No 4468 was present at Doncaster Works for the celebrations to mark 125 years since being founded. In the early 1980s thoughts turned to the approaching 50th anniversary of the locomotive achieving the steam world speed record. No 4468 had been inspected and found to be in quite good mechanical condition but still in need of attention. This raised the question of who would foot the bill for the work, and the NRM was unfortunately unable to do so. Scarborough Council stepped in and donated £35,000, which was enough for the majority of the work to be carried out but not all, meaning that the engine was only given half of a ten-year boiler certificate to run on BR's system. The work progressed swiftly and the boiler was tested in late summer 1985. Interestingly this was done in the frames without any boiler lagging or clothing plates, making this an event rarely seen. The remaining tasks had been finished by early the following year and *Mallard* ran under steam for the first time on 25 March 1986, going to Doncaster via Scarborough and Hull. The engine entered the works and had a fresh coat of Garter Blue livery applied and received a final check of all the mechanical components.

No 4468 was first employed on 9 July. The train was the 'Scarborough Spa Express' from York to Scarborough then Bridlington, Hull and Selby, before taking the ECML to York. The engine was late into Scarborough but otherwise kept close to the schedule and managed to sneak in some speeds over the maximum allowed. The next outing occurred on 25 August on the same service, although Scarborough was the limit of the excursion this time. *Mallard* headed south on 4 October with the 'South Yorkshire Pullman', travelling via Sheffield and Derby to London Marylebone. A few days later the engine was used alongside No 4498 on the 'Shakespeare Limited', which was a series of specials organised by BR to run from London Marylebone to Stratford-upon-Avon and back. The train was worked for a second time on 26 October with No 4472 *Flying Scotsman* and there was a final appearance on 2 November. No 4468 returned to York on 8 November with the 'Peter Allen Pullman' (to honour the president of the Transport Trust), capping a memorable first summer back in steam.

LEFT Roy Ardon (left) and David Pell (right) working on *Mallard*'s fresh coat of paint at Doncaster Works in May 1986.

ABOVE Staff at Doncaster Works pose proudly alongside No 4468 *Mallard* in June 1986. *Neil Daykin*

Mallard was used much less frequently in 1987 but again travelled to Scarborough and ran in Lancashire. The locomotive was also present for Doncaster Works' open day in early October. In 1988 the 50th anniversary celebrations began on 9 May (No 4468 was also 50 years old on 13 March) with a railtour honouring the 150th year of the Travelling Post Office. *Mallard* had begun the journey south from York the previous day but was held up through flooding at Sudbury and was unable to continue on the former GWR and GCR route to London Marylebone. The engine was then required to travel tender-first on the branch to Aylesbury to take the ex-Metropolitan and GCR joint line into the capital; this was the first time steam had been on these tracks since the 1960s. Quite soon after arriving in London No 4468 was back on the move, taking the train to Banbury where a Class 17 diesel returned the tourists to the capital. *Mallard* moved on to Newton Heath in preparation to work a second Post Office special – the 'Pennine Postal' – from Manchester to Scarborough on 10 May. This trip was not without incident as the engine's support carriage had to be removed from the train at Leeds so the coaches would fit the platform at Scarborough,

making the arrival at the latter nearly an hour late. The next outing occurred on 3 July 1988 when *Mallard* took to the head of a train from Doncaster to Scarborough, coming back later in the day. No 4498 *Sir Nigel Gresley* was present at York to join in the celebrations, as was *Bittern*. On board the special train, which had Driver Richardson at the regulator of No 4468, were members of the families of Driver Duddington and Fireman Bray, who were rightly very proud of their relatives' achievement. Afterwards, No 4468 was used on a number of 'Scarborough Spa Express' trains, in addition to the RCTS's 'Diamond Jubilee' special on 30 July. The last run for *Mallard* took place on 27 August when the engine travelled between York and Carlisle. Some problems occurred on the outward run but these were rectified and the return was made in fine style, with several high speeds near 80mph recorded. This was an appropriate end to *Mallard*'s return to steam, which people from all across the globe had come to witness and be a part of.

For *Mallard*'s big event *Bittern* had undergone a complete cosmetic makeover as class pioneer No 2509 *Silver Link*. Since being taken out of service in the early 1970s the locomotive had languished at Walton Colliery, near Wakefield, with 'A2' class Pacific No 60532 *Blue Peter*. Before the 1980s began both engines were moved to Dinting but a further lengthy spell of inactivity occurred before the North Eastern Locomotive Preservation Group stepped in and during 1986 took both on

ABOVE Setting out from Llandudno Junction on 28 August 1991 with the 'North Wales Coast Express' between Holyhead and Crewe is No 60009 *Union of South Africa*. *Bill Reed*

loan from Geoff Drury. *Blue Peter* was fully overhauled to working order but this left little attention available for *Bittern*. The NELPG did not see this as a fair situation and the locomotive was scheduled for a superficial restoration. At a Group meeting the suggestion as made by D. Fawcett that the livery applied should be the silver used in the 1930s instead of the Garter Blue selected. All present agreed that this would be an interesting variation given the length of time since an 'A4' class locomotive had been given such a scheme. The task (also including the provision of valances and a single chimney) was completed in June 1988 and the engine was loaned to the NRM for exhibition at York.

No 60009 *Union of South Africa* had not been able to support *Mallard*'s achievement as repairs were required and undertaken at the Severn Valley Railway. These took just under a year and the locomotive was able to be back in steam during 1990. Just prior to *Union of South Africa*'s return, No 4498 had to be taken out of service because of further boiler problems and would be under attention until autumn 1992. No 60009 headed north for the first special, which was the 'Forth Centenarian' on 4 March, but a change of name occurred and, after running briefly nameless, the engine became *Osprey*. Two trains were run between Edinburgh and Perth on the day and this was repeated a number of times throughout the year. In between these workings No 60009 was employed on the 'North Wales Coast Express' (which also used No 34027 *Taw Valley* and No

46229 *Duchess Hamilton* during the season), in addition to being at the head of the SRPS's the 'North Briton' from Edinburgh to Aberdeen on 5 May. In 1991 another renaming was afoot when the locomotive was given the identity of No 60004 *William Whitelaw* for the celebrations to mark 150 years since the opening of the Edinburgh to Glasgow route. Honoured soon after was No 60027 *Merlin* and this change lasted for a number of months, during which time the engine was again used on the 'North Wales Coast Express' and appeared on the SVR as a guest later in the year. On 19 September 1991 the engine reverted to being No 60009 *Union of South Africa* after a special ceremony was performed at Edinburgh Waverley and was capped by an excursion to Dundee. In December No 60009 returned to the SVR for more attention and this was completed in early 1992. The engine was back on the main line in April working again in the North West and Scotland for the SRPS.

No 4498's overhaul was drawing to a conclusion at this time and the engine would be in traffic at the end of August. However, a couple of setbacks occurred causing the locomotive to miss two engagements, including a railtour organised between the A4 Locomotive Society and Ian Allan Publishing to celebrate the 25th year of ownership of *Sir Nigel Gresley* and 50 years in existence respectively. No 4472 *Flying Scotsman* was able to step in so the day was not ruined. After being repaired No 4498 was present for a special weekend at the SVR and would revisit there early in 1993 to return *Flying Scotsman*'s favour as the engine failed prior to a gala. No 4498 would go on to work the Settle and Carlisle line with the 'Cumbrian Mountain Express' on 1 May and 17 July. At the end of the year the locomotive was hauling services between Loughborough and Leicester North on the Great Central Railway, which had been open as a heritage line since the mid-1970s. No 4498 was also used to teach senior drivers from Derby shed the intricacies of operating a steam locomotive as the number of originally qualified drivers was diminishing. Many had volunteered for the task after previously being firemen earlier in their careers. No 60009 was used similarly in Scotland during 1993.

No 4498 continued to be based at the GCR throughout 1994 and during this period boiler plaques of a similar design to *Mallard*'s were fitted to acknowledge the engine's post-war speed record. *Sir Nigel Gresley* did travel on the main line occasionally, in addition to being displayed at Doncaster Works open day in July. A major change occurred to the locomotive's appearance late in 1994 as the BR number was

LEFT No 4498 *Sir Nigel Gresley* was based at the Great Central Railway during the mid-1990s. The locomotive is seen close to Loughborough shed in September 1994. *Bill Reed*

BELOW No 60009 backs into Nottingham Midland station on 10 February 1992. *Bill Reed*

reinstated along with BR Blue livery with black and white lining. No 60009 was on the SVR in September after some minor mechanical work had been undertaken and joined in with the steam gala featuring No 4472 *Flying Scotsman* and 'King' class 4-6-0 No 6024 *King Edward I*, among others. In October *Union of South Africa* was working into London as the 27th saw the engine at the head of the 'Capital Streak' from Worcester to Ealing Broadway, then on the 29th the engine was given the great privilege of taking the first steam-hauled train out of King's Cross in 30 years, carrying the 'Elizabethan' headboard. No 60009 took the train north to Wansford, near Peterborough, on the Nene Valley Railway, where the locomotive was based for the excursion and back, then repeating the performance the next day. There was a great demand for spaces on the train and the tickets sold out very quickly. The engine also had the usual 60mph limit lifted and 75mph was allowed. No 60009 started off 1995 with a railtour from Shrewsbury to Newport on 7 January and the month finished with a run to Southport and back from Waterloo. In February the engine worked from Paddington to Exeter on the 18th, then from Exeter to Paddington on the 19th; during one of these trips the locomotive attained quite a high speed. More sedate running was the order of the day when No 60009 was on the SVR, and a relatively large mileage would be accumulated there during the year.

No 60007 *Sir Nigel Gresley* was at the East Lancashire Railway early in 1995, then, after hauling a Newcastle to King's Cross train on 11 June, the engine was on the Nene Valley Railway on the 16th, running with 18 goods wagons and a brake van. Over the weekend of 24/25 June both Nos 60007 and 60009 were employed by the West Anglia & Great Northern Railway for the Eastern Counties Steam Weekend, travelling between Bishops Stortford and Ely for a series of trains, but at a restricted speed of 40mph. From 30 September a set of steam trials were organised between No 60007, No 46229 *Duchess of Hamilton* and No 71000 *Duke of Gloucester* on the Crewe to Carlisle portion of the WCML, returning via the Settle and Carlisle. The tests focussed on the highest drawbar horsepowers produced on the ascents of the three notable climbs on the route – Grayrigg, Shap and Ais Gill. No 60007 was presented with the opportunity to show the other engines how these ascents should be performed by working first, but the locomotive struggled with the 11-coach train and the figures were the lowest of the three engines because of steaming problems. No 46229 went last and also experienced difficulties, in this instance with the injectors. No 71000 soundly beat the two others as the locomotive ran flawlessly on the second day.

During 1996 *Union of South Africa* was active around the network and also on the SVR and Nene Valley Railway later in the year before being removed from service to undergo an extensive overhaul at the SVR's shops. No 60007 continued on the main lines and found a new home at the North Yorkshire Moors Railway. In 1997 several tours at the beginning of the year were cancelled and *Sir Nigel Gresley*'s first excursion was not until 8 March with the 'Three Peaks Express'. The summer was spent at work on the NYMR and the engine's 60th birthday was celebrated by several tours organised for the end of the year. These began with the 'Cathedrals Express' on 28 September (with a 'Yorkshire Pullman' headboard) from Hull to King's Cross, then on 4 October a 'Flying Scotsman' train was worked from King's Cross to York and Edinburgh. The return the next day on the WCML was taken only as far as Carlisle due to the running being quite behind the timetable and a Class 47 diesel was used onward. A special dedicated to the memory of former A4 Locomotive Society Chairman Julian Riddick would be organised for the end of the month, travelling between York, Newcastle and Skipton. Another excursion from the period took the locomotive from Cleethorpes to Nottingham and Stratford-upon-Avon.

LEFT No 60007 is ready to leave Doncaster with the '40th Anniversary Jubilee' on 23 May 1999. *Geoff Warnes*

BELOW *Bittern* **spent time on the GCR, but was waiting for an overhaul to begin. The engine was still masquerading as No 2509** *Silver Link* **in June 1994 when photographed outside the shed.** *Bill Reed*

No 60007 started 1998 badly with a failure before a tour between Crewe and Nuneaton, resulting in a number of other excursions being cancelled due to repairs being carried out. The engine reappeared on 18 April when working the 'Royal Scot' from Nuneaton to Carlisle and later in the year *Sir Nigel Gresley* was travelling across the country to York from the latter and north to Edinburgh. Further mechanical problems were experienced before the boiler certificate ran out in 1999. One important tour that took place before this event was the '40th Anniversary Jubilee' from King's Cross to Doncaster on 23 May. There was no attempt at high speed on this occasion as the run up to Stoke summit saw a stop made at Great Ponton for a mechanical inspection. The final main-line run was on 6 June when a special was organised between King's Cross, York and Scarborough. A diesel locomotive attached to the rear experienced a mechanical issue and delayed the train by an hour, but No 60007 made this up to York. The locomotive's overhaul was performed at the NYMR and would take just under eight years to finish as a comprehensive repair was necessary, with the engine being completely stripped and major portions of the boiler replaced. Additionally, the engine was brought up to the increasingly rigorous safety standards of the new millennium. In 1999 the A4 Locomotive Society became a charity and a name change to The Sir Nigel Gresley Locomotive Preservation Trust Ltd followed. This made the

LEFT Former staff at Doncaster Works pose with
No 60009 *Union of South Africa* and No 4472
Flying Scotsman during an event in 2003.

RIGHT Coal is loaded into the tender of No 60019
Bittern at Doncaster Works before the engine
takes the return 'Christmas White Rose' to King's
Cross on 29 November 2008. *Hugh Parkin*

trust eligible for Heritage Lottery grants and
nearly £300,000 was received for the costs of
the repairs.

After being transformed into No 2509 *Silver
Link*, *Bittern* remained in that guise for some
time and later took up residence at the GCR where Geoff
Drury had a general overhaul started, but this was soon
delayed. In the mid-1990s Dr Tony Marchington bought 'A3'
Pacific No 4472 *Flying Scotsman*, then sought to purchase an
'A4'. All of the owners were approached – including those in
America – about relinquishing their steeds, but all declined
apart from Geoff Drury. In 1997 a deal was agreed for
approximately £325,000, and *Bittern* was relocated to the
Southall Railway Centre to continue the restoration to working
order. Unfortunately for the 'A4', Dr Marchington's priority
was *Flying Scotsman* and when the locomotive's overhaul costs
spiralled he was forced to sell *Bittern* to Jeremy Hosking. The
restoration of the engine was immediately put in hand to be
carried out at the Mid-Hants Railway, and the locomotive was
moved there in early 2001 for the process to begin.

No 60009 *Union of South Africa* returned to steam on the SVR
in the latter part of 2001 but was not ready for the main line
until 2002, when working the 'Mayflower' from Westbury to
Plymouth and back. Early in March the locomotive travelled
from Birmingham to Liverpool on the 'Liver Bird' and on the
30th was substituting for an unavailable engine on the
'Cumbrian Mountain Express' from Crewe to Carlisle. In June
the engine returned to King's Cross with the 'Robin Hood
Express', which travelled from Nuneaton to Lincoln, then joined
the ECML for the run into the capital. *Union of South Africa*
continued to be in demand throughout the year and worked all
over the country, including a service from Edinburgh to York, as
well as being employed on the SVR. The locomotive was the
only 'A4' in steam for the next few years and was consequently
in demand by tour operators. In mid-2006 John Cameron

bought Thornton shed to house the locomotive and his other
engine, 'K4' 2-6-0 No 61994 *The Great Marquess*, and a move
there occurred later in the year. Despite this No 60009 was kept
employed in England during late 2006 – working the 50th
anniversary special for the 'Talisman' on 23 September – and
into 2007. During April of the latter year both of John
Cameron's engines were employed on the 'Great Britain'
excursion from Glasgow to Perth behind *Union of South Africa*,
then from Perth to Inverness, with No 61994 piloting.

In mid-2006 No 60007's overhaul drew to a conclusion and
the first train was hauled on 23 July on the NYMR. Following
was No 60019 *Bittern*, which was ready in June 2007 and ran
on the Mid-Hants Railway in July. A test on the main line
occurred in September before the first railtour since the early
1970s was run on 1 December from King's Cross to York.
Then No 60019 returned south with the 'Christmas White
Rose' on 15 December. In the first half of 2008 the locomotive
was kept quite busy, running on the ECML several times and
from Euston to Guildford, in addition to King's Cross to
Cambridge and Norwich. *Bittern* was also present on the
NYMR in late March with Nos 60007 and 60009, this being
the first time the engines had been together for many years. *Sir
Nigel Gresley* did not get back out on to the network until mid-
April 2008, running a test around Carnforth. The first main-
line tour occurred on 31 May as the locomotive travelled from
York to King's Cross with the 'Cathedrals Express'. Many
people turned out on the fine day to catch a glimpse of No
60007's return. Soon afterwards all three 'A4s' lined up with
No 4468 *Mallard* to celebrate 70 years since the engine broke
the speed record, with the event being christened the 'Great
Reunion' by the NRM. On 5 July the first of two excursions of
the 'Coronation' were run from King's Cross to York, with Nos
60007 and 60009 from the latter to Edinburgh. Regrettably
Union of South Africa failed near Newcastle and a diesel had to
complete the journey. On 6 July No 60007 ran the train from

LEFT No 60009 is at the head of the 'Talisman' charter between
King's Cross and Darlington, which was organised by the A1
Steam Locomotive Trust on 23 September 2006. *Peter Alderson*

Newcastle to York and No 60019 travelled south to King's Cross. Also as part of the event No 4468 was put on display at the NRM's supplementary museum at Shildon.

Newcastle to York and No 60019 travelled south to King's Cross. Also as part of the event No 4468 was put on display at the NRM's supplementary museum at Shildon.

No 60009 was soon back in running order and was subsequently employed on several tours across the country, while No 60007 saw only sporadic use on the main line until later in the year when there was an intensive spell of employment. *Sir Nigel Gresley* and *Union of South Africa* were both present for an open day at Heaton depot on 14 September. The former was lined up with 'Deltic' No 55022 *Royal Scots Grey* and Class 43 HST No 43068, illustrating the development of ECML motive power over the decades; 'Deltic' No 55019 *Royal Highland Fusilier* and 'K4' No 61994 *The Great Marquess* were also present. Towards Christmas No 60007 ran on the ECML, from Scarborough to Crewe, on the Settle and Carlisle line and from Waterloo to Bristol.

No 60007 *Sir Nigel Gresley* was the first 'A4' on the main line in 2009 and was followed by No 60009. No 60019 was to make an appearance on the three-day 'Coronation' railtour with the engine's two classmates on 16 May but had to be replaced by new-build Peppercorn 'A1' class Pacific No 60163 *Tornado*. The locomotive worked *Bittern*'s portion from King's Cross to York where No 60007 took the train on to Edinburgh Waverley. On 17 May *Sir Nigel Gresley* hauled the excursion on to Dundee and No 60009 returned the train to the Scottish capital. On the final day of the tour *Union of South Africa* worked south to York where No 60163 finished the run to King's Cross. No 60007 was again with *Tornado* the following Saturday, which was also marked the 50th year since the

ABOVE *Sir Nigel Gresley* glides into Lincoln station with the 'Cathedrals Express' in the late 2000s. *Bill Reed*

TOP RIGHT No 4489 *Dominion of Canada* as restored in the Great Hall at York before the 'Great Gathering'. *Hugh Parkin*

BOTTOM RIGHT Returned to former glory – No 60008 *Dwight D. Eisenhower* shines at York. *Hugh Parkin*

engine achieved 112mph, and carried a 'Golden Jubilee' headboard for the occasion. No 60019 was based on the Mid-Hants Railway early in the year but was on the ECML on 4 July, and on the 25th was running non-stop to York with a second tender – No 5332 previously with No 60009 and No 4472 *Flying Scotsman*. This tender had been converted at Doncaster Works in 1966 to carry 9,000 gallons of water and no coal to eliminate the need for water stops as BR reduced the steam infrastructure. No 60009 had a number of obligations to fill before the boiler certificate expired at the end of the year and was present at an LNER gala held at Barrow Hill Roundhouse with Nos 60007, 62005, 60532 *Blue Peter* and 60163. The engine also stopped by at the NRM to pose with 'Coronation' class Pacific No 6229 *Duchess of Hamilton*, which had been re-streamlined. This offered a rare opportunity to see the two styles side by side. When No 60009 was taken out of traffic there was some uncertainty as to whether a repair would be carried out, but such fears were soon extinguished as the locomotive was booked into Crewe LNWR Heritage Works for a full repair.

No 60007 also underwent some attention in 2010 as a retube was carried out, and a return to steam was not made until late October. No 60019 was the lone representative of the class on the main line and was used on a number of railtours, including the 'Coronation' on the first day between King's Cross and Waverley. Later in the year *Bittern* was taken out of service for attention after running around 30,000 miles, and at this time underwent a livery change to Garter Blue and received a new identity, becoming No 4492 *Dominion of New Zealand*, complete with the type of whistle fitted to the original locomotive. No 4492 was officially renamed by the High Commissioner of New Zealand Derek Leask on 16 April 2011 before the engine took out the northbound 'Great Britain' railtour, travelling as far as Tyne Yard (just south of Newcastle), where No 60009 was waiting to take over. No 4492 also ran with the second tender, which had also been repainted in Garter Blue and had the New Zealand coat of arms on the side sheets. Although the locomotive was originally intended to run as No 4492 for three years, a reversion to *Bittern* occurred after a little over a year.

Sir Nigel Gresley was out of traffic again in early 2011 for new tyres to be fitted to the Cartazzi axle and the tender wheels. After working the 'Great Britain IV' No 60007 was used on the Bo'ness & Kinneil Railway and while in Scotland the engine also headed the 'Forth Circle' between Linlithgow, Dunfermline and Stirling, later working from Dalmeny on a similar circuit. No 60007 was soon back under repair with firebox issues and almost a year would elapse before these

were completed. When the engine returned to service in 2012 a highlight was transporting the Olympic Flame bearer from Grosmont to Pickering on 18 June. In July No 60009 was tested before a return on the 'North Wales Coast Express' from Crewe to Holyhead on 22 July.

As the 75th anniversary of *Mallard*'s achievement approached, the NRM – under the direction of Steve Davies – planned one of the biggest railway events in recent years. The staff at the museum worked hard over several months to secure the loan of the two 'A4s' based in North America and this was eventually agreed for two years, including the full cosmetic restoration of both locomotives for their appearance at the 'Great Gathering'. No 60008 *Dwight D. Eisenhower* was removed from the National Railroad Museum on 1 August 2012, then transported by rail to Ceres Container Terminal, Halifax, Nova Scotia. The locomotive arrived there in late August and was soon joined by No 60010 *Dominion of Canada*. Both were then loaded on to the ACL *Atlantic Conveyor* on 25 September and landed at Liverpool on 3 October. The two 'A4s' then travelled by road across the Pennines to Shildon and arrived on 5 October where a short period of display occurred before the restoration began. No 60008 was taken to the NRM for this to take place under the direction of Heritage Painting, but the task was not straightforward as the engine had been exposed to the elements while in America and the motion had to be stripped of silver paint that had been applied to stop weathering. *Dominion of Canada* was in a better state (even if the engine's external appearance did not testify to this) and the work was carried out

ABOVE All six 'A4' locomotives at the 'Great Gathering' - York National Railway Museum on 9 July 2013. *Jack Beeston*

BELOW No 4468 *Mallard* and No 4489 with the crowds during the 'Great Gathering', July 2013. *Hugh Parkin*

ABOVE All six 'A4' locomotives in a different light at the National Railway Museum, York on 1 November 2013. *Jack Beeston*

BELOW No 60009 at York – note the roof of the passageway on the right-hand side of the tender. *Hugh Parkin*

at Shildon to return No 60010 to original condition. This involved applying Garter Blue livery with stainless steel LNER number, lettering and trim to the valances, a single chimney, and the original bell and Canadian Pacific Railroad whistle. To aid the project the Friends of the NRM group generously donated £50,000 to the cost of the extensive work carried out on both locomotives. *Dwight D. Eisenhower* was finished first in February 2013 and was placed in the Great Hall at the NRM next to *Mallard*. No 4489 *Dominion of Canada* was on view to the public from late May and was briefly positioned next to No 6229 *Duchess of Hamilton* at Shildon before being transferred to the NRM in preparation for the 'Great Gathering'. No 4468 also had a fresh coat of paint applied for the special day.

No 60009 *Union of South Africa* was the busiest of the 'A4s' in the first half of 2013, being used several times on the 'Winter Cumbrian Mountain Express', the 'Forth Circle', and the 'Cheshireman' from Euston to Chester. The 'Great Britain VI' tour used *Union of South Africa* twice in late April: on the 24th from Aberdeen to Edinburgh and on the 28th from Waverley to York, with No 4464 continuing to King's Cross. The same pair would be used on the 'Cathedrals Express' on 24 June to start off a tour of Scotland. Undoubtedly the highlight of the excursions from this period came on 29 June when *Bittern* was rostered to head the 'Ebor Streak', which consisted of 10 carriages from King's Cross to York, and the service was authorised to break the 75mph speed limit for steam and travel up to 90mph for the first time since the 1960s. The schedule was relatively tight, allowing 4 hours 6 minutes for the 188 miles, and of these over 50 miles were chosen for the high speeds. No 4464 really began running impressively from Hatfield and was just under 80mph at Hitchin. Reaching Biggleswade at 90mph, there was a peak of 92mph three miles later at Sandy. A stop for water was made at Holme and *Bittern* passed Peterborough 1 minute late but managed to gain 5 minutes to Grantham and was 4 minutes early through the station. The locomotive was pushed for a second time on to Newark and reached a top speed of 92½mph through the station. A brisk pace was set on to York but no further highs were recorded and arrival was made some 7 minutes early.

The 'Great Gathering' began on 3 July when *Mallard* was pushed on to the turntable in the Great Hall amidst an orchestral accompaniment and the engine's whistle was then sounded to signal the start of the event. Later, No 4489 *Dominion of Canada* was named and the ceremony was presided over by the High Commissioner of Canada, Gordon Campbell, who, after giving a speech, rang the locomotive's bell and sounded the whistle. The event went on to break all estimates for attendances, and over the two-week period up to 140,000 people visited the NRM to see all six surviving 'A4s'. Unfortunately for HRH Prince Charles, who was a patron of the 'Great Gathering', two of the six engines had left when he visited on 22 July as part of a tour of Yorkshire. His arrival at

the museum was made on the Royal Train hauled from sidings a short distance away by No 4464 *Bittern*, and he went on to inspect *Mallard* and pose in typical fashion leaning out of the cab window.

No 4468 was given a change of scenery in early September as the engine was displayed at Grantham station for the 'Festival of Speed' exhibition over the weekend of the 7th and 8th. A number of road vehicles were also present, along with 'Deltic' No 55019 *Royal Highland Fusilier*. The event was particularly popular and attracted just under 20,000 people. The 'Autumn Great Gathering' followed soon after, beginning on 26 October, and on the day some 12,000 people attended to view the 'A4s', the total for the first weekend being 20,000. The event was initially to run until 8 November but owing to the volume of visitors three days had to be added. The 'A4s' also became the centre of the annual 'Locos in a Different Light' competition held by the NRM to support students of the performance arts. A number of interesting effects were conjured up to bring the engines to life over the evenings of 29 October to 3 November and the winner was No 4489 *Dominion of Canada*, which had been lit by students from the Da Vinci School of Creative Enterprise. The 'Autumn Great

Gathering' was as much a sensation as the preceding event and attracted over 100,000 people.

The year ended on a triumphant note with No 4464 *Bittern* again making high-speed journeys both north and south of York. The two trains had been postponed twice from the original dates of 19 and 27 July and the substitute days of 30 and 31 August because of dry weather bringing about restrictions on steam due to the risk of lineside fires. The 'Tyne Tees Streak' eventually ran on 5 December from York to Newcastle and back. Northbound the train was severely delayed as a result of gales being experienced, but the engine did manage to reach a top speed of 60mph. On the return the limits in force due to the weather were rescinded and *Bittern* flew through Darlington station at well over 90mph. Two days later No 4464 was hauling the 'Capital Streak' from York to King's Cross. The high speed began soon after departure and was sustained near the limit for several miles before a slight reduction was made for passage through Doncaster station. The train progressed swiftly onward and again reached 90mph north of Newark, later travelling up Stoke bank at around 70mph before a sustained period at 90mph running down to

ABOVE **A panoramic view of the 'Great Goodbye' at Shildon on 18 February 2014.** *Jack Beeston*

Peterborough. The early-evening traffic then prevented an uninterrupted dash to King's Cross.

After the great success for the 'A4s' in 2013 there were still events to look forward to in 2014. On 8 and 9 February Barrow Hill Roundhouse played host to No 60008 and No 4489 for the 'East Coast Giants' gala. All the engines were displayed in the yard with Nos 60163 *Tornado*, No 60532 *Blue Peter*, No 4464 *Bittern*, Ivatt Atlantic No 251 and two of the preserved 'Deltics'. While in attendance *Bittern* became the third 'A4' to have a plaque fitted to the side of the boiler commemorating achievement in high-speed running after the events of 2013. Around 10,000 people turned up to see the locomotives. Six days later the 'Great Goodbye' began at Shildon with all six 'A4s' present and on display outside the building. Nos 4464, 60007 and 60009 were in light steam and the footplates were accessible to visitors, giving many without first-hand experience a taste of the conditions. These engines were also used to take passengers on short trips in brake vans along a siding. Over the first weekend nearly 27,000 people attended and the total figure of approximately 120,000 comfortably surpassed all expectations and made sure that all three events were unqualified successes.

After the 'Mallard 75' events *Bittern* and *Sir Nigel Gresley* were soon back on the main line with tours over the Settle and Carlisle and from King's Cross to York respectively. *Union of South Africa* was working in Scotland on 27 April on the 'Forth Circle'. At this time both American 'A4s' were returned via Liverpool. *Dwight D. Eisenhower* was back on display in early August and *Dominion of Canada* was unveiled at Exporail in late June.

At the end of 2014 No 4464 was withdrawn from main-line service and ran for much of 2015 on the Mid-Hants Railway prior to entry into Crewe LNWR Heritage Works for a full overhaul. No 60007 was in steam until late September 2015 when taking up residence at the NRM for repairs to be carried out. No 60009 finished the year by transporting HM The Queen from Edinburgh to Tweedbank on the newly reopened Borders Railway on 9 September. The locomotive then ran several specials along the route for six weeks and the tickets were hurriedly snapped up by keen travellers.

BIBLIOGRAPHY

Allen, C. J. *British Pacific Locomotives* (1975)

The Gresley Pacifics of the LNER (1950)

The Locomotive Exchanges (1950)

Aylard, John, Knox, Tommy and Percival, David *What's on the 'Lizzie'?* (2010)

Bannister, Eric *Trained by Sir Nigel Gresley* (1984)

Bonavia, Michael R. *A History of the LNER: 2 The Age of the Streamliners, 1934-39* (1985)

A History of the LNER: 3 The Last Years, 1939-48 (1984)

British Railways Magazine: Eastern Region, various issues

Brooksbank, B. W. L. *Triumph and Beyond: The ECML 1939-1959* (1997)

Brown, F. A. S. *Nigel Gresley: Locomotive Engineer* (1975)

Clay, John F. (ed) *Essays in Steam* (1970)

Clough, David N. *British Rail Standard Diesels of the 1960s* (2009)

Coster, Peter J. *The Book of the A4 Pacifics* (2013)

Cox, E. S. *British Railways Standard Steam Locomotives* (1966)

Dyer, Malcolm *BR Class 40 Diesels* (1982)

Gourvish, T. R. *British Railways 1948-73: A Business History* (1986)

Grafton, Peter *Edward Thompson of the LNER* (2007)

Gresley, H. N. 'Address by the President' (*Proceedings of the Institution of Mechanical Engineers*, Volume 133, October 1936, pp251-265)

'Inaugural Address' (*Journal of the Institution of Locomotive Engineers*, Volume 12, Journal Nos 31/32, 1918, pp199-214)

'Locomotive Experimental Stations' (*Proceedings of the Institution of Mechanical Engineers*, Volume 121, July 1931, pp23-39)

'Presidential Address' (*Journal of the Institution of Locomotive Engineers*, Volume 17, Journal No 81, 1927, pp558-568)

'Presidential Address' (*Journal of the Institution of Locomotive Engineers*, Volume 24, Journal No 121, 1934, pp617-625)

'The Three-Cylinder High-Pressure Locomotive' (*Proceedings of the Institution of Mechanical Engineers*, Volume 109, July 1925, pp927-967)

Groves, N. *Great Northern Locomotive History Vol 3b: 1911-1922 The Gresley Era* (1992)

Guppy, Antony *BR Class 55 Diesels* (1981)

Hale, Don *Mallard: How the 'Blue Streak' Broke the World Speed Record* (2005)

Harris, Michael *Gresley's Coaches* (1973)

Hughes, Geoffrey *A Gresley Anthology* (1994)

Knox, Harry *Haymarket Motive Power Depot, Edinburgh* (2011)

LNER Magazine, various issues

McIntosh, David *Mallard and the A4 Class* (2008)

Mullay, A. J. *Non-Stop! London to Scotland Steam* (1989)

Streamlined Steam (1994)

Nock, O. S. *The Gresley Pacifics Part 1: 1922-1935* (1973)

The Gresley Pacifics Part 2: 1935-1974 (1974)

Pike, S. N. *Mile by Mile on the LNER* (1951)

Railway World, various issues

RCTS *Locomotives of the LNER Part 2A: Tender Engines – Classes A1 to A10* (1978)

Riddick, Julian *Great Preserved Locomotives: Gresley A4 No 4498 Sir Nigel Gresley* (1984)

Rutherford, Michael *Mallard: The Record Breaker* (1988)

Semmens, P. W. B. *Bill Hoole: Engineman Extraordinary* (1974)

Spencer, B. 'The Development of LNER Locomotive Design, 1923-1941' (*Journal of the Institution of Locomotive Engineers*, Volume 37, Journal No 197, Paper No 465, 1947, pp164-226)

Steam Railway, various issues

Steam World, various issues

The Engineer, various issues

The Gresley Observer 'The Silver Jubilee Commemorative Issue' (Autumn 1975)

The Meccano Magazine, various issues

The Railway Magazine, various issues

Townend, P. N. *Top Shed* (1989)

LNER Pacifics Remembered (2014)

Tuffrey, Peter *Cock o' the North* (2015)

Welch, Michael S. *Memories of Steam from Glasgow to Aberdeen* (2012)

Yeadon, W. B. *Register of LNER Locomotives: Gresley A4 and W1 Classes* (2001)

INDEX